War Comes to Long An

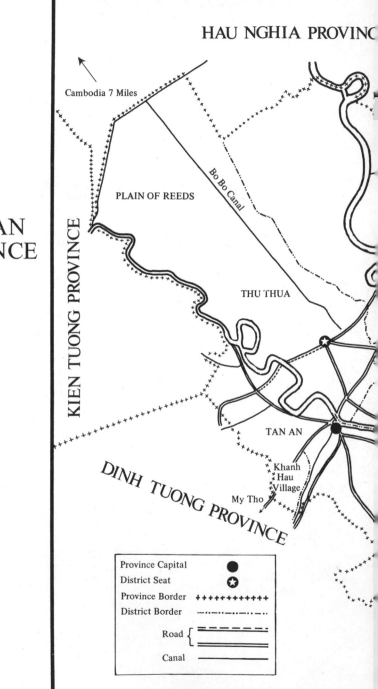

LONG AN
PROVINCE
IN 1968

HAU NGHIA PROVIN[C]

Cambodia 7 Miles

PLAIN OF REEDS

Bo Bo Canal

KIEN TUONG PROVINCE

THU THUA

TAN AN

DINH TUONG PROVINCE

Khanh
Hau
Village

My Tho

Province Capital	●
District Seat	★
Province Border	+++++++++
District Border	─··─·─··─
Road	══════
	──────
Canal	────────

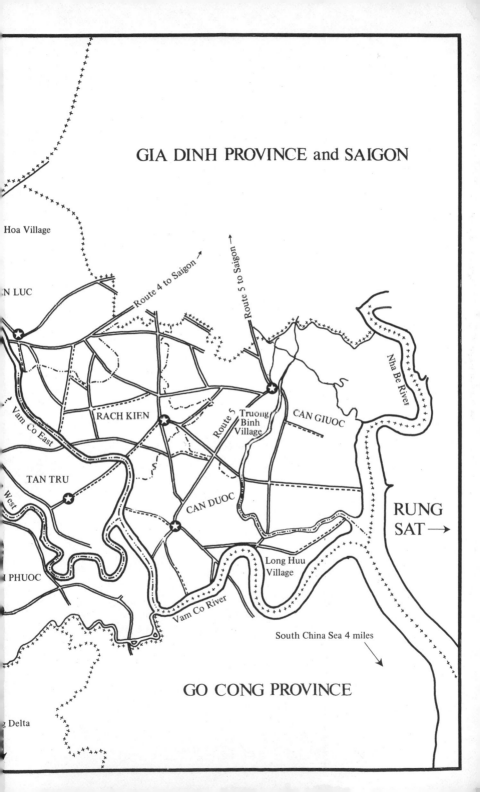

GIA DINH PROVINCE and SAIGON

Hoa Village

N LUC

Route 4 to Saigon ↗

Route 5 to Saigon →

Nha Be River

Vam Co East

RACH KIEN

Route 5

Truong Binh Village

CAN GIUOC

TAN TRU

West

CAN DUOC

RUNG SAT →

PHUOC

Long Huu Village

Vam Co River

South China Sea 4 miles

GO CONG PROVINCE

Delta

War Comes to Long An

Revolutionary Conflict in a Vietnamese Province

·

JEFFREY RACE

UNIVERSITY OF CALIFORNIA PRESS

BERKELEY · LOS ANGELES · LONDON

University of California Press
Berkeley and Los Angeles, California
University of California Press, Ltd.
London, England

Copyright © 1972 by Jeffrey Race
First Paperback Edition, 1973

ISBN: 0-520-02361-7
Library of Congress Catalog Card Number: 79-145793
Printed in the United States of America

8 9 0

The paper used in this publication meets the minimum
requirements of American National Standard for Information
Sciences—Permanence of Paper for Printed Library
Materials, ANSI Z39.48–1984. ∞

Know your enemy, know yourself,
One hundred battles, one hundred victories.

SUN TZU, sixth-century B.C. Chinese military strategist,
frequently quoted in Vietnamese communist documents.

We believe that now is not the time to conceal the truth, for
without removing the abscess how can the body be well? We know
that the truth may offend a number of people, who will condemn
us as antiwar, as willful traitors to the achievements of our
fighters who are sacrificing their lives for the survival of our
people. But we are determined to be faithful to reality, in order to
seek until they appear the reasons that have prolonged this
war and led to the impasse we face today.

LIEUTENANT COLONEL NGUYEN BE, commandant of the
National Training Center for Rural Construction Cadre,
in an essay written in 1968.

Contents

Tables

Maps

Preface

This is a study of the victory in a single province of Vietnam of a revolutionary social movement, led by a communist party, using the technique of people's war. The reader will find few evil or incompetent characters in this book, but rather an account of how such a revolutionary movement was able to gain victory despite the efforts of a considerable number of honest and conscientious men, acting according to their best understanding.

This book is in two parts. In the first four chapters, covering the years from 1954 to 1965, the main concern has been to analyze what factors were critical in the victory of the revolutionary movement. The principal focus is on developments during the important years from 1956 to 1960, during which each side laid the foundations for its subsequent victory or defeat. The last two chapters rely on the analysis contained in the preceding pages to evaluate the situation as it stood in 1968 and 1970, following the intervention of American combat forces and the adoption of several new programs by the Saigon government.

The desirability of making such a study as this occurred to me during 1967, while I was serving in the United States Army as an advisor to a Vietnamese district chief in Phuoc Tuy province, about sixty miles southeast of Saigon. It was clear from my army experience that my fellow officers and I frequently had to make decisions affecting people's lives with an insufficient understanding both of actual conditions and of the nature of the conflict itself of which we were a part. The models implicit in operational doctrines seemed inadequate to account for the events around us, just as the programs we were charged with executing seemed an inadequate response to these events. However, in just what way these doctrines and programs were inadequate was unclear. Here my own prior academic training in political science was of virtually no use, and indeed the ways I had been taught to think about the problem subsequently proved to be the greatest obstacle to understanding. In retrospect it is apparent that this widespread failure of understanding permitted a belief at higher levels of government in possibilities that did not actually exist, in turn leading to increased intervention and to the high costs which the failure of that intervention has subsequently entailed.

Such an insufficient understanding was just one consequence of the generally poor American preparation for dealing with Southeast Asia and the types of conflicts likely to arise there. This poor preparation also revealed itself in the contributions of both the press and the academic profession in Vietnam. If only because of its sheer size, the press community in Vietnam did a creditable job in serving as a transmission belt for statistics and reports of military engagements, or activities of civilian agencies of the government. Nevertheless, there was an obvious shortage of interpretive writing which might have served as the basis for evaluating the importance or even the relevance of the statistics and isolated facts which poured forth daily. Despite the presence of several "old Vietnam hands" during my military service in Vietnam, not a single member of the foreign press spoke Vietnamese, and as a consequence all the output of the foreign press had to be filtered through the limited part of Vietnamese society which spoke Western languages.

Ordinarily we could turn to the academic profession for the kind of analysis in depth that might give meaning to the outpourings of the daily press or to the flow of reports from the field crossing a military commander's desk. Regrettably, this has not been the case. Ironically, Vietnam is the most "researched" war in our history, but with the American government as the sole sponsor and consumer of the research. This effort has been handicapped in two important ways. First, the shortage of researchers qualified both in the Vietnamese language and in the understanding of revolutionary social movements has severely limited the reliability of the research effort. Second and equally significant is the fact that government research has been concentrated on trivial areas of study only marginally relevant to the basic issues of the conflict. Those engaged in the research effort have felt it either inappropriate or inexpedient to object to this preoccupation with triviality.

On the other hand, the part of the academic profession not involved in government research in Vietnam has not undertaken the kind of basic research that would settle some of the debated issues. This is illustrated by the fact that in 1968 there was, besides myself, only one privately sponsored foreign researcher in Vietnam —a student of Buddhism. As a consequence, the discussion of the war in the United States has consisted mainly of repetitious incantation of the same stale quotations from the works of the few individuals who have actually traveled to the scene.

I have chosen a province as my geographical area of study, since it is small enough to handle, yet large enough to give a reasonable idea of the diverse conditions and people on both sides. Moreover, on both sides the province level plays a unique leadership role. On the side of the Saigon government, the province is the most important administrative unit under the leadership of one man. Under a 1956 reorganization, the province chief was made responsible for the enforcement of law, the conduct of administration, and the maintenance of security, with authority to transfer officials within the province or to recommend their removal. He was also made responsible for the overall supervision of the provincial offices of the central ministries. Moreover, in June 1956, the elective village councils established in 1953 were abolished and replaced by administrative committees appointed by the province chief. Finally, in Long An in 1957 the province chief concurrently assumed command of all provincial military forces. Thus to the extent that events can be controlled at all, they are responsive largely to the will of one man with extensive military and civil powers. Similarly, on the side of the communist leadership, the province is the level at which the general policies of the Central Committee are interpreted in terms of local conditions and converted into specific missions for execution by the Party's village-level apparatus.

In tracing the development of the revolutionary movement in Long An and the government's efforts to deal with it, I have relied primarily on interviews and captured documents in an effort to depict events through the eyes of the actual participants themselves. The interviews took place mainly in Long An from late 1967 to mid-1968, and ranged from casual contacts of ten minutes to prearranged meetings stretching over several months. In all, several hundred individuals were queried, including former and present province, district, village, and hamlet officials, former members of the revolutionary movement—communist and noncommunist—rural construction cadre, American advisors, and ordinary citizens. About thirty interviews were tape-recorded in whole or part, the typed transcripts of which total about 1,000 pages. Of these, two principal interviews run over 70 pages each—one with the individual who was province chief of Long An from 1957 to 1961, the second with a communist defector of equivalent rank.

In general I have tried to let the Vietnamese tell their own story. This is not simple in many cases. It is indeed an unusual situation which does not have at least three sides and perhaps more: that of officials appointed by the central government in Saigon; that of the local officials whose views tend to coincide more closely with those of the villagers; and that of the revolutionary forces and their sympathizers. Where possible I have tried to match up all three perceptions. I have also relied to a considerable extent on captured documents to fix dates and to describe the policies of the communist leadership more clearly than the memories of those interviewed allowed. Some of these documents were supplied by the Joint United States Public Affairs Office in Saigon, and some were supplied by Vietnamese sources. Thanks to the latter, I obtained access to a number of important documents, previously unpublished, from the 1956–1960 period. Almost all the primary sources used in writing this book have been deposited with the Center for Research Libraries in Chicago. Because these materials are available only in the original Vietnamese, I have quoted interviews and documents at greater length than would have been the case if these materials were more accessible to other scholars.

The difficulties of the interview technique must be frankly acknowledged. Primary among these is the suspiciousness of the Vietnamese villager, despite his hospitality, of anyone outside his family or friends. Twenty years of violence and betrayals, even within families, have taught him *khon thi chet, dai cung chet, biet moi song*, or "If one is too clever, he won't survive; if he is foolish, he won't survive; the only way to survive is to know when to seem clever and when to seem foolish." The general reaction to authority is a desire to avoid involvement, and "long noses" automatically mean authority. Moreover, any foreigner who speaks fluent Vietnamese is considered (not without justification) to be a CIA agent. Thus answers to direct questions generally are extremely conventional, if they even get beyond the "I don't know" stage. Another frequent problem is the villager's poor conception of time. His memories of events that took place five, ten, or twenty years ago are often selective and inaccurate. This in itself is significant, however, because an individual's memories, even if inaccurate, nevertheless are reality for him, and they are the basis on which he makes his judgments and comparisons between today and yesterday.

Paradoxically, Vietnamese will often be more candid with a Vietnamese-speaking foreigner than they will with other Vietnamese, if they can trust that the information given will not be traced back to them. This was frequently demonstrated to me while I served as a military advisor. Village and hamlet officials would provide me with information they would not dare give to the district chief or to other Americans through an interpreter, because the latter would certainly pass it on to the district chief. On occasion, one also comes across individuals who "tell all." Such people may feel secure enough to think they can afford to tell the truth; more often they are disgruntled and are anxious to obtain a hearing regardless of the consequences. Such sources are invaluable, since the disclosures they make may often serve to jog the memory of others.

To overcome the disadvantages in interviewing, I have relied on written records to resolve many issues that were cloudy in people's memories; and I have tried to tap all possible sources—local and central government officials, American advisors, former members of the revolutionary movement, ordinary citizens—to determine whom to believe and to what extent. The reader must be the final judge of how well I have succeeded.

A special question concerns the interviewing of former members of the communist leadership, whose testimony some would reject completely as "contaminated" by "communist ideology." Further on more will be said on the subject of "ideology," but it is appropriate at this point to mention my own view of the credibility of former communists. While it is true that those interviewed still adhered to a Marxist scheme of social analysis, all had abandoned the revolutionary movement and made their peace to a greater or lesser degree with the Saigon government. Thus their testimony might reasonably be viewed as their "dying words," because they no longer had any motive to consciously distort the facts. Indeed, in the case of the high-ranking defector mentioned above, "dying words" was a true term in a literal sense: before the interviewing was completed, he died from the effects of tuberculosis and leprosy, contracted during twenty years of life in the jungle.

Thus I believe that the defectors interviewed recounted reality as they saw it. Nevertheless, it is fair to ask whether their perceptions of reality were accurate. My own conviction is that the former members of the revolutionary movement were far more accurate observers of the social scene than were the government officials interviewed. It was possible both to compare the replies of the two groups on certain issues with actual records from government files and to compare the predictions and analyses made by both sides in government reports and captured documents from five, ten, or fifteen years ago. In both these areas, as the reader will see, the observations and predictions of communist observers were generally far more accurate than those of government officials.

Yet in a sense, there were different realities, depending on one's position. However, while former members of the communist leadership were able to envisage reality as it looked to government observers, the reverse was seldom true. For example, government officials uniformly dismissed the significance of land ownership as an issue in the conflict, while former members of the revolutionary movement uniformly emphasized its importance. When asked to account for this difference, government observers attributed it to "communist ideology," while communists attributed it to the government officials' lack of contact with the people, and to the fact that those for whom obtaining land was not important tended to cluster around the government, while those for whom land was critical clustered around the revolutionary movement. This fact of multiple realities was demonstrated to me by my own experience, because my understanding of the revolutionary movement changed considerably after I left the army, where I had talked only with government officials, and began to meet individuals who had lived on the other side.

Finally, I should note that the former communists interviewed were not the "bloodthirsty killers" or "ideological fanatics" ordinarily portrayed. Instead, they were, like their government counterparts, simply good people who had done what they believed to be right.

Three things I have tried to avoid in this book. First, I have tried to avoid such general statements as, "The people just want to be left alone to make a living," since these fail to take into account the diversity of Vietnamese rural society. Common sense tells us that we should be sensitive to the different motivations and interests of the various elements of a society, but this is particularly critical when one is confronted by a revolutionary movement whose tactics and strategy are based on decisive distinctions between and even within social classes. One of the most striking aspects of my interviews was the great disparity in perception between different groups. As we shall see, the government's failure to take this element into account has brought it untold grief.

Second, while trying to bring out the real pattern of events, I have attempted not to impose a rigid logic of progression which exists only in my own mind. Aside from those derived from faulty memories, contradictions and inconsistencies also derive from regional differences. Where contradictions and inconsistencies have been apparent, I have endeavored to point them out, rather than suppress them, in the hope that others may come forward with additional information.

Third, I have minimized my reliance on public pronouncements of the revolutionary movement. Even a cursory study of communist internal documents makes one aware of the importance the communist leadership attaches to public opinion as an "objective factor" which must be manipulated. Several examples of completely opposite attitudes on various issues, depending on whether the communist leadership is addressing its own followers or outsiders, will be cited. This should make us treat all public pronouncements and intended disclosures of information by the Party and its instruments as suspect, if not completely false.[1]

On the other hand, readers will note in the following pages a deliberate selectivity of focus. Because the purpose of the first four chapters is to account for the communist success and the government failure in Long An, I have generally concentrated on what the former did right and the latter did wrong. To gain victory, the revolutionary movement did not need to be "good" or "effective" by any absolute standard; it needed only to be better than the government. My goal is to show what provided this margin of superiority. I could equally have cited policy mistakes and organizational problems within the revolutionary movement, but that would not have been germane. Its mistakes were not fatal, but those of the government were. Despite all the problems within the revolutionary movement (and there were many), the fact remains that by 1965 it had won in Long An, and the government had lost.

A few words are also appropriate on the methodology employed in this study and on the logic of presenting the material as I have done. The main issue addressed in this study—how the revolutionary movement was able to win—concerns two principal questions. First, what were the objective facts of the situation in which the movement developed, i.e., the "data"? Besides such quantifiable data as force levels, tax rates, training periods, and landholding patterns, an equally significant category of data comprises the atti-

---

1. Sadly, experience dictates the wisdom of an identical skepticism regarding the public pronouncements of the various governments involved.

tudes and judgments of the participants. The second question—and this became apparent only after some time—was, what scheme of analysis did each side employ?

In dealing with these two questions, I have written a good deal of journalistic material. While some of this material may seem merely amusing or entertaining, even boring, it has a serious purpose, namely, to reveal the attitudes and judgments of the participants, the reasoning behind their decisions, or the factors they considered significant. In some areas, a quantitative response would clearly have been more persuasive, as, for example, where I note the general low level of motivation in the government's local apparatus. Nevertheless, to a single individual like myself, statistical data of this type was unobtainable, as it probably would have been for anyone, given the current conditions in Vietnam.

The ordering of materials in the first part of this book—three chapters of history followed by one chapter of analysis—parallels the evolution of this study in my own mind. When I began, my effort was focused on such issues as force deployment, allocations among types of forces, weaponry, and training, or, in other words, the issues which I had been led to believe were important during my army training and military experience in Vietnam. When I began to meet high-ranking defectors several months later, an entirely different conceptual approach emerged. The line of investigation I had been pursuing now seemed trivial. Consequently, I gradually redirected my inquiry into the areas of social and economic policies and power relationships which now appeared more fundamental. As a result, I had to interview several individuals a second and even a third time. At this point an interesting development occurred: I simply could not get responsive answers from government officials to many questions in the new areas of inquiry. This development, which I call the "blank areas of consciousness" phenomenon, marked a kind of intellectual turning point in my study: it became clear that the fundamental failure of the government had been a conceptual one.

The point I wish to emphasize is that the analysis developed in Chapter Four derived from more than a year of interviewing and of poring over captured documents and government files—and not the reverse. It has seemed worthwhile to preserve this order, although admittedly it represents a compromise. I might have placed the analysis first, thus easing the reader's puzzlement at the contradictory accounts in the historical section, but I have felt it more appropriate to ask the reader to work through confusing historical material first, to give perspective to the analysis described in Chapter Four, and to show how this analysis was in a sense forced on me by the logical and factual inadequacies of the conventional explanations of events recounted by the government decision makers in the first three chapters.

Chapter Four contains in addition a number of conclusions on factual issues. These are simply reasonable deductions from the logic of the situation and from the data now available, above all, the judgments of the participants themselves. While I believe that these conclusions are correct and will stand the test of time, I concede that they may have to be revised as additional information becomes available—a situation not immediately in prospect due to the paucity of substantive research in Vietnam. Moreover, these conclusions apply only to Long An, which differs in many respects from other areas of Vietnam. The degree to which the experience of Long An may be relevant to other areas of Vietnam, or to other cultures, may be verified only by research yet to be carried out. Nevertheless, since each side followed identical policies nationwide, the process described occurred in the same way throughout the country as it did in Long An, although at differing rates depending on local conditions. From talking to individuals close to the situation, my impression is that, of all areas of the country, the events in Long An most closely followed the communist leadership's projections, while elsewhere, particularly in central Vietnam, events moved at a much slower pace. On the other hand, the scheme of analysis in Chapter Four cannot be judged as true or false, but only as more or less helpful in aiding our understanding of events and our predictions.

Moral views on the issues addressed in the following pages are unavoidable. However, I have attempted to prevent my own outlook from interfering with an understanding of events. A certain selectivity is inevitable, but it has been guided by the criterion of whether it aids understanding, not by whether it scores points for one position or another. This approach will perhaps prove unacceptable to a number of people. I may be condemned by some for not taking a vigorous anticommunist stand, and by others for not taking a vigorous stand against the actions of the Saigon and the American governments. However, by trying to present the situation with a minimum of personal coloration, I hope to serve not only students of Vietnamese affairs but all interested readers. It should be noted in line with my position only as a reporter and interpreter of other people's views, that I have not felt obligated to comment, at each quotation, on the biased, incomplete, and sometimes bizarre views expressed. My failure to comment should not be interpreted as implied agreement. The subject matter of this study—a war—and the duty of a scholar —to speak truth—have similarly required me to report many brutal actions and many unpleasant conclusions. The reader will, I trust, restrain the urge to flay the messenger who brings the bad news.[2]

Related to the ethical question is the problem of terminology. To use the term "Vietcong" is hard to justify. It means literally, "Vietnamese communist," whereas most of those who oppose the Saigon government are outside the Lao Dong Party (since 1961 in the South called the People's Revolutionary Party). On the other hand, the term "insurgent" is equally misleading. The term implies an uprising against a legally constituted authority, when in fact because of a whole series of fraudulent elections and coups d'etat neither the Diem regime nor its successors through 1965 could have been considered any more "legally constituted" than could the leadership of the Lao Dong Party in the South. Likewise, the term "insurgency" carries the misleading connotation of an uprising against an "established" authority. Yet successive central governments have been "established" only in the sense of occupying a number of buildings in the principal cities and in the province and district capitals. A study seeking to understand why the "established" government declined is thus misdirected from the start. The question is, why one of two competing leaderships was capable of establishing a stronger movement in the rural areas.

The term which I have selected—revolutionary movement— has its own drawbacks. It is somewhat longer, and it may offend some who prefer not to think of an adversary of the United States in this way. Nevertheless it points directly to what created the success of the movement—the fact that it represented a social revolution. Moreover, it permits an important distinction between the leader-

---

2. I would also like to note that I conducted this research as a private citizen, without the sponsorship of any program, group, or official organization. While this was not my desire, it was necessarily so, since no organization saw fit to support research of this type.

I first traveled to Vietnam in the military service, and during my nineteen months in this capacity studied the Vietnamese language at my own expense. Shortly after my release from active duty I returned to Vietnam via a United States Department of State Vietnam study grant, which was unilaterally rescinded immediately after my arrival. Research on this project was thereafter supported from my own funds.

During the summer of 1970 a grant from Harvard University permitted me to return to Vietnam to complete the research for Chapter Six.

ship of the movement (the Lao Dong Party) and the great majority of the membership, which is noncommunist.

While one aim of this study is to suggest some alternate ways of analyzing conflicts such as that in Vietnam, it is not intended to suggest any alternate policies or strategies. All the information contained in the following pages has long been available to policy makers. If they had been persuaded by its implications, or had been able to act on them, then they would have done so long ago.[3] Consequently I consider this work principally of academic interest, to scholars and to members of the general public desiring to know more about revolutionary social movements, or about recent events in Vietnamese history.

Researching this book has meant continual discoveries for me. When I began in September 1967, it was with a determination to have an open mind and to share these discoveries with others, whatever they might be. In what follows I have tried to let documents and records, and the Vietnamese people, speak for themselves. Having proceeded thus I find I have reached conclusions which surprise even myself.

---

3. For two divergent hypotheses why they did not, see Daniel Ellsberg, "Escalating in a Quagmire," and Jeffrey Race, "American Intervention Abroad: Systematic Distortions in the Policy-Making Process," papers delivered at the Sixty-sixth Annual Meeting of the American Political Science Association at Los Angeles, September 8–12, 1970 (available from University Microfilms, Ann Arbor, Michigan).

Acknowledgments

O nly when an author sets down the final page of a work such as this, and sits back to contemplate what he has completed, does he realize how much he is indebted to others for the words he has put to paper. This debt is particularly great where those who assisted were often under the enormous stresses of war.

First I would like to record my debt to my friend and teacher, Huynh Kim Cuong, who started me on the study of the Vietnamese language. Throughout the time when we were comrades in arms, and later when I began this project, he enlightened me in the complexities of the Vietnamese language and the Vietnamese people, and performed countless other acts of assistance to ease the way of a foreigner in his country.

This study of Long An province would have been impossible but for the patience and enthusiasm of Colonel Nguyen van Nguu, province chief, and Colonel James A. Herbert, advisor to Colonel Nguu. Their exceptional cooperation cannot be acknowledged too highly. Dozens of members of their staffs cooperated to provide documents, statistics, explanations, and hospitality; in particular I would like to mention Robert V. Craig, Larry Crandall, Bruce Kinsey, Robert Rintz, and Thai Quoc Thanh.

Special thanks are also due to Lieutenant Colonel Nguyen Be and Major Jean Sauvageot, who despite their extremely crowded schedules provided generously of their time in elucidating the rural construction program.

I would also like to express my gratitude to the staffs of the National Press Center of the Ministry of Information, the General Political Warfare Department of the Ministry of Defense, and the Office of Information of the United States Military Assistance Command Vietnam. These individuals were unfailingly courteous and helpful in providing visas, introductions, advice, and information. Special thanks are due to MACV for the exceptional logistical facilities it provided, greatly easing the work of gathering the information presented here.

For access to the documents quoted herein, I am indebted to the Joint United States Public Affairs Office, and to the following

Vietnamese agencies: the Special Branch of the National Police, the J-2 branch of the Joint General Staff, and the Central Intelligence Service.

To the many individuals not mentioned here whose interviews appear in the text, I am obviously also much indebted. Their willingness to cooperate in this endeavor was a sign of their confidence in me. While some of those interviewed may not agree with my interpretations, I hope that I have fulfilled their trust by reporting their views accurately.

Throughout the period of this research Gerald C. Hickey was generous with his time, as he is to all scholars of Vietnam.

H. Lee Braddock, Everet Bumgardner, Jack Riggs, and Lieutenant Colonel William N. Thomas all have my appreciation for furnishing data and documents used in this study, as does Earl Young for contributing several photographs from his collection on Long An. Michigan State University has kindly granted permission to reproduce the map shown opposite page 1, as has Lieutenant Colonel David E. Shepherd for the map shown on pp. 138–139.

In Saigon Le thi Sang and Tran thi Duyen struggled to transcribe what must have seemed endless reels of Vietnamese-language interviews onto paper, while in Bangkok Katherine Rader and Susie Smith labored with equal grace to transform my difficult handwriting to admirable typed copy. Also in Bangkok Robert Behnke, Richard T. Borden, and Dennis Holoviak gave both moral support and the facilities of their offices for typing and copying.

Many individuals have read all or part of this work in manuscript and offered valuable suggestions. Here I wish to record my gratitude to Suzanne D. Berger, John D. Caldwell, Philip Dion, Jerrold Milsted, Charles A. Murray, Michael Pearce, Samuel Popkin, Katherine Strelsky, and William S. Turley. In reviewing the manuscript for publication both David Marr and Robert Scalapino offered numerous valuable criticisms. I would also like to extend thanks to William J. McClung and Margery Riddle of the University of California Press, for their assistance in producing and editing this work, and for tolerating my eccentricities in both.

Finally I must acknowledge my debt to my mother. Like all mothers whose sons go off to war, mine endured the agony of waiting for the knock announcing tragedy. Each of the four times I went to Vietnam she endorsed my decision and did all she could to make this project succeed, despite the pain she felt. Unlike so many who have left their homes—of brick, wood, or thatch—to confront this war,

I was favored to return safely, to complete the work presented here. My mother's tireless efforts, in searching citations, purchasing books, and typing drafts during my four years abroad, contributed immeasurably to the success of this project.

For such accuracy and completeness as this work possesses, these people are responsible. As for the interpretations, and the errors, they are my own.

Location of Long An province within Vietnam south of the 17th parallel (1960 boundaries)

17TH PARALLEL

QUANG TRI

THUA THIEN

QUANG NAM

QUANG NGAI

LAOS

KONTUM

BINH DINH

PLEIKU

CAMBODIA

PHU YEN

DARLAC

KHANH HOA

QUANG DUC

TUYEN DUC

PHUOC LONG

NINH THUAN

BINH LONG

LAM DONG

TAY NINH

BINH DUONG

BINH TUY

LONG KHANH

BINH THUAN

BIEN HOA

KIEN TUONG

LONG AN

PHUOC TUY

KIEN PHONG

AN GIANG

DINH TUONG

SOUTH CHINA SEA

VINH LONG

KIEN HOA

PHU QUOC

KIEN GIANG

PHONG DINH

VINH BINH

BA XUYEN

AN XUYEN

From *The Study of A Vietnamese Rural Community*, by Lloyd W. W
Michigan State University Viet-Nam Advisory Group.

The Physical Setting

L ong An, Sino-Vietnamese for "prosperous and peaceful," is the name of a province which lies to the south and west of Saigon. Its 350,000 people occupy 540 square miles of typical Mekong Delta land, most of it only two feet above sea level. This land is very fertile, and, with double-cropping, Long An until 1966 produced some 260,000 tons of rice annually, more than half of which was exported outside the province. It also produces considerable quantities of sugar cane and *nuoc mam*, a high-protein fish sauce without which no Vietnamese meal is complete. From the standpoint of its contribution to the economy of Vietnam, Long An occupies a prominent place.

Strategically, Long An is even more important. In 1957 the province of Cholon was divided in two, one part being annexed to the capital city of Saigon and the remainder joined to the province of Tan An to create the new province of Long An, its seven districts stretching from the Rung Sat (Jungle of Death) on the east coast to the Dong Thap Muoi or Plain of Reeds on the Cambodian border in the west. The Rung Sat is an almost impenetrable swamp through which the various branches of the Saigon River flow from the interior down to the South China Sea. All international shipping must pass through the Rung Sat. Formerly, it was an important center of Vietminh strength, as it has become for their successors as well. In the west the northern part of the Plain of Reeds extends up into Long An from Kien Tuong province. Unlike the Rung Sat, the Plain of Reeds is relatively open, but movement is slow and tiring in the waist-deep mud. Surprise is almost impossible to achieve. Over the years this has allowed various antigovernment forces to turn it into a relatively secure base area.

The security of the capital thus demands that Long An be secure to prevent enemy forces from striking out across it from their bases in the Rung Sat and the Plain of Reeds to attack Saigon itself. Even more significantly, Long An cuts almost completely across Vietnam, from Cambodia to the South China Sea,[1] dividing

---

1. Until 1963 Long An actually did reach the Cambodian border. In that year the government position had become so precarious that an additional

the provinces north of Saigon from what is called the "Western Region"—the vital rice-producing provinces of the Mekong Delta which contain the majority of the South's rural population and which make the rest of the South, including the capital, viable. Two vital land routes stretch south from Saigon through Long An: Route 5 in eastern Long An connects Saigon with Go Cong province, and Route 4 in central Long An travels on through Dinh Tuong province to the heart of the Mekong Delta. The interdiction of these routes is sufficient to interrupt the vital flow of food to Saigon. From the strategic standpoint, then, whoever dominates Long An is in a commanding position either to attack the capital or to starve it, or both.

---

province, Hau Nghia, was created on the Cambodian border from portions of Long An, Tay Ninh, and Binh Duong provinces to concentrate additional resources in this area. For the same reason in 1961 the Rung Sat was removed from the jurisdiction of Long An and became a special military zone.

CHAPTER ONE

Long An at Peace

Peace is concluded to procure advantages for us, not for the purpose of ceasing the struggle. Peace as such is not unconditional. We love peace and do not want war which causes bloodshed, but we are resolved to maintain our fundamental point of view, which is independence, unity, democracy, and peace. If the political struggle does not permit us to accomplish this essential aim, we are resolved to continue the war in order to support our just cause and to achieve total victory.

1954 document on post-Geneva strategy, apparently issued by the Lao Dong Party Central Committee.[1]

In July of 1954 the long war was over. Although it had brought its share of grief to Long An, there had been little of the large-scale destruction which had taken place in northern and central Vietnam, where the decisive battles of the Resistance had been fought. Sufficient forces had been available locally and on call from Saigon to protect the major roads and government buildings, but not to eliminate the presence of the Vietminh. Although the Vietminh had held large areas such as the Plain of Reeds, these were relatively unpopulated. Ho van Si, province chief at the time of the armistice, felt that the situation had been relatively good. "The Vietminh had their areas, like the Plain of Reeds, which we just abandoned. Whatever the Vietminh wanted to do, we did not bother them, but in the rest of the province it was relatively peaceful. The district chiefs and village council members, even I as province chief, could travel anywhere at all, as long as we had four or five armed men along."[2]

---

1. Excerpt from Document 200 of the appendices to *Working Paper on the North Vietnamese Role in the War in South Viet-Nam*, released by the United States Department of State in May 1968. In subsequent notes this will be cited as *Working Paper*.

For the sake of simplicity, throughout this chapter the name Long An is used, although until 1957, when it was joined with part of Cholon, the province was known as Tan An.

2. A village is a self-contained community, ranging in population from several hundred to several thousand families, and sharing a common leadership, a communal house, and probably a market. It is the largest unit of social significance to the rural population of Long An. Each village is divided along

Bui van Ba, from 1952 to 1954 chief of Can Duoc district and later province chief, was even more complacent. "The situation in Can Duoc was quite good, since each of my fifteen villages had an outpost with police and soldiers, and each had a village council. I had three canton chiefs to help me supervise the village councils, so the administrative work was fairly easy. The Vietminh operated very weakly, except for two villages in the northeast [adjacent to the Rung Sat], where it was difficult for us to travel." At night all the troops and the village council members would withdraw into the outposts, but even then there was little difficulty. "From time to time the Vietminh would just come into the villages at night and harass the outposts so they could collect taxes from the people, that's all."

From the peasants' viewpoint, however, the situation looked quite different. Each village had had its own Vietminh "Committee of Resistance and Administration," just as the Saigon government had had its village council. Outside the market areas the Vietminh cadres and sympathizers had been constantly moving about, propagandizing, recruiting, and taxing—enough so that for the most part landlords had no longer dared to leave their exile in the towns to collect rents, for fear of assassination. On the other hand, the village council appeared only fleetingly, in the company of an armed escort, to collect taxes. Occasionally the French would conduct a "sweep" operation, surrounding a hamlet and rounding up Vietminh suspects as well as any potential draftees, but they would always depart in a few hours and the Vietminh cadres would return. Even in the more populated areas near the outposts the situation was not basically different. One shopkeeper who lived at the market in the district town of Thu Thua recalled, "The Vietminh were very strong here. The government troops just operated a little bit right around the market, and in the evening they withdrew into the outpost. Then the Vietminh would come up and move around freely." Another individual, a Vietminh village chief at Thu Thua for nine years, found it very easy to move around. "When I was with the Vietminh I was the chairman of the Binh Thanh village committee. I lived about fifteen miles away, but I operated near here constantly. In spite of the French outpost, I was able to travel up here to work with the people any time I wanted to."

geographic or residential lines into several hamlets, or what might better be described as neighborhoods.

Canton, district, and province mean progressively larger administrative and geographic subdivisions.

Actually the government and the Vietminh had reached a tacit modus vivendi in Long An, while the decisive events of the war had been taking place elsewhere. Given its troops and its tactics, there was little more the government could do than to concentrate on protecting its roads and offices. From the point of view of the Vietminh, who were being hurt very little by government activities, there was nothing to be gained in mounting large-scale attacks. Long An was a rich source of rice and of manpower for the Vietminh, and at little cost.

The signing of the Geneva Accords meant different things to different groups in Long An. For the soldiers in the outposts it meant an end to nervous nights of waiting for the Vietminh. For the village officials perhaps it meant a return to the pleasant prewar days when a position on the village council meant power and prestige instead of the perpetual threat of death. For the landlords it meant a chance to return from their exile in the province capital of Tan An and in the district towns to collect nine years of back rents. For several hundred Vietminh soldiers and sympathizers it meant a trip to the North. Many of these were members of Vietminh military units, moving under orders, but a substantial number were young peasants, who had been told of the new life being built in the North and of the education they would be given there—something they could not get in the South. No doubt most were very homesick ón leaving—the Vietnamese are particularly attached to their place of birth—but they were consoled by the knowledge that they would be returning in two years. And finally for the majority of the inhabitants of Long An—the peasants in the areas under Vietminh influence—it meant either a resumption of land-rent payments (though an end to Vietminh taxes) or else the outright loss of the land they had been told was theirs by the local Vietminh committee, and a return to the uncertain existence of tenant farmer. But for all who remained, it meant an end to violence and a return to normality.

Yet what was a "normal" life in Long An? A widely distributed government propaganda poster depicting a "typical" village scene shows two attractive young women wearing the *ao dai*, a traditional Vietnamese costume ordinarily worn by the middle and upper classes, watching their younger brothers playing at a New Year's celebration. The caption reads, "Without the communist rebels, life in the village would be peaceful and happy." While the picture itself projects a happy image, it nevertheless typifies the government's failure to understand the countryside, for it depicts what the life of only a few people would be like without the "communist rebels."

It must be admitted that for everyone, poor or rich, life in the Mekong Delta is much easier than in central or northern Vietnam. In most areas of the Mekong Delta the land is so fertile that a family of six can survive with less than two hectares of riceland.[3] Southern peasants are fond of saying, with only some exaggeration, that one really only has to fling rice into the fields, wait six months, and there will be enough to eat for the coming year. To supplement his rice diet, the peasant need only drop a line into the stream or canal going by his house to have fish for dinner, and he can plant vegetables in the front yard or buy them cheaply from one of his neighbors who grows extra. Even in a bad season there will still be enough rice for local consumption, and there is always plenty of fish.

On the other hand, in central and northern Vietnam the less fertile land and the cold season make life in general much more difficult, so that with a good crop stomachs are full, but with a bad crop death by starvation is a real possibility. During 1944–1945, for example, between one and two million people died in the North after the wartime destruction of the transport system prevented the import of rice from the South. Such contrasting economic circumstances between the South and the rest of the country produce very different outlooks on life. Southern, central, and northern Vietnamese alike will all tell you that if a northern or central Vietnamese peasant earns a hundred piasters, he will spend thirty and save seventy, but a southern peasant will go out that same day and spend the whole hundred piasters eating and drinking with his friends, for he knows that tomorrow he can always earn more. But while a northern or central Vietnamese repeats this with scorn, a Southerner says it with pride. Among themselves Southerners frankly acknowledge their easy, even lazy, attitude toward life and express contempt for the sharp and crafty ways of the northern and central Vietnamese.

Enjoyment of the general prosperity of the Mekong Delta, however, is tied closely to access to its source: the land. No other factor looms so large in the consciousness of the peasant. Aside from the economic precariousness of owning no land, a peasant also feels a rootlessness particularly strong in Vietnamese culture, because the land has a special ritual significance for the Vietnamese: it is the focus of life and family activity. Closeness to ancestral graves and the fields the family has worked for generations provides the emo-

---

3. One hectare equals 2.47 acres.

tional security and strength which Westerners generally draw from prophetic religion.

While renting land in the Mekong Delta was preferable to being an agricultural laborer, it had its own difficulties and uncertainties. Land might be rented either from the village itself or from private landowners. Theoretically at least, a portion of the village communal lands were reserved by the village council for the poorest members to farm, either permanently or for a term of years. Yet at the same time the rental fees from communal lands were a principal source of village income. Thus the village council had the impossible task of reconciling the contradictory objectives of low rentals for the poor peasants and high rentals for maximum village revenue. This conflict was frequently "resolved" by letting the communal lands out for bid, with the result that the poor peasant, if he won the bidding at all, had to top the higher rent which the more well-to-do bidders could afford, using fertilizer and other modern techniques beyond the resources of the poor peasant. Or, depending on the conscience of the members of the village council and the degree to which they were supervised by higher authority, they might simply rent the communal lands to themselves or their friends.[4]

The remaining landless peasants had to turn to private individuals for land. Again, the system worked satisfactorily if the landlord was a man of good will, but the ordinary situation was fraught with difficulties, and at worst the system, until 1945, amounted in many places to virtual slavery. The tenant and landlord might agree, for example, to rent a parcel of land for five years at a fixed annual percentage (commonly 50 percent) of the expected yield. In the event of crop failure, the landlord might still insist on full payment of the agreed rent, conceivably exceeding the actual crop harvested that year. Should the tenant not pay the full amount, the agreement could be canceled and the tenant's house and possessions seized. Frequently the landlord might require one or more of the tenant's daughters to live in his house as servants, as security for the payment of the annual rent. Should the rent not be paid, the girls would be

---

4. The reader will find it worthwhile to refer to Gerald Hickey's *Village in Vietnam* (New Haven: Yale University Press, 1964), for a detailed view of the workings of a Mekong Delta village. Khanh Hau, the village described in Hickey's book, lies on Route 4 in Long An just a few miles from the border of Dinh Tuong province. Hickey notes that in 1958 two members of the Khanh Hau village council, both already landowners, were renting communal lands.

retained, possibly becoming concubines or minor wives for the land-lord's sons. Moreover, an unscrupulous landlord could extort additional rent when the contract was about to expire, not only because of the difficulty of finding new land to farm but also because the tenant would ordinarily have made improvements, such as irrigation or buildings, during his tenure.

An even worse fate befell those who farmed land of absentee landlords where rent collection was usually turned over to an agent known as *trung gian bao ta*,[5] probably the most hated word in the peasant vocabulary. Ordinarily the landlord required only a specific amount each year from the agent, who retained anything he collected over this amount. On larger estates the only law was that of the land-lord or his agent, and the peasant was reduced to a perpetual sub-sistence living, without any hope that even his children might escape by education, because they had to work in the fields for the family to survive. Though the large estates have been broken up since 1956, the bitter memories linger on.[6]

The local organization responsible for maintaining the state of "normality" just described was the largely autonomous village council, the *ban hoi te*. Until 1945 it was a self-perpetuating body of twelve members responsible for all aspects of village life such as administration, finance, justice, religious rites, and welfare. Vacancies were filled by the council itself from the local landowners or from resident mandarins or military officers. With the Vietminh seizure of power in 1945 the village councils were disbanded and their members either imprisoned or executed, but the French re-established the ban hoi te a short time later. During the next seven

---

5. Literally, "middleman who takes care of tenants."
6. Long An never had any of the large estates which existed deeper in the Mekong Delta. One individual recalled a relative who before World War II owned over 3,000 hectares in Dinh Tuong (then My Tho) province, im-mediately south of Long An, and who owned a Ford automobile at a time (1926) when even high French officials were fortunate to have a French vehicle. Although at that time 3,000 hectares represented a colossal fortune, many estates were much larger. The most extensive landholding by a single family (excluding that of the former emperor) lay in Bac Lieu province. It consisted of over 23,000 hectares of riceland and almost 4,000 hectares of salt flats.
    Hickey records that one of the wealthy landowners in Khanh Hau formerly acted as rental agent for another landowner and that "a number of villagers, particularly tenants and former tenants, continue to harbor resentment against [him] for his actions" (p. 253). In 1968 the practice of *trung gian bao ta* still survived, though its excesses had been reduced, partly by government legis-lation and partly by the threat of assassination.

years its size and method of selection changed with the succession of French-sponsored governments in Saigon. Nevertheless, in the countryside it was seldom possible—even with eased property requirements—to select a complete council, because membership carried with it such a high risk of assassination.

Ideally, the ban hoi te was composed of the wisest and most honorable among the village elite, who would rule fairly and impartially, with little accountability to higher authority. Prior to the French occupation of Vietnam, the emperor dealt only with the village council, never with individual villagers, and the French maintained the practice of working only through the ban hoi te. Even today the peasant deals primarily with his hamlet chief and village council, and for the rare times when he must have direct contact with district or province authorities, he must first have a certificate from the village council. Thus for the overwhelming majority of the Vietnamese population, "government" has always meant simply the village council—the peasant has little experience of any other.

While the village council was theoretically an impartial body, in practice throughout the Mekong Delta and particularly in the provinces distant from Saigon, the village council became an instrument of the landlords to maintain a privileged status above the law, with positions bought and sold as investments. Abuses were so widespread and so flagrant that they were a major subject of discussion in progressive circles, even within the colonial administration. For example, Ho Bieu Chanh, an official who had achieved the highest administrative rank of *doc phu su*, was famous for his realistic novels describing the situation in the countryside. One of his novels, *Loi The Truoc Mieu*, published in 1938, recounted the life of leisure of village officials in Can Giuoc district (now a part of Long An province) and how one official was preparing to sell his position for 200 piasters, at that time more than a year's income for an average tenant farmer.

The peasants of Long An still remember the period prior to the Geneva Accords with anger. Nguyen van Ben, in 1968 a hamlet chief in Thu Thua district but formerly an agricultural laborer, described the pre-1954 period:

It's difficult to remember the details about that time—just mostly that the people here were poor and life was very difficult. The village authorities squeezed the people and made life very hard. We'd have to go on guard, and everyone had to pay the *thue than* [body tax] of four and a half piasters a year, but a lot of times poor people didn't have the money and they'd be put in jail. . . . Whoever wanted to be on the ban hoi te had to pay a bribe, and he would get the job. But in those days the village officials were the "father and mother of the people"—whatever they wanted we had to obey them. If the village chief wanted to go visit some friends somewhere, he would order us to get a boat and row him there. Or if he came to someone's house, they would have to be very humble and respectful, maybe kill a chicken or a duck and make *chao* [a popular kind of soup] for him. . . . We just had to do whatever they told us, if not we'd be called communists and sent to Catinat[7] to be tortured. Really, in those days people were afraid just to look at a council member.

A shopkeeper from Can Duoc district replied as follows to the question whether there were ever any average or poor peasants on the ban hoi te:

Ha! Where would they get the money to pay the bribes? It cost a thousand piasters [about $500 at that time]. Only if you were rich would you have money like that. Otherwise you were just lucky to make your living and pay your taxes. But being on the village council was very "tasty" indeed. Whenever we met a council member, we clasped our hands, bowed, said *bam*, and then left as quickly as we could.[8]

In 1953 the ban hoi te was replaced—at least on paper—by the *hoi dong huong chinh* (village administrative council), composed of six members, without property qualifications, elected by universal suffrage.[9] It was a negligible improvement. Though the decree called for elections, in practice in Long An they were held only in relatively

---

7. The name of the main street in Saigon, on which the office of the *Cong An*, Vietnamese counterpart to the French *Sûreté*, was located. Even today many superstitious Vietnamese avoid the building, since they believe there are many angry ghosts still wandering about the area.

8. The term *bam* was formerly used to address high-ranking mandarins; thus he means that the villagers looked upon the village council members as if they had been appointed by the emperor himself.

9. This discussion applies only to the South, since village government organization developed differently in central and northern Vietnam. Throughout this text the general term village council refers to whatever Saigon-sponsored organ was responsible for village affairs, whether elected or appointed.

Viet My, III:2 and III:3 (June and September, 1958) contains two articles entitled "Village Councils—Yesterday and Today" by Diem's Minister of the Interior, Lam Le Trinh, which describe the changes in village government for the three regions. Readers should note that the Vietnamese original is more detailed and accurate than the English translation. Both are included in *Viet My*.

secure areas, while in the rest of the province members were simply appointed, often in accordance with the system of payoffs described for the ban hoi te. Even in those areas where elections were held, no observers were permitted when the votes were counted, and the "approved" candidates invariably won. Many people felt, however, that there was some improvement, because the most oppressive individuals were intimidated from holding positions.

Thus the signing of the Geneva Accords, ending the war in July 1954, did not have the same significance for everyone in Long An. For a large part of the population the war had actually meant an immediate, or at least a prospective improvement in their condition, although at the cost of occasional violence: many had obtained their own land, and the oppressive activities of the discredited village councils had been limited by Vietminh threats of assassination. For others, particularly centrally appointed government officials, the return of peace was a pleasing prospect. For them a peaceful village meant a contented village; they had little awareness that the prewar peacefulness had been out of resignation and not contentment.

In 1954, then, the end of violence was welcomed by all, but the "return to normal" was not. A significant part of the population was either indifferent or strongly embittered toward the new government, both as sponsor of the returning landlords and village councils, and as the successor to the French. While we have no statistics on how many were among this group, it is reasonable to believe that the major criterion was economic position—and, as Vietminh propaganda constantly pointed out, "the poor are the great majority." What this group might do in the future would depend largely on the extent to which its traditional grievances would be resolved: land, abuses by the *cuong hao ac ba* or "local tyrants," and exclusion from power over decisions affecting their own lives.

The two years from the signing of the Geneva Accords until the summer of 1956 were a period of physical recovery and relative peace for Long An. In Saigon the Diem government was occupied in relocating refugees and in consolidating its position: reducing French influence, bringing the national army under control, and eliminating the armed power of the Cao Dai and Hoa Hao religious sects and the Binh Xuyen bandit gang. There was little attention to spare for events in the provinces, where organization, administrative procedures, and personnel remained largely the same as during the time of the French. Since the threat of violence had subsided (except for occasional incidents of personal vengeance), the administrative system of village councils was extended to areas where its grip had previously been weak or nonexistent.

The governmental system which the Bao Dai regime inherited from the French had concentrated power in the Governor of Cochinchina, subsequently replaced by the regional delegate and the Ministry of the Interior. Subordinate levels—province, district, canton, and village—were merely executive in nature, carrying out policies established in Saigon and researching and passing even minor problems up to Saigon for resolution. Province and district chiefs were centrally appointed from a list of civil servants and were never allowed to serve in their home province or district. Canton and village officials, on the other hand, were appointed (the latter in some areas theoretically elected) from among the local elite. District and canton were both simply supervisory echelons, having no legal character and no budgets. Villages were considered juridical persons and had their own budgets, but in fact they had very little autonomy and had become little more than instruments by which the provincial government collected taxes and retained administrative contact with its citizens.

The system the Diem regime inherited was essentially a hybrid of Chinese mandarin and French administrative concepts designed to rule a subject people. The only concession to popular participation was the theoretically elected village council, which would indeed have been the most logical starting point to build a popularly based government, because it was in practice the only level of government with which the peasant had any significant contact in his daily life. But the elitist character of the councils, and their actual functioning principally as instruments of manipulation and of tax collection, only reinforced the peasants' traditional indifference toward them, or even hostility.

An important obstacle confronting the Saigon authorities in stirring enthusiasm in Long An was the attitudes of their own administrators toward what constituted a just society. How these attitudes distorted their perception of the motives for antigovernment activity is exemplified by the recollections of Ho van Si, the province chief quoted earlier. Si was born in Ben Tre province, where his family had long been part of the local elite which traditionally ran village affairs, and his father had been a canton chief. Si left Ben Tre early to obtain a French education at the Chasseloup-Laubat School in

Saigon,[10] but illness caused him to leave school during his last year. When he recovered, he became a clerk in the colonial administration, and by studying in his spare time he was able to pass the examinations to become an administrative civil servant, eventually rising to the highest rank of *doc phu su*. He served as district chief in several districts of the Mekong Delta, then deputy province chief in Soc Trang and Gia Dinh, finally becoming province chief of Long An (then called Tan An) in April 1953. Now retired, he lives in a small house near the Saigon racetrack. In talking to Si, one notes how well he exemplifies the bureaucratic mentality which pervaded the French provincial administration. To questions about military or policy matters, Si repeatedly replied that one would have to ask the "politicians" or the military experts—he was an administrator who just "did what they told me."

Si recalled that prior to the Geneva Accords there had been occasional annoying demonstrations during the day.

Usually the people would demonstrate about taxes. At that time, as I remember, the village collected a lot of miscellaneous taxes: there was a land tax, and a house tax (everyone had a house, even if just of thatch), a tax on people who used the market, and a vehicle tax. They were not very high, but the people would come up in a demonstration and say, "Why do you make the poor people pay all these taxes? They are illegal. We're not going to pay." And then the district chief or someone else would have to go out and explain to the crowd, "These taxes are all just to help you people, they are used for the good of the village, like the maternity ward which you women use when you have babies. The government is here to help you, to provide you security and prosperity. Everything you have is thanks to the government." We would very seldom arrest anybody—just one or two people who were the leaders of the demonstration. The rest had just been stirred up by the Vietminh.

[After the truce] the people were able to go back to making an easy living and could return to their fields without being threatened by the Vietminh. Before they would be working and the Vietminh would come along and force them to go out and dig up the roads so they could plant mines. But now they could work in security—that was the only thing they really wanted.

Si also felt that the ban hoi te, although not "democratic," was nevertheless more effective than the elected hoi dong huong chinh, and that the people had actually been better off previously.

---

10. Later named for Jean Jacques Rousseau; at the time it was one of the finest schools in the French Empire.

In the old days only well-known, older, respected people were chosen for the ban hoi te—people who already had land and money, so there was no problem of corruption. The council members had a lot of personal power and prestige with the people in the village, because in those days there were no Vietminh—everybody just paid attention to making a living, and whatever kind of problem came up, the village council would settle it. So even though it was not "democratic," as you call it, nevertheless the people were able to make their living peacefully and happily without being bothered by the Vietminh.

The only problem with the ban hoi te, according to Si, was that "every so often there might be a member who would worry more about his own interests than those of the community." But this was minimized by the careful process of selection:

One didn't just ask to become a council member and then become one. The canton chief would have only three or four villages in his canton, so naturally he would suggest the names of the best people to the district chief, who would submit them to the province for approval. But if the district chief didn't trust his canton chief, he could go around and get the opinions of the various village elders himself. Of course, out of ten people, one or two bad ones might get in, but the district chief would replace them if he found out. . . . If you had good council members, the people would support them. It all depended on how good the council members were.

It was too early for elections then, first because the people didn't understand about elections[11] and second because of the Vietminh threat. . . . The peasants only know about making a living, they don't know anything about politics. The communists are very clever and they deceive the people. . . . For example, the communists promised they would give the people land for nothing. Naturally the peasants liked to hear that. But they are very simple people, they don't know anything about politics, how could they know that the communists would just exploit them in some other way? Unfortunately, we had very little money then to hire cadres to go and educate the people about politics. If we had been able to make the peasants understand, the communists would not be as powerful as they are now.

While considering other questions, Si said, however, that the government's propaganda efforts were weak:

Each village had an information office, where we would have pictures

---

11. Si said this despite the fact that village elections in various forms have been practiced in Vietnam for five centuries.

and mimeographed stories about government activities in other parts of the country. Each village council had one member in charge of information who would go out to the hamlets and explain what the government was doing to help the people. But the means were very limited compared to the present—now they have speakers and all kinds of other devices. In those days we just had the mimeographed articles and posters, and our propaganda was not too effective.

Although Si declined to answer the question, "What makes a government strong?" by saying that one should ask the politicians, he did later explain what he thought were the strong and weak points of the government while he was province chief.

The strong point was helping the people to enjoy a better living, for example, by distributing seed or by lending plows. In particular I emphasized education, so that I worked for every village to have a school, even if it was just in a borrowed building. I also tried to arrange for every village to have a maternity ward, a reading room, and night reading classes. In those days officials were chosen for their ability and integrity, and when the people saw us working for them, they supported the government. . . . I really didn't see any weak points, just that we didn't have enough weapons and ammunition, although I requested them often enough. Our political cadres and the local officials had no way to protect themselves, so when they were moving around there would occasionally be an assassination. That was the only weakness.

Si said that each echelon had "adequate" authority to do its job, but the actual allocation of authority between local officials and Saigon-appointed officials appears in his reply to the question, why were local people not appointed to the positions of district and province chief:

District and province chiefs are civil servants appointed by Saigon. That is the way it has always been organized right up until now. If you are a civil servant, you must serve all over the country. You can't have someone just work in one place all the time and eventually get to be district chief. [But why not?] That would make a lot of difficulties. It's much better to have a person come from somewhere else to be district chief. If you let a local person be district chief, naturally he would have his family right there, and it would be nothing but cliques and factions. [But why doesn't that happen with canton and village chiefs, since they are local people?] It does happen occasionally, but it is not much of a problem, because they have no authority at all. The canton chief, for example, is just like a liaison between the village and the district, he just keeps track of the village councils and reports to the district chief, who is the one with the authority. The same with the village councils, they are responsible for only a small area, and they just carry out the decisions of the central government, make up rosters, birth and death certificates, etc.—they really just do what the district chief tells them to do.

In July 1955, Si was succeeded by Do van Doan,[12] a man with a similar social outlook but a stronger and more independent character. Like Si, Doan gradually worked his way up in the colonial administration. Also like Si, he took an "idyllic" view of Vietnamese rural life.

Before 1945 there was little strife in the countryside, because the land was fertile, the people had plenty of money, and life was easy. Landlords could easily cultivate the land, and they would often lend money to help the tenants buy seed and water buffalo, build houses, or even aid in family matters, like weddings and funerals. As a consequence, the relationship between landlord and tenant had been warm and cooperative for many generations, and there was no reason at all for any trouble between them. Landlords easily collected land rents and paid their agricultural taxes to the government, the price of agricultural produce was maintained, and much was exported every year. There was no disorder in the countryside, and few disputes between landlord and tenant.

In 1945, however, the Vietminh disturbed this rural tranquility with a policy of "scorched-earth resistance and class struggle, killing landlords and unsettling the countryside, so that the landlords had to flee to the cities and abandon their fields to the tenants." By 1954, when the landlords returned to their estates "with the hope of returning production to normal," the peasants had a contemptuous attitude toward them, no longer evincing the respect for landlords which they had displayed before the war.[13]

While Doan was province chief, the rural situation was beginning to return to "normal":

Order in the countryside was relatively good. Most of the tenants were paying rent at the rate of 15 percent to 25 percent of the crop as established by the government, with most of the disputes between landlord and tenant concerning either the owner's abuse of the right to re-

---

12. A pseudonym at his request.
13. Doan and his wife own some land in Go Cong province, but he noted with regret that after a few years it was no longer safe to return to collect rents, and impossible to take legal action against the tenants who refused to pay.

cover his land to farm himself, or failure to respect the legal option of the tenant currently farming the land to buy it, or else the tenant's failure to pay rent. The majority of these disputes were resolved amicably and speedily by the province Agricultural Affairs Committee, chaired by myself or my deputy, according to the report of the chief of the province Land Service. In this way it was unnecessary to bring suit in the Land Court, and by awakening both sides to their proper interests we in some measure succeeded in conciliating the interests of landlords and tenants and in avoiding communist influence over the peasantry.

Doan considered that the Diem regime's land-reform program, planned but not yet carried out during his tenure as province chief, later aggravated the stabilizing rural situation, by creating hatred and bitterness between landlord and tenant.

By Ordinance 57 of October 22, 1956, the House of Ngo[14] expropriated any landlord's property over 100 hectares, with the declared intention of giving land to the landless peasants and directing landlords into industry in order to speed the industrialization of the country. But in fact this was just a demagogic scheme to gain the peasants' good will at the cost of alienating a small number of landlords who, Diem claimed, had concentrated control of too much land.

It appears that this policy was not well received by the peasants, because under it they had to pay for the land as well as pay agricultural taxes to both the government and the Vietcong. But the communists had already confiscated most of this land and distributed it free, one-half to one hectare to each family.

As for actual reforms during his tenure, there were none, "because the central government was too busy repressing antigovernment elements (Vietminh, Binh Xuyen, Cao Dai, and Hoa Hao) and organizing the referendum to remove Bao Dai and establish the republic." There were, however, certain limited programs of rural assistance.

In some of the larger towns, the government was able to construct, thanks to American aid, a number of school buildings, and to enlarge some others, as well as to provide additional medical supplies and instruments for the dispensaries. Several orphanages and old people's homes were also aided. There was a program to provide inexpensive and good quality fertilizer for the peasants, and they could also borrow money

---

14. For reasons clarified below, Doan continually referred to the Diem regime by terms formerly used in describing the imperial family, such as the House of Ngo and the Ngo Dynasty.

from the government on easy terms for seed and agricultural tools such as water pumps. These measures were welcomed by the people, but nowhere were they near sufficient. Their effectiveness was also limited in part by Vietcong terrorism and anti-American propaganda, particularly in the remote villages.

Listening to Doan, one is impressed by his emphasis on justice and uprightness, within the limits of his social outlook, and his strong southern regionalism. These aspects of his character proved to be his undoing in the National Assembly election of March 1956 and also explain a puzzling aspect of previous interviews: that no one mentioned fraud in the 1956 elections, although many did so regarding those of 1959 and 1963.

According to the official typed instructions I received from Saigon, the election was to be completely free, just, and impartial. But several days before the day of the election [March 4] a special envoy arrived from Saigon with verbal orders for myself and Major X, the sector commander,[15] to do whatever was necessary to ensure that one particular candidate was elected. If these instructions were not carried out, I would be removed immediately. But not only was the government candidate not as qualified as the others, he was a downright undesirable character. Major X came over and asked me, "What are we going to do?" I told him I had written orders to carry out a fair election, so let each person follow his own conscience. On the evening of the 4th, I announced the outcome of the election, in which the government candidate was defeated. The next morning an envoy arrived from Saigon and informed me that by order of President Diem I was to leave the province within forty-eight hours and return to Saigon for further instructions. There was not even to be a change-of-office ceremony.[16] Major X was the only one who dared even to see me off.

When I returned to Saigon I was given a desk at the Ministry of the Interior with nothing to do. There were three separate investigations in Tan An and My Tho [where Doan had formerly been province chief] to find some evidence of wrongdoing to try me, but after six months they came up with nothing, and I was given a minor job at the ministry for the

---

15. "Sector" is the military equivalent of the province level in the administrative system. During this period the province chief was the senior civil servant in charge of all administrative organs in the province, and the sector commander was the senior military officer in charge of the military forces belonging to the province, at that time consisting of the *Bao An* (Civil Guard), organized by districts, and the *Dan Ve* (People's Self-Defense Force), organized at village level.

16. Long An in fact had no province chief for the next three months.

next seven years. I hardly even dared to look around in the office with
all the Can Lao people there watching me, and in those days it was impossible to resign—many others had tried—they were just led off in the
middle of the night by Diem's men dressed as VC, taken to P-40 or
Poulo Condore, and never heard from again.[17]

Almost certainly because of this fate, Doan was one of the first
to be sensitive to important shortcomings of the Diem regime. Thus,
in accounting for the subsequent development of the opposition, he
emphasized what he viewed as the dictatorial and discriminatory
nature of the regime.

Under the Diem regime, the majority of people were employed because of their loyalty to the Ngo family rather than their ability or their
willingness to serve their country. If one wanted to have a position, one
had to be a member of the Can Lao party, a Catholic, and a central
Vietnamese. As a result, in the army as well as the civil administration,
the majority of the leading officials were opportunists, bootlickers, and
incompetents, and the effectiveness and initiative of the army and the
administration were destroyed. But without a good administration no
policy, good or bad, can be carried out. . . . The Diem regime's blind
anticommunism . . . its antipopular policies, such as strategic hamlets
and agrovilles, Madame Nhu's family law, the special military courts of
Law 10/59[18] and the Communist Denunciation Campaign . . . forced
many noncommunists into the underground, where they joined the communists in the National Liberation Front. Their grievances were skillfully
exploited by the communists to win popular support and expand their
power.

Thus from Doan's viewpoint the subsequent vast increase in
antigovernment activity after he left Long An was caused principally
by abuses of government officials and by general administrative in-
competence, rather than by underlying conditions in the rural society
itself, which Doan viewed as satisfactory to both peasants and landlords. In any case Doan's observations, however correct, could not
be expressed during the Diem period, and even in 1968 he hesitated
to discuss them, because he saw the same "opportunists, bootlickers,
and incompetents" of the Diem regime still in the government.

Doan's removal as province chief was among the first of many

---

17. "P-40" is the number of a room at the Saigon Zoo used during the
Diem regime for the torture of political opponents.
18. Law 10/59 was promulgated in May 1959, and provided harsh penal-
ties for virtually any type of involvement with the revolutionary movement.

steps the Diem regime was to take in Long An to streamline the bureaucracy and to tighten its hold on the countryside. By early 1956 the regime's control of the central government was assured: it had eased out the French, broken the armed resistance of the religious sects and the Binh Xuyen, arranged for a properly docile National Assembly, and obtained what subsequently proved to be an almost unconditional commitment from the United States. It was now in a position to turn its attention to the provinces and purge the country-side of communists and other disloyal or "nonresponsive" elements, such as Doan.

In June 1956, Memorandum 802/BPTT/VP was sent by the Ministry of the Interior to the provinces. It definitively abolished the elective village administrative councils (hoi dong huong chinh) established by Bao Dai in 1953 and prescribed new procedures for organizing local military and security organs. In part the memorandum read:

> While awaiting a general statute [to regularize village government], province chiefs are requested to replace existing village administrative councils with administrative committees.
> An administrative committee will consist of three persons:
> —One chairman, concurrently in charge of administration,
> —One deputy chairman, concurrently in charge of financial, social, and economic matters,
> —One police commissioner.
> In large villages, with substantial budgets, it is encouraged to appoint two additional personnel, one for finance and one for administration.
> Individuals appointed to the administrative committee must meet the following requirements:
> 1. born and currently residing in the village;
> 2. anticommunist and antirebel background;
> 3. loyal to the republic;
> 4. energetic in performance.
> Province chiefs should coordinate with the various security, military, civilian, Civil Guard, Civic Action, and other agencies in carefully investigating and selecting members. Province and district chiefs bear full responsibility for selection.
> Naturally, former village officials meeting the above conditions may be selected. The commander of the village People's Self-Defense Force will concurrently be the police commissioner, so that his mission may be more clearly understood and security better maintained.
> In cases where it is not possible to select a police commissioner, the province chief will coordinate with the province Civil Guard to select a

noncommissioned officer to fill this position, in which case the birth and residence requirements will not apply.

Thus reform of village government should proceed together with the organization of the People's Self-Defense Force.

That little regard was being paid to legal technicalities during this period is shown by the fact that this memorandum did not have sufficient legal authority to supersede the decree under which the previous village administrative councils had been established—hence the reason for noting that a "general statute" was forthcoming. It took seven years, however, for the "general statute" to appear. It is also noteworthy that this memorandum only ratified an existing situation: in large areas of Long An councils had been appointed because elections could not be held under the 1953 (or earlier) legislation, and such councils as had been elected had for the most part disappeared by 1955.

This memorandum also mentioned a number of matters pertaining to security. In one section it emphasized that the province chiefs were to proceed expeditiously with the establishment of the Dan Ve, as provided in a previous directive, and that responsibility for their recruitment, administration, and employment rested with the province chief, not with any branch of the central government. It also stressed a previous decision that all organizations pertaining to security were to be placed under the direct operational authority of the province chief. In another paragraph it foreshadowed the future agroville program:

Because of the scattering of the population over large and remote areas, causing difficulties for the maintenance of security, province chiefs are requested to investigate the usefulness of establishing small towns to resettle the population in several more easily defensible places, naturally having adequate conditions for living and economic development.

Four months later, in October 1956, a major change in provincial administration was brought about by Ordinance 57a, which made the province chiefs the principal agents of the central government outside Saigon, and placed them directly under the president's authority. Henceforth province chiefs were to be appointed by the president and would be charged with the direction of all government agencies operating in a province, including the various ministries, the regular police and the Cong An, and the Dan Ve and Bao An. In exceptional circumstances a province chief even could order into action elements of the national army stationed in his province. The regional delegate was reduced to an advisory and inspection role. In a memorandum accompanying Ordinance 57a, President Diem stated:

> By Ordinance 17 of December 24, 1955, the status of juridical person and independent budget of the regions was eliminated and the reorganization of the Vietnamese administrative system was begun. I wish now to inform you that with Ordinance 57a of October 24, 1956, I have completed that reorganization process, with the following objectives:
>
> 1. to expand the powers and responsibilities of the province chief;
> 2. to fix the new duties of the regional delegate.
>
> This completes the reforms that the government had planned in order to increase the effectiveness of administration.
>
> The province chief is to be the representative of the central government and not of any particular ministry. In the future he will have to bear many more responsibilities than before, but at the same time he will have more means at his disposal.

In the opening months of 1957, however, another significant step was taken. The positions of province chief and sector commander were combined in one individual, henceforth to be a field-grade military officer. This was symbolic of the approach the regime was to take in dealing with disgruntled elements. It was also partly motivated by an attempt to force discipline on the administrative system, necessitated, for example, by Doan's disobedience in failing to rig the March elections.

The last civilian province chief of Long An was Bui van Ba.[19] Unlike his predecessors, Ba was born in Saigon rather than in the provinces, but to a large extent he shared their paternalistic attitude toward the peasantry. Ba recalled that during the last six months of 1956 the situation in Long An was still "full of hope." Antigovernment activity, though slightly increasing, was still at a low level and was limited mainly to tax collections and propaganda, particularly against the government-sponsored land-reform program. The peasants themselves were quite content, Ba felt, and if any dissatisfactions existed, they were minor, concerning perhaps some difficulties in making a living, or personal grievances against individual soldiers or village council members. Although the central government had not provided for village elections, Ba believed that it would have been

---

19. In 1968 Secretary General of the Ministry of Social Welfare.

possible to carry them out in all regions except a few hamlets near the Plain of Reeds, where travel was difficult and antigovernment activity was greater.

During Ba's tenure as province chief there was no program to strengthen local government, as, for example, by training appointees or increasing manpower at the local level. Ba felt, however, that the situation had improved somewhat over that of the French occupation, because canton and village officials were now more easily approachable by the people and were less "mandarinal and feudalistic." Moreover, "Democracy had been established by then—we already had the republic set up. We had National Assembly elections, so the people had representatives." Responding to a remark that electing a single National Assembly representative did not yet mean democracy for the villagers in Long An, Ba seemed rather pained: "No matter how you look at it, we had had elections, so the situation was perfectly all right. That was a good start toward the later elections."

Ba replied in much the same way as Si to an inquiry, why district and province chiefs were not elected.

There is no way that district and province chiefs could be elected—they are civil servants. [But why?] In my opinion the people have not yet reached the point where these officials could be elected, as in other more advanced countries. . . . If a local person were to be district or province chief, there would be the problem of his relatives and family—it would be hard for him to speak plainly and to work for the public good. [But why don't you have that problem with canton and village officials?]. . . . Canton and village officials do not have broad powers like those of the district chief. Their role is only as a liaison between the people and the higher echelons, like district and province, so it is not necessary to employ nonlocal people.

According to Ba, the best way of dealing with communist influence was to develop true democracy, which he interpreted as helping the people toward economic self-sufficiency.

We must truly help the people to have a good life. If we just talk all the time but don't do anything, then the people will see that and say: the government makes a lot of promises but doesn't help us. . . . Only if we help the people, worry about their problems, will they follow us. . . . [As for specific programs while in Long An] we helped the people by selling fertilizer and rice seed at low prices. Agents also traveled around to show them how to plant rice, fruit trees, etc. In this way the people would have a good income and they would not be thinking about the communists.

Ba also felt that the land-reform program, which was just beginning in Long An when he was province chief, was "very effective," because "many former tenants became owners of their own land." Despite these assistance programs, Ba noted that the major effort to overcome opposition to the government was military, involving either small sweep operations or else the use of Cong An agents to seize communist cadres. After he became province chief, two extensive military operations were carried out in neighboring provinces over a period of many months. These consisted of sweeps by military forces into formerly strong opposition areas, followed by groups of information, youth, public-health, and assorted other cadres. "Usually the people wouldn't come to us, so we had to go to them." Ba carried out similar smaller operations in Long An, coordinating military sweeps with activities by various civilian cadres. He noted, however, that their effectiveness was questionable: "You just can't have a campaign one year, skip it the next, then abandon it permanently, and expect to have results. . . . It is necessary to have a continuous campaign." Theoretically, it was the responsibility of the appointed hamlet chiefs to carry out this function on a permanent basis, but as Ba noted, "they worried mostly about paperwork."

Ba attributed the increase of antigovernment activity, despite these military and civilian programs, to the fact that "the communists were close to the people." When asked why, even though there was security in the countryside, Ba replied: "That is a question I have never been able to answer." Later, however, he ascribed increasing communist strength to two factors: first, their propaganda was more effective (although he did not know why), and second, their policy was harsher than the government's:

> Because of their kind of regime they must be harsh, and the people fear them. For example, they may announce that there will be no more gambling. Then if anyone is caught gambling, he will be shot on the spot. But the government is democratic, we cannot just go and shoot anybody —we have to send them to court, then release them, arrest again, and so forth. That is the difference.

While this represents the view from the province chief's office, we may gain a different perspective on the reasons for antigovernment activity in the countryside, and on some of the shortcomings in the government program to "disinfect" the countryside of communist influence in the 1955–1956 period, from the comments of one of those people directly involved in carrying out the program. Nguyen van Long[20] began working as a Civic Action cadre in Tan Tru district of Long An in 1955, after coming to the South from Hanoi. The Civic Action program began in 1955 as a government effort to "get close to the people." The program, Long felt, was good in concept, because the cadres did not fall under the regular administrative chain of command but were responsible directly to the president. Moreover, they were to live close to the peasants, right in their homes, and most were young people not identified with the government. Arriving at Tan Tru, they were met and briefed by the district chief, then they consulted the council in the village where they were to work, and henceforth they dealt directly with the people, individually and in small meetings, to propagandize and to develop plans for local development, self-help projects, schooling, and so forth. When the six-man team first arrived, the villagers were skeptical and withdrawn, as they usually are with government officials, but after a short time confidence began to grow, owing to the obvious enthusiasm of the cadres and to the fact that they were not working for the local government.

There were numerous problems, however, and some grew worse as time went on. First, most of the cadres came from northern and central Vietnam. Initially, this created language problems in dealing with the peasants and hampered confidence. In time, however, those cadres who were effective were accepted, despite their accent. A second difficulty was the general quality of the cadres. Long said that his team was an exceptional one, but that the great majority of the cadres working in Long An should have been "thrown out," for they were ineffective and undisciplined, having obtained their jobs through family influence (at this time cadre pay was exceptionally high). The remainder were acceptable, and a few were outstanding. Another kind of problem had to do with inadequate support from above. Long described one incident at Tan Tru to illustrate this.

In one of our meetings with the peasants several people complained that the police chief was behaving very badly with some of the local women. Not that he was molesting them—rather he was associating with some of the less reputable ones and spending a lot of time carousing. They

---

20. A pseudonym.

didn't think a government official should behave that way. I was very noncommittal, just saying that I would investigate, and, if what they said were true, I would suggest action. That night I went to visit a friend in Tan An. When I got back the next day, I found that seven men had come during the night to the house I had been living in in the village. They mistook one of my friends for me and beat him up very badly.

Long reported this incident through his own channels, and eventually the police chief was transferred. He was not punished, however; he had relatives in the police directorate in Saigon. Because of occasional incidents such as this, and also because a number of less disciplined cadres got into trouble (for example, by getting local girls pregnant), the province chief wrote consistently bad reports to Saigon about their activities. In 1956 the cadres received instructions from Saigon to "stop all the investigating" and carry on with their work.

Theoretically, the Civic Action cadres were supposed to gain the people's favor by direct assistance at the local level, and then to trade on this influence to propagandize against communism. Long found that the villagers were pleased with the assistance provided by the cadres, but this did not help them with their propaganda mission, which met one insuperable obstacle: "We were supposed to explain why the communists were bad and why the people must follow the government. But during the Resistance the communists had been the only ones in the village to fight against the French, so when we tried to explain that communists were evil people, the villagers just didn't listen to us." Long also noted that in 1959, when they were working in a different area, the Civic Action cadres were responsible for falsifying the National Assembly election returns. It was no secret, and subsequently it became impossible to preach the evils of communism and the virtues of Diem-style democracy.

Together with the overt "denunciation of communism" campaigns carried out by the Civic Action and information cadres, there was another, less publicized effort to apprehend communist cadres and their supporters. In practice, however, this campaign was not carried out with the attention to democratic niceties which Ba suggested distinguished communist methods from those of the government. One village official from Long Huu Island in Can Duoc district described his own experience:

After Diem came to power, anybody who had had a relative with the Vietminh was arrested and beaten up. . . . Look what happened to me. . . . Lieutenant Ba[21] had me interrogated. They poured water in my nose, and then later hooked up a generator to my fingers and toes and cranked so hard I collapsed and wanted to die. . . . I told them, "Stop, stop, I confess, I haven't done anything but I confess anyway. . . ." After that they sent me down to Go Cong province, where a colonel interrogated me. I told him the truth, and he believed me and let me go. But all the rest of the people who had been involved with the Vietminh were sent to prison.[22]

According to this man, most of the people he know who were arrested were innocent, but it was still necessary for them to pay bribes to the village council to obtain their release. Moreover, a number of people, estimated by one former Civic Action cadre at about forty in Can Duoc district alone, were forced to flee to avoid arrest, imprisonment, or worse. They obtained refuge with the few communist cadres still operating in remote areas of the province.

A much more complete view of the situation during these years may be gained by considering the testimony of Party members themselves. Events within the Party[23] from the signing of the Geneva Accords until about 1960 remain largely unknown. Research in Vietnam has been handicapped by the earlier obsessive secrecy of the Diem regime and by the continuing strictures of military classification, as well as by the lack of area specialists qualified in the Vietnamese language and of financial support for independent scholarly work. Conditions within the revolutionary movement itself during the same period also have made research exceedingly difficult. From 1954 to 1959 there was no mass front, and thus the active cadres were almost entirely long-term Party members. The only ones who could reveal to us the Party policies and deliberations, and the vacillations of the "line," during those years were defectors from this hard core—and there have been very few. There have been many defectors from the group which began to work for the Party in 1959

---

21. Like the province chief, also named Bui van Ba. This individual was later promoted to chief of Can Giuoc district. He is now retired.

22. Political suspects were not tried in the regular courts, but were judged by a "Security Committee" consisting of the province chief or his deputy, the public prosecutor, the chief of the provincial police, and one private citizen appointed by the province chief "to preserve democratic forms." The accused did not have defense counsel.

23. For continuity with the quotations from captured documents and from interviews with former members, the Lao Dong Party will be referred to simply as "the Party," the term its members invariably use.

and after, but in keeping with Party practice these individuals initially worked entirely at the village level and thus were not privy to events within the higher councils of the Party. Furthermore, documents from the period before 1960, when the Party's organization was scant, are extremely rare. The period from 1954 to 1956 is especially obscure, because many Party members who might have defected later simply did not survive.

It may be useful to begin by describing the organizational structure of the Party—a structure that has remained remarkably constant for more than twenty years. The Party in Vietnam is organized as a hierarchical system of committees consisting of six echelons, stretching from the Central Committee in Hanoi to the village level in the South. Subordinate echelons have the task of transmitting decisions of the Central Committee, adapting them to the specific situation in their own areas, supervising their execution, and reporting back to higher echelons, much as in a conventional military organization. The Party organization is sharply different from conventional military organization, however, in its provision for leadership by committee at each level.

Party committees vary in size, depending on several factors, such as an area's degree of development and the number of directly subordinate committees. Typically, they range from ten to twenty members, headed by a secretary and a deputy secretary. Ordinarily, committee members are drawn from two sources: committee secretaries from the immediately subordinate echelon, and chiefs of the committee's own specialized branches, such as finance, propaganda and training, military affairs, and so forth. The committees meet for only a short period each month to discuss policy and reach decisions by majority vote, after which members return to their own areas of responsibility to carry out decisions. A small current-affairs committee and a housekeeping staff remain at the physical location of the committee to handle routine matters.

A few comments are in order on the special characteristics of each of the committee echelons. The Central Committee is the supreme continuous policy-making body for the entire Party, although it is subordinate to an infrequent Party Congress. During the initial period of the war against the French, the echelon in the South immediately beneath the Central Committee was the Nam Bo Regional Committee (*Xu Uy Nam Bo*). In 1951, due to the great distance between the Central Committee and the Nam Bo Regional Committee (then located in Ca Mau at the extreme southern tip of Vietnam), and to the need for more rapid decision-making as the war entered its conclusive phase, the Nam Bo Regional Committee was reorganized into *Trung Uong Cuc Mien Nam*. This is ordinarily translated as the Central Office for South Vietnam (COSVN), and for the sake of consistency with other writings the term will be retained here. However, this translation masks an important organizational shift, which is clear in the original Vietnamese: Central [Committee] Southern Branch. In other words, the status of the Nam Bo Regional Committee was altered from that of a subordinate echelon to that of a forward element of the Central Committee itself, by the assignment of a number of Central Committee members to permanent duty in the South.[24] As the regroupment to the North was completed early in 1955, COSVN reverted to its former status as the Nam Bo Regional Committee, charged with carrying out Central Committee policy in the special conditions of the South. (Seven years later, as the conflict in the South again intensified, the Nam Bo Regional Committee was to be reorganized a second time into COSVN by the addition of a number of members of the Central Committee from the North, empowered to make decisions on the spot which formerly would have to have been referred to Hanoi.)

Subordinate to the Nam Bo Regional Committee (now again COSVN) are three interprovince (or zone) committees for eastern, central, and western Nam Bo, each charged with supervisory responsibility over five to seven provinces, and one committee for the Saigon-Cholon Special Zone.[25] Interprovince committees have limited policy functions: their principal purpose is the serve as a liaison with the province committees. Without them COSVN's span of control would be stretched too thin to direct the activities of a score of province committees.

The most important function of the province committee is to adapt general Party policy to the specific circumstances of each province, and to develop plans for executing the policy appropriate to the local situation. In supervising the actual execution of policy by the village committees, the province is assisted by district committees. They perform for the province the same role of expanding

---

24. Details on the formation of COSVN in 1951 are contained in *Working Paper* Documents 11 and 211.

25. The provinces of central Vietnam lying south of the 17th parallel are supervised directly from the North as Interzone (sometimes Region) 5. For a comprehensive treatment see *Viet-Nam Documents and Research Notes*, Nos. 23 and 93.

span of control that interprovince committees perform for COSVN.

Finally, the basic organizational unit of the Party, the one directly responsible for carrying out Party policy, is the *chi bo* (usually translated as the Party chapter or branch), consisting of from a half-dozen to several hundred Party members, organized into cells of from three to seven members each. The chi bo may be organized in an industrial enterprise, an urban neighborhood, a military unit or, most importantly in rural Vietnam, at the village level.

From what can be pieced together more than a decade later about the Party apparatus in the South, it appears that the two years from the signing of the Geneva Accords until the summer of 1956 were a time of unparalleled disaster. The following description of this period is extracted from extensive conversations with Vo van An, a Party member for nineteen years and one of the highest ranking Party members to defect under the government Chieu Hoi program.[26] It is a sign of the Party's strength in Long An that of more than 4,000 communist and noncommunist defectors in that province during the decade of the sixties, not one was a Party committee member of higher than village level. An's only direct contact with Long An was a period of several months he spent there in 1964 recovering from a serious illness. However, at the time of his defection in 1965, he was a full member of the Tay Ninh province committee, responsible for the consolidation of the base area of COSVN. Because COSVN was located at that time in Tay Ninh, An had considerably more opportunity than did Party members from other provinces to learn of events at the higher levels within the Party, and to learn about activities in other areas of Vietnam from cadres traveling to Tay Ninh on business with COSVN. Nationwide, of approximately 75,000 Chieu Hoi returnees from 1963 through 1968, only three besides An were members of province committees.

During interviews An answered each question with the clarity and precision of the professor he probably would have been had he not joined the Party at the age of twenty-one. He described his own entry into the Party as follows:

---

26. The Chieu Hoi program offers amnesty and rehabilitation to individuals who voluntarily surrender themselves to the government. Returnees are indoctrinated for one or two months, after which they are released. Many receive technical training, others simply prefer to return to their homes, and a small number enter one of the many military, paramilitary, or armed propaganda units, where they frequently distinguish themselves. For many, however, finding employment is difficult.

At the very beginning of the Resistance I was a student in a French secondary school. Like almost every other youth at that time, I took part in armed activities, with the patriotic intention of liberating my people. After a time our organization, a suicide squad, was smashed, and in the reorganization I was selected to carry out political activities, because they saw I had ability in that area.

An became a Party member in 1946, and subsequently rose through the hierarchy, serving at village and district levels, and finally as an alternate member of the Tay Ninh province committee at the time of the armistice in 1954.

An's decision to leave the Party was based on a combination of personal and idcological factors. On the ideological level, An had long thought that the Party's strategy of armed conflict was unrealistic and was only bringing purposeless suffering to his country. On the personal level, he was unhappy with the Party's discrimination against him because of his class background as a "petty bourgeois intellectual," which meant that promotion was much more difficult for him than for a member of worker of peasant origin.[27] The catalytic incident occurred while An was recuperating from his serious illness in 1964. An was informed that he was to go to Russia, at the Party's expense, for medical treatment and for further ideological training. Unknown to An, however, the province committee wrote to his family requesting them to sell their remaining property to help defray expenses. An was furious when he found out: he felt that his family had contributed enough during the Resistance by selling all but one hectare of his inheritance. The one hectare now demanded was of *huong hoa*, the income of which must be used for ritual worship of the family's ancestors. The escalating recriminations growing out of this incident, coming on top of long-standing personal and policy disagreements, led An to break with the Party.

Although An's own responsibility during the Resistance had been political agitation and organization (*dan van*, literally "action among the people"), he admitted that the decisive element of the struggle before 1954 was the military effort, because the French and their clients had effectively accomplished the "propaganda work" for the Vietminh already. In An's words, "The people who sided with

---

27. Even getting into the Party is more difficult. Persons of worker and peasant origin must pass a three-month probation before admission to the Party. Intellectuals may be required to spend nine months or more on probation.

the French were just doing it for money, not an ideal: we knew it, and they knew it, and the people knew it. Thus the people were already with us." In this situation, the immediate task was very clear: a military effort proceeding through three stages from a defensive guerrilla struggle, through an intermediate stage of conventional confrontations, to the final general counteroffensive. In this military program, the strategy was "seize the forests and mountains, contest the open country, surround the cities."

The Party foresaw, however, that in the period following the Geneva Accords the situation would be more complex. Before 1954 the government had clearly been a tool of foreign powers; after 1954 the government would appear superficially to be independent. Thus political action would be the principal effort required in the post-Geneva situation, and this effort would be most decisive, so the Party initially believed, in the towns and cities, either in the event of elections, of other opportunities for seizing power such as a coup d'etat, or of anarchy resulting from the outbreak of fighting within the government armed forces. Because Saigon was the South's political and military nerve center, considerable manpower and resources were devoted to developing an organization in Saigon itself.

The process of regrouping individuals to the North was carried out selectively in accordance with the needs of this new policy emphasizing political activity. According to the slogan the Party brought forth at the time of the regroupment, either to remain in the South or to move to the North was equally honorable and desirable: "To go North means victory, to remain in the South is to bring success."[28] Said An:

In general the individuals regrouped were the military forces—that was the first criterion. The second category regrouped were specialists, because a certain number of people with special training were needed to build up the North. Third were what was called "special cases." For example, if I had been in the [Vietminh] security service and had incurred the enmity of the local population, I would be regrouped. A certain number were also sent to the North to keep a potential hold on certain families or regions [i.e., people who were to be sent back South later]. Those retained in the South, generally speaking, were the political forces. Also a

---

28. *Di la thang loi; o lai la thanh cong.* Party practice is to develop a simple slogan (*khau hieu*) for each of its current objectives among the masses or among its own members, using this slogan as a starting point in its study sessions and as a simple way of keeping the mission clear in everyone's mind.

great many military personnel with political abilities were ordered to remain in the South.

The military units regrouped to the North took only old weapons, leaving their newest weapons concealed in the South.

The mission of the individuals remaining behind was as follows:

The overall goal of those remaining behind was to develop a readily available force to carry out the Geneva Accords, i.e., to propagandize for the general elections. In reality, they were to develop both political and military forces, the latter being absolutely secret, to provide against any developments in the revolutionary situation in the coming years. Thus the slogan "to remain is to bring success" meant that they were to develop political and military forces to take advantage of any situation to gain power in the South— if by general elections, fine, but if not, then by whatever means were necessary.

Party members had operated fairly openly in most areas of the country during the Resistance, so with the regroupment, steps were taken to protect the structure remaining in the South, whose effectiveness would depend on the continued existence in each village of the Party's basic executive organ, the chi bo.

As regroupment started, the Party began a complete reorganization. For example, say that in village A there were 125 members. These were broken down into two groups, those who had been exposed and those who had maintained their secrecy. The unrevealed Party members might be only ten or twenty—10 or 20 percent unrevealed was good. These would be grouped into cells of three members each, and all the village cells organized into one secret chi bo charged with responsibility for that area. The remaining hundred or more who had been revealed as Party members would be dispersed to other areas where they were not known and controlled individually as single-contact members [*don tuyen*] by special cadres. These dispersed members could then begin to organize cells of their own in their new area.[29]

---

29. The dispersion movement was known in Vietnamese as *dieu lang*, a compound word of communist creation, meaning "to arrange so that things become peaceful again." Dispersed members were known only to one cadre responsible for controlling perhaps up to 100 of these single-contact members. This method of organization was used in preference to the cell system, as it provided greater security in case part of the organization was exposed. The disadvantage was that, if the controlling cadre were apprehended, the members he controlled would all be cut off from the Party, because they were not in contact with the local Party organization.

While at the village level almost all the members presented themselves to the authorities to obtain identification papers and take up a
legal existence, at higher levels, such as district and province, part
of the organization stayed underground. At higher levels still, such
as the Nam Bo Regional Committee, all members maintained an
illegal existence.

Under the new conditions in the South after the Geneva Accords, carrying on even the simplest Party administrative work was
much more difficult than it had been during the Resistance. Formerly, instructions from the Central Committee in the North could
be relayed to the village level in the South in two or three days,
because radio communication was maintained between province
(sometimes even district) and higher levels. Now, according to An,
only the Regional Committee maintained radio contact with Hanoi.
Contact with lower levels was by written message and could no
longer be openly written as an official message, as had been done
during the Resistance. Communications were instead disguised as
individual letters. This was difficult enough, and government efforts
to disrupt the Party apparatus seriously worsened the situation, particularly because of the security precaution that only one person at
each level ordinarily knew how to reach other levels. As a result,
instructions sometimes took months to reach the village level, and
thus the Party's ability to react to events was seriously hampered.

The Party maintained this extensive apparatus in the South
because of its attitude toward the Geneva Accords and its evaluation
of the chances of their being implemented. According to An, higher
level cadres (province and above) were certain that general elections
would never take place, although this was not discussed at lower
levels to maintain morale and so as not to conflict with the Party's
public stance that the Geneva Accords were a great victory for the
Party. By the summer of 1955 it became apparent to everyone what
the higher echelons in the Party had felt all along: there would be
no general elections and no steps toward reunification talks. The
leadership was not surprised. "We just considered Diem as a debtor
who refused to pay—we would force him to pay."

The likelihood of this outcome had been clearly perceived by
the Party in 1954, and hence in the regroupment a number of hard-
core military units had been retained in the South, in addition to the
political operatives who had also stayed behind. The Party's reasoning was, as An put it:

Why should the Party proclaim political activity as the main line but retain military forces? From a revolutionary viewpoint, the South was still a backward agricultural country, without any democratic tradition in which parliamentary struggle could be effective: it was still in the "national liberation" stage. In that stage, if one wants to carry out what we call the "revolutionary mission," force is the decisive element. Without it nothing can be accomplished.

These units were not to appear, however, for several years, during which time they were cut off completely from any contact with the world except through the Party. For these hard-core units, to endure for any length of time without combat was a great hardship, because shared sacrifice on the battlefield is the cement which holds such a unit together. Conditions of total isolation and inactivity, except for constant flight, were a terrible hardship which seriously affected their morale, particularly after the two-year period specified in the Geneva Accords passed. An described their situation thus:

After 1954 there were theoretically no communist armed forces left in the South, but in reality from province on up, each echelon maintained its own armed units. These were hard-core units, all members of which were at the very least Labor Youth, if not actually Party members. There were no mass forces at all. . . . These units were extremely well armed, and their main activity was in preserving the secret of their existence. . . . According to the Geneva Accords, there were to be no armed forces remaining in the South, so naturally it was necessary to show the masses, or, speaking more generally, to show the world, that the communist camp was correctly carrying out the Geneva Accords. Therefore it was necessary to preserve absolute secrecy. These units lived deep in the jungles "fleeing from people as if they were tigers." That is why I say they had to be Party members or at least Labor Youth, or they never would have been able to do it. They maintained no bases, no camps. . . . Each soldier had a hammock which was his home. . . . They were constantly on the move, avoiding contact with anyone, using every means of camouflage, covering their tracks, leaving absolutely no sign at all.

Five years later the remnants of these forces were to form the skeleton of the developing Liberation Army, as it was to be called. Intelligence reports from 1957 and 1958, for example, show the existence of seventeen major Party-controlled units in the South, variously called companies, battalions, or regiments, and varying in strength from fifty to two hundred. These were located principally on the Cambodian border and deep in the Delta, and were fully armed, including substantial quantities of light and heavy machine guns and even bazookas.[30]

A good illustration of both the Party's attitude toward the Geneva Accords and its difficulties of coordination and communication was its handling of the Binh Xuyen crisis in 1955. An estimated that at that time the Party had the capability of supplying up to eight fully armed regiments (6,000 men), which would have fought under the Binh Xuyen name without identification with the Party. Publicly, then, the Party would have avoided responsibility.

When the Binh Xuyen first opened war on Diem, we should have supplied arms and men and provided support. . . . But the responsible cadres failed to seize the opportunity and take full advantage of the situation. . . . If we had done so the armed conflict between the Binh Xuyen and the Diem regime would have been expanded and prolonged and so produced great benefit for the Party. Instead we allowed the Binh Xuyen to be smashed and only then did we begin to introduce supplies and men and take hold of the Binh Xuyen forces in order to preserve them.[31]

I was not responsible for this operation, and do not know all the details, but afterwards in the evaluation sessions the cadres who were responsible were reprimanded for their "mechanical interpretation" of the provisions of the Geneva Accords forbidding military activity. . . . Higher levels had not been able to provide timely leadership to overcome these errors in outlook because, after the Geneva Accords, all activity was carried on in secret, and the means of communication were extremely limited.

In 1954, then, the Party had prepared, it thought, against all contingencies in the coming years by maintaining secret military forces, extensive arms caches, and a widespread network of politi-

---

30. Contained in *Ban Tran Liet Viet Cong* [Vietcong Order of Battle], a classified intelligence document produced annually and later semi-annually during this period by the Cong An. Excerpts from these reports, copied by the author from Cong An archives, are included in the material deposited with the Center for Research Libraries.

31. Aside from the leverage it obtained over these units by providing their necessary supplies, the Party also ensured effective control by placing members in key positions. One battalion operating in 1958, for example, was nominally Binh Xuyen, but of the three key positions of commander, deputy commander, and "political officer," only the commander was of Binh Xuyen origin, whereas the other two were Party members. See *Ban Tran Liet Viet Cong*, cited in the previous footnote.

cal operatives. The latter in particular was to be the key element in the Party's eventual take-over, operating either alone in a purely political strategy, or as the local eyes and ears for the reserve military forces should events require their use. Although the Geneva Accords provided that no action could be taken against Resistance members for their former antigovernment activities, the Party had taken steps to protect its political apparatus, as well.

What subsequently happened, however, far exceeded the Party's worst expectations, as the government proceeded unhindered with an extensive manhunt in the cities and the countryside, ultimately destroying almost the entire political apparatus that the Party had concealed in the South. In Tay Ninh, An's home province, 50 percent of the cells were smashed by the summer of 1955, and 90 percent by the summer of 1956, with the members either imprisoned or killed. A similar ratio prevailed in other parts of the South, according to An's talks with cadres traveling to Tay Ninh from other provinces, and in central Vietnam the situation was even worse. An's own experience in Tay Ninh is worth quoting:

According to the Geneva Accords, there would be no revenge against former Resistance members, who were to return as ordinary citizens. But the problem was not so simple. Returning cadres did not become faithful citizens by any means, but were still "revolutionary fighters." Likewise, on the government side they were treated on paper just like ordinary citizens, but in reality the government employed every means to track them down and arrest them. This took place everywhere, but particularly in the areas where the movement had formerly been strong. . . . After arrest, the cadres would be liquidated. For example, in my area two village cadres were arrested in the middle of the night, walked out to the corner and then given a shove. As they started to run they were shot in the back. The police said later that they had orders only to arrest them, but that the cadres fought back and tried to escape. Actually, it was all arranged that way just to liquidate them. . . .

Like these two village cadres, I had been a cadre in the Resistance. Because I was well known in the province, the police had a full file on me when I turned myself in and applied for government identity papers. They supplied me with the papers just like everyone else, but secretly they were following me. At the time of course I was still an active cadre responsible for the leadership of the Party in my area. My wife had a small store in our village, and I just worked as a farmer, planting peanuts and sugar cane on our family's plot of land.

We lived right next to the military outpost in the village, and during the day I would sit and drink coffee with the soldiers and the village officials. Everyone knew that I had been in the Resistance, but that I had now returned and was just an ordinary citizen. Yet at night I always had to slip off and sleep somewhere else. . . . Less than three months after I turned myself in, I got word that the Cong An had received orders to liquidate a number of important cadres, so I was particularly on my guard. The night before they attempted to seize me, they got the district secretary by making it look as if a gang of thieves had broken into his house and shot him. The next afternoon when I was riding my bike home, I saw a number of people riding after me who I knew were Cong An. That evening I turned up all the lanterns in my house so they could plainly see I was home, and then I climbed out the back window and followed one of my agents into the forest. About twelve or one o'clock the Cong An burst in, thinking I was still at home, but I had actually crept out at eleven. After that I had to live secretly.

The government's attempts to ferret out and destroy the Party apparatus were made easier by the negligent manner in which Party members handled the matter of secrecy.

Party activities took place in absolute secrecy. But to meet in hiding was difficult, so ordinarily members would rely on public or semipublic events to conceal their activities. For example, each week the three members of a cell would have to meet. They might choose to get together for a drinking party or for some family anniversary—these things were very common activities in the village, which the authorities did not officially sanction but which they didn't forbid either. . . . However, we must face the fact that Southerners are not very good at keeping secrets. Although the Party has had much experience in secret activity, here in the South since 1945 Party members in general were experienced only in armed resistance against the French. Except for some special branches in the cities and towns, they operated openly and hence were not accustomed to secret activity. Trying to reorganize these exposed members into secret units was like trying to turn an elephant into a mouse—they were very easily exposed. Whenever a number of members collaborated for a few months, they would be revealed. Then the ones who had been exposed would have to be dispersed and the rest reorganized again. . . . In this way from 1954 to 1956 every chi bo was exposed and reorganized at the very least from three to four times, creating enormous difficulties in communications.

Thus by the spring of 1956 it was clear to the Party that its plans for seizing power in the South within two years had failed. The Diem regime had not yielded on the point of reunification talks or general elections, although this had come as no surprise. Yet neither had the South fallen into chaos, allowing the Party, as the only organized force, to seize power with the extensive military and political apparatus it had left in readiness. On the contrary, its underground apparatus had been extensively damaged. Moreover, pressure on the Party was clearly about to increase as the Diem regime, having consolidated its control over the central government, turned its attention to the countryside. Thus sometime around the middle of 1956 the Party made the decision to rebuild its apparatus in the South, but now with a new strategy for seizing power summed up in the slogan it passed down to its cadres with instructions to rebuild: "*Truong ky mai phuc suc tich luc luong don lay thoi co*," or "To lie patiently in ambush, gathering one's forces, waiting to strike at the right moment."

In looking back on the Resistance period, one is not surprised that the government lost the countryside to the Vietminh. The great difference between ruler and ruled in their perception of the rural situation almost guaranteed that the steps the government took would be the wrong ones, because its understanding of the rural situation was so badly flawed. To high officials, the countryside was basically happy, and grievances were ipso facto communist-inspired and thus to be ignored. Yet from the viewpoint of the peasantry, the rural situation was by no means happy. How to reconcile these conflicting views? Perhaps the official view of a contented countryside was once true in a sense, with authoritative and respected village councils ruling locally, and peasants quietly farming the lands and paying their rents without complaint. But the reality behind this picture was well expressed by a Vietnamese encountered in Long An: "If you are a tenant farmer whose family has worked the same land for the same landlord family for the past century, keeping just enough to live and paying the rest to the landlord, and if you and your father and his father had always been told that this was right, and nothing had ever challenged this, then it is likely that you are going to think like an obedient tenant farmer, and so are your sons." This fatalistic passive attitude of the peasantry was for a time a terrific stumbling block to the Vietminh; but one of their most enduring accomplishments in the South was the decisive destruction of this fatalism. It was as if they had given eyeglasses to a man nearsighted since birth. The peasantry had *seen* the landlords run, they had *seen* the village councils forced to sleep in outposts and to move in the countryside with armed escorts. As night fell in the countryside, the peasants saw where lay the power of the conflicting sides: the Vietminh slept with the people, the village councils slept with the soldiers in the outposts. The nine years of the Resistance had destroyed the sense of inevitability which had kept the "contented peasants" quietly farming the fields.

Except for the midnight shots marking the execution of former Resistance members, the period from 1954 to 1956 was one of relative peace for Long An. Doubtless the government had gained some credit for the removal of the French, and many followers of the Vietminh turned from communist leadership to cooperate with the regime in Saigon. There had also been a noticeable change in the composition of the village councils, a permanent consequence of the Resistance. Traditional village notables now no longer wished to serve on the village council in such numbers as before. They generally explained this by saying that the posts—whether on the ban hoi te, the hoi dong huong chinh, or the appointed post-1956 councils—no longer retained their previous "prestige." In reality, however, this "prestige" had been a monopoly of power to protect their position in a society whose day had passed forever. The daily sight on the village roads of those who had killed landlords was a powerful reminder of that fact.

Yet this modest improvement in the social composition of the government village councils was small compared to the enormous shift in the locus of local power effected by the Vietminh during the Resistance. For in fact in Long An the overwhelming, immediate, and practical significance of the Resistance had not been the elimination of the French presence, which had not been significant, but rather the overthrow of the power of the local elite, which the French had employed to carry out the functions of the central government in the countryside. In terms of actual impact on daily life, the Resistance had meant an economic revolution to the peasant, and only incidentally was it anti-French. The genius of the Vietminh had been their skillful synthesis of these two aspects of the Resistance. Indeed they described their movement as *phan de bai phong*: anti-imperialist and antifeudal. One could not succeed without the other. By bringing an antifeudal revolution to the countryside, they motivated the peasantry to serve an anti-imperialist revolution as well. The organizational key to their success had been the relative strength of their village organization: the chi bo. The absence of any comparable government organization to do battle on the crucial level of the village meant that much of the population went to the Vietminh almost by default.

Thus the return to the countryside of the exiled government village councils in 1954 under the Geneva Accords was regressive in its impact, as if the eyeglasses had suddenly been taken from the nearsighted man. The village councils always found themselves in the position of making demands on the population: for annoying paperwork, for taxes, for "volunteers" for the Dan Ve, for rents for the landlords. By 1956 they had no more resources than had the ban hoi te of the French, and they were now more than ever an instrument of the central government. Local government thus had no firmer foundation than a leaf floating on the ocean. The only thing that had changed since 1954 was that the ocean had temporarily abated its violent churning.

By 1956, then, it could not be said that anyone "controlled" Long An, politically or militarily. The mass of the peasantry felt no loyalty to the government-sponsored village councils; nor was the government strong enough to exercise unchallenged "control." Its forces were sufficient to deal with the local tipplers and hooligans, but the politically disaffected could always pick up and move a few miles to an area where government influence did not reach. The open areas in the Delta are too large to "control"; government opponents were simply driven out to where they could plot in secret. Neither did the Party exercise "control": its underground apparatus had been severely damaged, though in such a clumsy fashion that considerable resentment had been created even among those who had not fled or been imprisoned. The Party was retaining its vestigial military forces in absolute secrecy, well realizing that without an underground apparatus they were useless. In this situation the government appeared to have "control" only in default of overt violent opposition. Thus to say that the government later "lost control" is misleading, and any analysis which proposes to answer the question of why the government "lost control" or why there was an "erosion of mass support for established institutions" is addressing the wrong question.

By 1956 both the Party and the government had begun to develop their rival holds on the countryside. Both sides had advantages and disadvantages. The government's simple but immensely important advantage was that it could operate openly, while the Party's need for secrecy greatly hampered its work. Because it was the internationally recognized legal authority in the South, the Diem government was also free to use its military forces, as for example, in the large sweeps of rural areas begun in 1956. The Party, on the other hand, was limited in this respect, because a resurgence of organized armed activity against the Diem authorities would clearly be identified with the regime in the North. The government was also in a position to draw openly upon extensive foreign resources, economic, technical, and military. Finally, the government, with the departure of the French, could claim itself a legitimate nationalist alternative to the Party. Thus the Party had lost a unifying symbol of first importance, although it was still able to draw on its nationalist reputation made during the Resistance, especially in the rural areas where the majority of the population lived. Both the government and the Party, as we have seen, had the structure of a ruling organization, especially at the higher levels. The government had its system of village councils, district and province chiefs, and the regional delegate and central ministries leading up to the Presidency—all now theoretically invigorated by the reorganization of 1956. The Party retained its pre-1954 organization of hierarchical executive committees, stretching from the chi bo in each village up to the Central Committee, now established in Hanoi.

Yet the village structures of each were weak. The Party's once strong local organization had been smashed by the government, while the government's local organs had never been strong. It was here that the Party held its decisive advantage. In terms of actual composition and the interests it served, the government was a melange of urban middle-class and elite elements, landlords, and mandarin remnants, generally French educated if not actually with French citizenship, whose breadth of social vision was typified by the three former province chiefs quoted above. While the technical skills of this group were considerable, its organizational skills at the local level had been poor compared to the Vietminh, and it had ruled in the rural areas through social elements whose interests in practice were hostile to the interests of the people they ruled. The Vietminh, on the other hand, had built up a strong local organization based on landless or land-poor elements; thus from its experience in the Resistance the Party had both a better rural organization and more actual and potential sympathy. By dominating the villages, it had rendered the central government helpless. In the words of one former Vietminh cadre: "You have the central government, then the province, district, and village. But the lowest of the four is the level that lies with the people. If the village level is weak, then I guarantee you, no matter how strong the central government is, it won't be able to do a thing."

In 1956, then, the government "declared war" on the remaining elements of opposition in the countryside through a combination of efforts: tightening the administrative organization and extending it to the family level, increasing the efforts of its civilian programs to win over the uncommitted, and intensifying its military and police efforts to root out the opposition. The Party also decided to destroy the Diem regime and complete the revolution interrupted in 1954. It moved more quietly, simply keeping up a steady stream of anti-government propaganda while secretly ordering the rebuilding of its Party structure.

Nguyen van No and Mac van Minh had fought together in the Resistance. For nine years No had been the chairman of the Binh Thanh village Committee of Resistance and Administration, while Minh had been the chairman of the village Vietminh front committee and a Party member. In 1955 both returned to the government, but after a few months Minh fled to avoid seizure by the Cong An, while No became a village information cadre for the government. From time to time they saw each other, and No would inquire what Minh was doing. Minh answered that he was just avoiding the Cong An, trying to keep from getting arrested. Then in the fall of 1956 No received a letter from Minh. "Diem is a tool of the Americans," the letter said; "The Americans trained him for years. Now they have made him president, and he has refused to carry out the elections for reunification with the North. We are now rebuilding the movement to topple Diem and bring about general elections. You accomplished much for the revolution during the nine years of the Resistance—we want you to rejoin us." No ignored the letter, merely turning it over to the district chief. In January 1957 he received a similar letter, which he also ignored. Finally he received a third, again asking him to return, but warning, "If you do not, the revolution cannot guarantee your life and property."

Long An's days of peace were drawing to an end.

CHAPTER TWO

Preparations for War

The Province Chief's View

I was very democratic.

MAI NGOC DUOC, Province Chief 1957–1961

To understand the government of Long An from 1957 to 1961, it is necessary above all to understand the personality and attitudes of Mai Ngoc Duoc.[1] Quite simply, he was the government. It is no exaggeration to say that for most of his tenure his authority in the province was exceeded only by that of the president. On those issues Duoc chose to contest, he did not hesitate to go directly to President Diem, bypassing the Minister of the Interior, the corps commander, and even, it seems, Diem's brother Nhu.

Duoc is the type of individual who generates strong reactions, favorable or unfavorable, in those who encounter him. Duoc's character is complex, and the record of his tenure as province chief is marked by contradictions. Personally honest, he was plagued by corrupt subordinates; although "close to the people" in his own mind, he was uniformly considered to be the most remote and forbidding province chief in Long An's history; although decisive and hardworking, under his leadership the government in Long An collapsed. The key to Duoc, if there is one, may be the temperament of his birthplace, Hue, for centuries the seat of the Vietnamese emperors.

Hue is the center of Vietnamese traditionalism, and its people consider themselves as the only true preservers of the Vietnamese heritage.[2] Central Vietnam, where Hue is located, never became a colony like the South. Instead, French power was exercised through the imperial government, which continued its tradition of a small ruling elite emphasizing rank, formalism, elaborate ceremony, proper signs of submission to authority—or what is known in the West as

---

1. Pronounced Zuoc.
2. Hue has also, it should be noted, been a center of revolutionary and anticolonial activity as well. The Quoc Hoc, attended by Ngo dinh Diem as noted below, was also attended by such leading revolutionary figures as Ho Chi Minh, Vo Nguyen Giap, and Pham van Dong.

the mandarin mentality. The language of central Vietnam is also different from that of the South, both in vocabulary and in pronunciation, so that a person raised in central Vietnam often finds it difficult to be understood by Southerners. The people of Hue are the "puritans" of Vietnam, differing considerably from their countrymen in the South in language, dress, manners, and attitudes. They feel that Southerners are lazy, undisciplined, and hopelessly corrupted by foreign influences. Southerners, in turn, feel that central Vietnamese are narrow and outdated.

It was in the mandarin atmosphere of Hue that Mai Ngoc Duoc grew up as the son of a member of the imperial service. Duoc attended the Quoc Hoc, a nationalist school founded by the father of President Diem and later attended also by Diem himself. Duoc joined the imperial administration and became successively chief of the districts of Cam Lo, Gio Linh, and Vinh Linh in central Vietnam. In 1952 he entered the Vietnamese army as a lieutenant, assigned to combat units in the North. Under the Geneva Accords, his unit returned in 1954 to Quang Ngai province, where Duoc became sector chief of staff.

Duoc was brought to the attention of Diem, then prime minister, as an honest officer with previous administrative experience, and he was appointed to replace the chief of Quang Ngai province, who had been removed in a rice scandal. Because of Duoc's success in reducing corruption in Quang Ngai (one of his early moves was to replace six district chiefs at one time), he was appointed by President Diem as province chief of Long An. He held this position for more than four years—an exceptionally long tenure at that time, and a record still unmatched by any other province chief of Long An.[3]

When Mai Ngoc Duoc became chief of Long An in the latter part of 1957, he was both the senior military officer and the senior civilian official in the province.[4] Under Ordinance 57a he had extensive civil powers as province chief, and he reported on most mat-

3. In 1968 Duoc was again a civilian, having been removed from the army in one of the upheavals following his fall from favor. His circumstances at the time were a considerable come-down from his days as "king" of Long An —he had no car, no home, no powerful connections. He was living with a friend in a crowded one-room apartment in the center of Saigon and working for one of the large American construction firms under contract to the United States Army.
4. Duoc was the third military province chief in Long An. His two predecessors held office for only about two months each.

ters directly to President Diem. As an army officer, however, he was also commander of all military forces organic to the province. These legal grants of authority were reinforced by his friendship with President Diem.

Like his predecessors, Duoc felt that life in Long An was fundamentally satisfying—much more so than in his native central Vietnam, where making a living is so much more difficult—and any grievances were the result of abuses by government officials. When he arrived, he regarded this as the major factor which the opposition would exploit. Recalling his views during his early years in the province, he said:

Only when the communists have developed their political apparatus will they begin their military activity, with ambushes and assassinations. But the very best fertilizer for the communist apparatus is injustice and corruption. If a country can eliminate injustice and stamp out corruption —if it can clean out its government—then the communists cannot develop.

To illustrate the situation he found, Duoc recounted the following story:

On my third day in Long An I put on civilian clothes and went out to the market, where I saw one of our Cong An agents eating lunch with his pistol on the table. I went over to the owner of the shop and asked what was happening. He explained that the fellow with the pistol had been eating there for two months, but whenever the owner tried to ask for money the fellow just took his pistol out of his holster and put it on the table. I went over to the Cong An agent and asked him if he knew me. When he said no, I told him that I had the authority to make him pay for the two months' worth of meals he had eaten there. The man replied that he didn't know who I was and he was not paying. When I heard that, I got his name, then went back to my office and called the chief of the Cong An. I told him to order all his men to pay their debts within twenty-four hours, no matter if they had to sell their families into slavery to do it.

Anticorruption was thus the first of several programs which Duoc advanced, but he frankly acknowledged that when he left the province in 1961 the situation was only somewhat improved. Corruption was widespread, especially in the Cong An, of which about 10 percent, according to Duoc's estimate, was dishonest. The nature of its work—antisubversion and public security—offered many opportunities for extortion and bribery, but it is important not to oversimplify and describe the whole organization as rotten. Rather, the

Cong An represented the problem of the government in general: good and bad elements coexisted, because neither could eliminate the other. Frequently, because of its extensive network of agents, the Cong An itself was the source of information on corrupt and abusive practices. For example, during one three-month period in 1959, the Cong An's daily reports to the province chief revealed three significant incidents:

1. In Binh Phuoc district the chief of the regular police, who were at that time organized separately from the Cong An, was using his position to force local merchants to buy firecrackers from him, while forbidding others to engage in the wholesaling of firecrackers in the district.
2. Two Dan Ve soldiers had raped a girl in Duc Hoa district.
3. A long report by a special investigative team visiting a village in Ben Luc district stated in part: "Since the day Mr. X took over the job of village police representative, he has committed many improper actions. Mr. X still has a feudalist-colonialist mentality [the contemporary expression for arrogance], and as a consequence the people in the village are very upset."

How did it happen that the province chief himself could not put an end to this situation? It was partly a problem of authority and partly one of communication. Under the basic Ordinance 57a establishing the powers of the province chief, Duoc had authority to remove summarily any hamlet-, village-, or canton-level administrative official. His authority over provincial branches of the central ministries (such as the Cong An, the regular police, or the public works) allowed him only to transfer personnel within the province, or else to return them to the ministry or department in Saigon with recommendations for disciplinary action. Thus he could and did discharge village and canton officials (or inflict lesser punishments), but offending Cong An members could only be "exiled" to an undesirable location or else sent back to Saigon for action. Undesirable locations were considered to be areas of revolutionary activity, so "exiling" had the practical consequence of concentrating abusive officials in the areas where the population was already seriously alienated from the government. As for returning officials to Saigon, Duoc commented:

Naturally, I would try to salvage as many corrupt officials as I could, and I was frequently successful in setting offenders on the right road.

Hopeless cases I would send back to Saigon with the reasons why I refused to have such an individual in my province. But frequently the very reason these people were in the government was that they had relatives or friends back in Saigon, who would just "lose" my reports, and the individual would end up getting a better assignment than he had in the first place. It often happened that in the place of a corrupt official I would receive a corrupt official who had been thrown out of another province and then assigned to me.

Duoc felt that the growth of the Can Lao, the National Revolutionary Movement, and various other organizations set up by Diem and his brother Nhu to consolidate their grip on the administration, made the situation worse. Duoc thought that many good appointments had been made prior to 1958, but subsequent appointments were strongly influenced by personal connections with these organizations. In one instance Duoc received a number of Can Lao "testimonial letters" for several government cadres being prosecuted for extorting money in Thu Thua district. "It was already getting dangerous to punish Can Lao people, but I just tore up the letters and sent their files to the Court."[5] In 1961 he was less successful in prosecuting his deputy for security.[6] The latter had secure connections in the Can Lao, and when Duoc attempted to begin the legal paperwork, the public prosecutor implored him to "forget" the case. Duoc abandoned the prosecution but succeeded in having his deputy transferred.[7]

Closely related to Duoc's anticorruption program were his measures to become "close to the people." It is in his relations with the population that Duoc's mandarin outlook caused the greatest difficulties and reduced the impact of some worthy measures that he took. Duoc's conception of his role as province chief is clearly indicated by the two images he used to describe the need for closeness to the people: at one point in the interviews he compared himself to a father who must understand the needs of his children so that he can take care of them; in a second image he likened himself to a doc-

---

5. Duoc denied that he was a Can Lao member, although this seems inconceivable in view of his position.

6. Duoc himself was removed a few months later. He was certain that there was a connection. For further discussion of Duoc's removal, see below.

7. This individual has since been promoted from captain to full colonel, and in 1968 was mayor of an important city. His continued financial manipulations as well as his questionable competence are confirmed by numerous persons who have worked with him.

tor who cannot treat his patient's disease without a knowledge of the symptoms.

Duoc insisted that he was entirely approachable, by anyone, anywhere, at any time. He also noted that there was never a crowd outside his office waiting to see him, which he attributed to their easy admission. Others, however, attributed this to his forbidding aloofness.

A second means Duoc employed to be "close to the people" was a genuine innovation: the setting up in each district of several complaint boxes, opened once a week by a special committee from the province headquarters. Duoc felt that these boxes were successful because the people knew that the local officials could not open them.

Duoc's principal method of "keeping close to the people," however, was inspection visits previously announced.

I went on inspection very often—perhaps twenty-five days out of thirty—because I felt that being close to the people was more important than sitting in my office doing paperwork. On each trip I would bring along all the chiefs of the province technical services, as well as the district chief concerned, so that if the people had any problems the appropriate official would be present to answer questions. In this way the people would not have to make a long journey to the province or district headquarters.

On these trips I would usually visit three or four locations in one day, each one covering two or three villages. I would inform the district a day ahead, in order that the people could assemble to wait for my arrival. In this way I could easily cover a number of villages in one day.

On my arrival I would explain any important points I had for the people, such as matters pertaining to public security and order or to the Denunciation of Communism Campaign. Then I would tell the people that I was there to help them, and if they had any problems, they should come up to the microphone and tell the whole truth. If not, how could I help them?

Ordinarily, the people complained mostly about abuses by the local authorities, or about the soldiers stealing chickens and ducks—a lot of little things like that. They would also complain about land problems, about the slowness of handling paperwork, about borrowing money from the agricultural credit organization, about the lack of schools, etc. . . . Many times the communists would get in and stir up the people to make a lot of spurious complaints about people getting killed by mortar fire, etc., even though we weren't even firing mortars.

We may get a better idea of how these visits actually progressed, and the impression they made, from the following report submitted by the Cong An in its daily summary of activities:

Yesterday, February 28, 1959, at 8 A.M., the province chief arrived with a delegation of civilian and military officials for an inspection visit at Thanh Phu Long village, Binh Phuoc district. A reception had been organized at the Thanh Hoa hamlet communal house, with the presence of the district chief, the village council, retired village officials, and approximately 300 local residents.

The province chief entered the communal house and expressed his best wishes to those assembled. He discussed the dictatorial communist system, and then inquired about the wishes of the people in regard to the government.

At 9:00 the village chief presented a briefing on the accomplishments of the village in community development.

At 9:15 Mr. Vo van Dung requested the province chief to repair Routes 18, 12, and the section of Route 21 passing through the village. The province chief turned this problem over to the chief of the public works department for investigation.

At 9:30 the Tan Long hamlet chief requested the province chief to construct a dike in the hamlet, at a cost of about 5,000 piasters, to protect about fifty hectares of hamlet land from salt water; to construct a communal house in Tan Long hamlet, at a cost of about 40,000 piasters; and to move the local primary school to a new location, in order to ensure better sanitation for the school children; and to resurface the hamlet roads. The province chief turned these projects over to the local authorities for investigation.

At 9:45 the province chief passed out gifts to fifteen poor families.

At 10:00 the province chief left the communal house to visit the home of the Thanh Muc Ha canton chief for tea.

At 10:20 the province chief visited the Ba Ky bridge in Tan Long hamlet, to see how the repair work was progressing under the community development program.

At 10:45 the province chief and party returned to province headquarters.

The inspection took place solemnly and in good order.

The Cong An reports also noted that the question of land came up on a visit to Can Giuoc district in January 1959.

Three peasants stood up and asked the province chief to reconsider their situation. They had just finished clearing a section of communal land over several years, and now it had been taken back from them. The province chief explained this situation clearly and the three peasants agreed and did not ask further.

Several peasants got up to say that the government should give out one hectare of land for each poor family in the village to live on. The province chief explained that this was impossible because most people in the province were poor.

Because of his innovations—for example, the complaint boxes and the caravans of officials—Duoc felt that his administration was both democratic and close to the people, and that its principal weakness was that he did not hear of all abuses or that he was not able to resolve all he did hear of. Certainly his measures did open another channel of communication between the people and the province chief, but they also clearly indicated the paternalistic nature of the government. One can imagine the doubtful satisfaction of a poor villager at being handed a gift and then seeing the province chief go off to tea with the local notables and landowners. Duoc, of course, did not pretend that he was in touch with everything. For example, while he was able to remedy some cases of arrests for personal revenge, there were "very many" others that he did not catch. It is hard to conceive of an aggrieved person standing up in public at one of Duoc's inspections to denounce the local Cong An agent, who was right there making a detailed report of the meeting. While Duoc's innovations may have brought improvement, they still had only a limited impact since even Duoc was frequently powerless to remedy abuses. On one point there is general agreement, however. Duoc stated that "everyone knew my face in Long An." While the daily reports from that period indicate he did not travel twenty-five days out of a month, he did travel a great deal, and as a consequence seven years later Mai Ngoc Duoc was still remembered more clearly than some of his successors. Yet the impression he left is not the one intended.

Duoc also took several steps meant to strengthen local government in Long An. When he assumed office, village administrative committees were organized according to Memorandum 802/BPTT /VP, as described in the previous chapter. In practice, members of the village committees were selected by the district chief from among the *than hao nhan si*, or "local notables," and ratified by the province chief. On the subject of local elections, Duoc said:

Naturally, if one wants real democracy, one should organize elections, and I agree with this idea for other countries that are not harassed by communists. It is difficult to have this kind of democracy in Vietnam, because the communists operate everywhere, and it would be difficult to control the elections to prevent them from getting their people in.[8] . . . At that time [1957–1961] it would have been very dangerous to organize village elections, because the communists could propagandize and threaten the people to make sure their people got elected, which would have been the most dangerous thing conceivable, because then they would have had a legal base of operations. It was better to have honest and reliable people chosen by the government, so that if anything happened, they could easily be replaced. Had there been elections and it became necessary to remove elected officials for some reason, the government would have been criticized.[9]

It was the policy of the government ultimately to hold elections, but the people themselves never demanded them.

Hamlet chiefs were nominated by the village councils, approved by the district chief, and appointed by the province chief. Duoc described the function of the hamlet chief in this way:

At that time the task of the hamlet chief was to keep track of any occurrences in his hamlet and to report them to the village council. To do this the people were organized into family groups, each headed by a family group chief, who reported to the hamlet chief. . . . Aside from the job of controlling the people in the hamlet, he received instructions from above, for example, to make reports on how many poor there were in his hamlet and so forth. His main job was just to keep his eyes and ears open and make reports back to the village council.

The principal functions of the village council, as Duoc described them, were to control the people in the village, to collect taxes, and to be responsible for "miscellaneous administrative tasks." Prior to Duoc's arrival as province chief, local officials had received no training in their jobs. One of Duoc's improvements was to institute a training center for all village and hamlet officials.

I believed this very necessary. In 1959, when an American delegation was visiting Long An, I requested funds, and late in 1959 I set up a

8. It is worthwhile to note that Duoc did not hesitate to fix national election returns in Long An in 1959. He justified this step by claiming that every country has dishonest elections, that it was necessary to get the best people elected, and that he first tried to "encourage the less qualified candidates to withdraw."

9. The appointment of local officials still does not seem to have been sufficient to prevent communist agents from infiltrating the government. The Cong An reports reveal numerous arrests of appointed hamlet and village officials as communist agents.

training center. This covered such subjects as administrative procedures, hamlet and village management, security, finances, and tax collections.

Duoc also made certain suggestions for simplifying paperwork, many of which had to be approved by President Diem. He also encouraged his officials to use the telephone to obtain concurrence on actions, instead of wasting time in preparing a report for his approval.

Another problem was the weakness of the propaganda efforts at the local level, which Duoc contrasted with the extensive communist attention to propaganda. Duoc distinguished between information and propaganda, and noted that most governmental efforts were devoted to just passing out news. Propaganda programs were handicapped, "because personnel and other resources were so limited. We had very few public address systems, for example."

Duoc also discussed at some length the various assistance programs carried out during his tenure. His idea was that the province chief was like the "father and mother of the people," who would love the government only if it helped them. The vehicle for much assistance was the so-called "community development" program, under which projects might be supported partly by the central government and partly by the local government. Frequently sufficient funds for a specific project were not available at the village level, in which case the villagers contributed labor instead. The Civic Action cadres played an important role in organizing the local population to take part in these programs, or, as Duoc put it, "to educate the people to their duties as citizens." Under the community development program such projects as schools, markets, dispensaries, and irrigation systems were completed throughout the province. Government records indicate, for example, that during the first four months of 1959 two schools, one market, and one dispensary were completed.

The largest and most ambitious community development project in Long An was an agroville begun in 1959 in Duc Hue district, a sparsely inhabited area near the Cambodian border. President Diem told Duoc that this was the most important project he had to carry out. In Duoc's words:

The agroville had two purposes: first, to bring government benefits to the people, and second, to provide a strategic barrier on the Cambodian border to prevent communist infiltration. At that time I divided Duc Hoa district in two, setting up Duc Hue district to have an administration to look after the people up there. Previously the people were scattered all over, their houses 500 or 600 meters apart. If one person were sick or dead, the nearest family would not know it, and there weren't any hospitals anyway. In that area the people had had a difficult life for generations. They had never seen an automobile, they did not know the government, and the government did not know them. The purpose of the agroville was to gather all these people together, to urbanize them, to bring the light of civilization to them. In this way they would understand that the government cared for them and wanted to help them, so they would not follow the communists.

About one thousand families were relocated in the agroville. The government provided money to build hospitals, schools, and so forth, and also lent money to the families to start cultivation in the new area. The people themselves contributed their labor. As the population of Duc Hue was small, I arranged for people from other districts to come, each for a few days, to help in the construction. I carefully explained the program to them and resolved all their questions beforehand.

The agroville program was very effective.

President Diem himself visited the agroville at its completion. The Cong An report of the event gives an idea of the spirit of the occasion.

President Diem arrived to find about ten thousand people waiting for him at the agroville. The district chief of Duc Hue read a speech expressing gratitude to President Diem for providing the resources to construct the agroville so as to protect the life of the people and to preserve security in the district. At the conclusion of his speech, the audience enthusiastically called out, "The people support President Diem." Next a representative of the local residents read a speech to this effect: all the people of Duc Hue district are determined to support the government under the leadership of President Diem. At the conclusion of his speech, the entire audience enthusiastically shouted, "The people support President Diem." Next President Diem described clearly to the people the nature of the feudalist, colonialist, and communist regimes, and then the nature of the Republic of Vietnam.

He explained that the desire of the government is to ensure that the people have their own piece of land, in order to ensure their economic independence and security. The government wants to help all the people, in the city and the country, but especially the rural people, to whom the government constantly pays more attention in order to ensure that the rural people have a full life, as in the cities. The president spoke for one and a half hours. The people approved of the president's speech and vigorously supported the government policy he described. At the conclusion the people enthusiastically called out, "Long live President Diem."

Further on we will learn of some of the feelings of the residents of other districts who went to work on the agroville project in Duc Hue. It is not possible, however, to ask the residents themselves, because the agroville ceased to exist several years ago. It failed in its goal of securing the sparsely settled area adjacent to the Cambodian border, and this region became so insecure following the collapse of the Diem government in 1963 that the population of the agroville was dispersed to other areas. By 1968 all that remained was a long access road and some abandoned buildings, partially occupied by an American Special Forces detachment.[10]

In connection with government aid programs, it will be useful to consider land reform and agricultural assistance. Although Long An's population lives almost entirely by rice farming, strangely enough Duoc paid very little attention to this subject in his account of his tenure as province chief—in fact, he never raised the subject. When questioned, he replied in generalities on several points, but when pressed for details, he replied, "If you wish details, I suggest you approach the Ministry of Agriculture, which will be able to give you more exact information than I can, for this was not my specialty."

Several agricultural assistance programs were in effect during Duoc's tenure. Civic Action cadres helped establish agricultural cooperatives, whose main function was to sell fertilizer and pumps to members at slightly below market prices and to disseminate technical information on planting, seed, fertilizers, and so forth. An agricultural credit organization was also established to provide seasonal loans. Duoc recalls that he was among those who vigorously objected to the initial form of the loan program, which would have permitted loans only to landowners. Subsequently the program was altered to provide a second type of unsecured loan for tenant farmers.[11]

The core of the government agricultural assistance effort, however, was the land-reform program, consisting of land redistribution and rent control, which Duoc thought created considerable good will toward the government.

Previously, tenant farmers or agricultural laborers worked their

10. For a contemporary description of an agroville in another province, see Joseph J. Zasloff, *Rural Resettlement in Vietnam: An Agroville in Development* (Washington: Agency for International Development, n.d.).

11. The program was later abandoned, since so little money was recovered, partly because of the decrease in rural security, and partly because much money disappeared under corrupt village councils.

whole lives but had nothing to show for it. Thanks to the land-reform program, the government expropriated holdings over one hundred hectares, and thus each tenant obtained his own piece of land. That was a historical first step for the tenant farmers . . . it achieved good results, because the government provided land for the people, as opposed to the communist policy of seizing land from the people.

Duoc had no detailed information on the execution of land reform in Long An. The following information was obtained, on Duoc's advice, from the ministry in Saigon and from the province land office in Long An.

The first governmental efforts toward land reform consisted of rent reduction and security of tenure, embodied in Ordinance 20 of June 4, 1953, and Ordinance 2 of January 8, 1955. Land rent was to vary from 15 to 25 percent of the main harvest each year, as agreed by tenant and landlord. Certain additional payments were allowed for agricultural implements or seed furnished by the landlord. The rental rate and other conditions were to be defined by a mandatory five-year contract, to be automatically renewed, should neither party act to terminate it. The landlord was authorized to recover his land at any time during the life of the contract, should the tenant abuse it or fail to pay rent. The landlord could also recover the land to farm by himself or by a member of his family, but only after the first three years of the contract had passed. Contracts had to be registered at the village where the land was located. The enforcement of contracts and the resolution of disputes were entrusted to canton and district Agricultural Affairs Committees, composed of representatives of the landlords and tenants, and a province Agricultural Affairs Committee composed of the province chief, the presiding judge of the province court, and the appropriate district chief. It should be noted that the rent limitation did not apply to village communal lands, which were let by the bid system. These rents, calculated on a percentage basis, frequently reached 50 percent of the harvest.

Under the registration provisions of Ordinance 2, a total of 28,364 rental contracts were recorded for Long An province, covering a total of 60,372 hectares. This figure compares favorably with the estimated rented area totaling 78,000 hectares, and it indicates that the great majority of the rented land was brought under at least the theoretical control of the law. So far as could be determined in 1968, the security of tenure provisions had been well enforced. Frequently, however, landlord and tenant privately agreed on a higher rent than was specified in the contract. Tenants seldom took recourse to the local Agricultural Affairs Committees; as one peasant remarked, "Vietnamese peasants hate to get involved with the law or with the village council." Certainly a contributing factor was the composition of the canton Agricultural Affairs Committee: two landlords, two peasants, and the canton chief (i.e., a member of the local elite and almost invariably a landlord himself).

A potentially more progressive effort was the previously mentioned program for land redistribution promulgated in Ordinance 57 of October 22, 1956. Under Ordinance 57 the maximum holding of riceland was fixed at one hundred hectares. Areas over this limit were to be purchased by the government for resale in small parcels. Land used for other purposes—such as industrial crops and grazing—was exempted from expropriation, and landlords were given one year in which to convert the use of their land, should they wish to do so to avoid expropriation. Landlords were allowed first choice of the hundred hectares they were permitted to retain, and were allowed an additional plot of fifteen hectares of patrimonial land for maintaining family graves and for ancestor worship. Payment to expropriated landlords, at rates established by the government, was fixed at 10 percent in cash and 90 percent in twelve-year, 3-percent bonds, convertible to shares in enterprises to be developed as part of the government's industrialization program.

The following groups, listed in order of priority, could purchase expropriated lands: (1) tenants or laborers currently working the expropriated land; (2) individuals wounded, or relatives of those killed or wounded in the war against the Vietminh; (3) refugees; (4) unemployed; (5) small landowners having more than five children and less than three hectares; and (6) others without land. Landlords would continue to collect rents until the season in which they were expropriated, when the purchaser would begin to make payments to the government. The total payments by the purchaser were to equal the government's purchase price from the landlord (not including interest) and could be made over a maximum period of six years. Until payment was completed, the legal ownership of the land remained with the government, with the purchaser receiving a temporary certificate of title. Under the prevailing rice prices, annual payments to the government were less than the previous land rents.

The distribution of expropriated lands involved a complicated bureaucratic process stretching from the village council to the ministry in Saigon. Because the land records were so inaccurate, the initial step was a declaration by each individual owning over one hundred hectares. These declarations were collated and examined for accuracy and completeness. Surveying was then carried out by province officials. The results of the surveys of the expropriated lands were sent to Saigon, together with applications for purchase. At the ministry all papers were verified, and temporary certificates of title were issued and returned to the province land office for issuance to the purchaser, who only then ceased rent payments to the landlord and began making payments to the government.

A few general comments on this land-reform program are in order. First, the retention limit of one hundred hectares was very high compared with the average farming unit in the South. In Long An, for example, the average farm holding is two and one-half hectares (100,800 hectares of riceland operated by 39,300 family units).[12] By comparison, Japan, Korea, and Taiwan, which also carried out extensive postwar land reforms, limited retention to only three to four hectares. Considerable leeway was also allowed to landlords to minimize or escape the impact of expropriation: the

---

12. The following data on land use as of 1968 were provided by the provincial land office in Tan An:

Land Ownership

Village-owned (communal) land	9,566 hectares
Central-government-owned land	2,331 hectares
Expropriated under Ordinance 57	7,370 hectares
French-owned land	578 hectares
Privately owned land	108,503 hectares
Other land area (canals, cemeteries, etc.)	12,000 hectares
Total land area	140,348 hectares

Land Use

Total land area	140,348 hectares
Cultivable land area	107,800 hectares
Riceland	100,800 hectares
Rented riceland (estimated)	71,400 hectares

Farm Population

On rented land only	30,800 family units (est.)
On partly rented, partly owned land	4,500 family units (est.)
On wholly operator-owned land	4,000 family units (est.)
Total of estimated family farm units	39,300

NOTE: These figures represent the situation as it probably existed from a legal viewpoint in 1965, although at that time the majority of the farming families were not actually paying rent to the owner of their land. After 1965 large areas of the province were abandoned owing to the increase in military activity.

additional allowance of fifteen hectares for ancestor worship; the right to keep lands converted to industrial crops; the right to select and retain the best land. Finally, the beneficiaries of the program were required to repay the government on harsher terms than those the government allowed the expropriated landlords.

In Long An the land-reform procedures began in 1957, and the first group of surveys and purchase applications was sent to Saigon at the beginning of 1958. Because of the limited number of teams, surveying continued through 1963, although it dropped off sharply in 1960 with the decrease in security. A total of 7,370 hectares of riceland belonging to thirty-four landlords fell under the expropriation provisions of the law.[13] Although both good and bad land was included, in general the expropriation comprised the worst land, in the remotest areas, belonging to each landlord.[14]

How long and involved the bureaucratic procedures were may be seen from the fact that in Long An the first land distributions took place in mid-1958, or almost two years after the signing of the land-reform law. Moreover, this first group of temporary titles comprised only a small part of the total number of applicants entitled to land. Of the 7,370 hectares of expropriated land, 5,022 hectares were finally surveyed; 3,613 people filed applications for purchase. Only 973 titles were returned from Saigon by 1960, and none in 1961.[15] The security situation was already beginning to deteriorate

13. The figure of thirty-eight expropriated landlords cited by Hickey, *Village in Vietnam*, differs from the figure of thirty-four cited here, because of the land of four expropriated landlords in the districts of Duc Hoa and Duc Hue removed from the jurisdiction of Long An in 1963.

14. According to the scale established by the government, the most valuable land in the whole country was located in Long An province. Prices paid ranged from 250 to a national high of 15,000 piasters per hectare ($3 to $140 per acre). These figures for various grades of land are cited in *Luat-le Cai-cach Dien-dia tai Viet-Nam* [Land Reform Laws in Vietnam], *Bo Dien Tho va Cai-cach Dien-dia* [Ministry of Land and Land Reform], Saigon, n.d., p. 85.

15. According to records in the province land office, temporary titles received each year from the ministry in Saigon were as follows:

Year	Temporary titles
1960 (and previous years)	973
1961	0
1962	2,558
1963	40
1964	13
1965	9
1966	0
1967	20

seriously in 1960, as seen from the fact that the government received only 82 percent of the scheduled 1960 payments. A larger distribution was made in 1962, on which 70 percent was collected. The corresponding figure for collections for 1963 was 31 percent, and for 1964, only 8 percent. The latter figure is in fact deceptively high, for some advance payments had been made in previous years. As of mid-1968, only 1,573 temporary titles had been distributed; the remainder lay in the district offices, but had not been given out, because the land was in insecure areas.

What conclusions can be drawn about the government land-reform program in Long An? The first and most striking is that the maximum impact of the program was limited, even on paper. Of some 78,000 hectares of rented riceland at the time the program began,[16] only 7,370, or less than 10 percent, came under the expropriation provisions of Ordinance 57. This was because only thirty-four individuals owned more than the legal maximum. Moreover, by 1960 when the government was already in serious trouble in Long An, only 973 temporary titles had been distributed, that is, less than 3 percent of an estimated 35,000 tenant families profited from the program in time for it to benefit the government. The 1,573 titles distributed by 1968 represented less than 5 percent of the 35,000 renters. Government figures indicate that in 1968, 79 percent of the farm families in Long An had no land of their own, and an additional 11 percent rented some land; only 10 percent farmed their own land exclusively.[17] Even if the deterioration in security had not interfered with the execution of the program, these figures would not have been appreciably different. Thus it is hard to see how the government's land reform could have fulfilled its announced purpose of turning a dissatisfied peasantry into a satisfied one, even if it had been implemented to the fullest.

These facts show that Duoc's belief that "each peasant was able to obtain his own piece of land" was seriously mistaken. Most landless peasants in Long An did not obtain land; in fact, even the majority of those entitled to land under Ordinance 57 got none.

---

16. Obtained by adding the estimated rented riceland of 71,400 hectares to 7,370 hectares of expropriated riceland. Not all of the latter was rented, however; some was too poor to cultivate and some had been abandoned during the war against the French.

17. Thus inequality of land ownership in Long An was considerably worse than the national average, for which the corresponding figures were 49.2 percent, 11.0 percent, and 34.8 percent respectively, according to figures supplied by the Ministry of Agriculture and Land Reform.

While the system of rent limitation and security of tenure was moderately successful, the program of land redistribution was clearly a failure both in concept and in execution. When Duoc left the province in 1961 it had had only a negligible impact—a fact still true in 1968. Thus the evidence does not support his opinion that the program achieved good results. However, government policy was based on Duoc's judgments and the judgments of people like him.

Looking back on the government assistance programs in general (aside from land reform), Duoc considered that the results were limited, and for three reasons:

First and foremost, we must admit that the cadres were corrupt. If ten bags of cement were given out in Saigon, only one or two would actually be distributed. Second, assistance was frequently so limited that it was just symbolic and not really of practical use. Third, it was often inappropriate. For example, Vietnamese like to eat rice, but we sent barley. Another example—mechanical plows are good for plowing dry soil, but they don't work in marshy fields. Rather than supplying mechanical plows, it would have been better to supply a good buffalo-drawn plow and some water buflalo.

During the last two years of Duoc's tenure as province chief, the opposition's military activity increased, and so his attention turned more to military matters. His view on this is summed up as follows:

According to a saying of Confucius, if the people do not have peace and prosperity, they will rise up in revolt. That is exactly my view, but we must first of all provide peace, for without peace there can be no prosperity. Just as a father and mother who love their children must take care of their children, so a government which cares for its people must provide for their security first of all. If the people have peace and prosperity, they will not demand anything at all of their government except to be left alone to make their living. In this stage whatever makes trouble for the people must be eliminated, whether it be communists or corrupt officials.

At the time of the increased revolutionary military activity in 1959 and 1960, Duoc had four types of forces available to him. First was the Cong An, consisting of approximately a hundred agents and numerous "contacts" spread throughout the province, to follow opposition activities in secret. Each village also had a post of Dan Ve, a poorly paid, poorly equipped, part-time military force which operated only within village limits. Theoretically, the Dan Ve were "citizen-soldiers"; they were expected to perform military duties part of the time and to carry on a normal life as well. Thus their pay (when they got it) was merely symbolic—"not enough to buy cigarets," as Duoc put it. The Dan Ve were trained for one to three months within the province and were provided with old rifles such as the American M-1 or French MAS 36. Their mission, according to Duoc, was "to preserve order in the village, to protect the village office, and to guard the village officials when collecting taxes or performing other administrative jobs." Membership in the Dan Ve was voluntary, although, as Duoc put it, "it was required to volunteer" when one reached a certain age.

The next level of military force was the Bao An, or Civil Guard, one company of approximately 100 men in each district. In all respects the Bao An was a stronger military force: its men were full-time soldiers, their pay was adequate, their weapons were better, and their training was for six months. The Bao An company performed for the district chief the same security function as did the Dan Ve for the village chief. In addition, the Bao An was responsible for conducting offensive operations and for supporting the Dan Ve in the event of attack.

When the Party stepped up its assassinations, kidnappings, and guerrilla attacks, there were no regular army forces stationed in Long An; only a limited number of army personnel were assigned to training men for the Dan Ve and Bao An. Duoc admitted that he was perplexed about how to cope with the increased violence. The tactical problem was that the guerrillas could at will mount greater forces against the static Dan Ve outposts. Duoc concluded that the Dan Ve could not abandon the outposts and take up mobile tactics like the guerrillas, because of both their duty to protect the village offices and officials and their inadequate training in mobile, small-unit tactics. His solution was to request conventional army units, to be used as mobile relief columns in the event of an attack on an outpost. In response he received one battalion to guard the two strategic bridges at Tan An and Ben Luc along Route 4, one artillery platoon, and two Ranger companies. Because of rigid limitations on the use of the infantry battalion, only the two Ranger companies could be used as a mobile reserve, and Duoc found this inadequate to halt the expansion of the guerrilla forces. Local officials—even the village police commissioner—had no weapons. Instead they had to rely on the Dan Ve to provide security, but by 1960 this was no longer sufficient. As a consequence, "some local authorities and Dan Ve outposts had to be withdrawn from outlying areas." For this Duoc did not feel responsible; he had warned the government of what was coming:

> I am sure that if you go to the Ministry of the Interior you will still find my reports. I warned them very clearly that if they did not give me enough troops to pacify the province, then whole divisions of troops would not help later on. But they just gave me two Ranger companies. How can you pacify a province with two companies?

Duoc was removed as province chief in October 1961, a fact for which everyone has a different explanation. Some point out that Duoc's habit of bypassing higher officials and going directly to President Diem created many enemies. Others emphasize the need of appointing a professional military man to cope with the decline in security. The incident which precipitated Duoc's removal, according to Le Tai Hoa, in 1968 one of the National Assembly representatives from Long An province, was his own arrest for suspected complicity in the attempted coup in 1960. Duoc vigorously defended Hoa, who had been his Information and Youth chief. Hoa was finally released on condition that Duoc be removed from office so that he could not use his position to present evidence of Hoa's torture while in jail. Probably all these explanations are true in part. Duoc's replacement as province chief was a skilled professional military man—later the commanding general of the Fourth Corps Tactical Zone—which lends credence to the view that Duoc was removed because of the decline in security. Before he had been called to military duty, Duoc had actually been an administrator and self-made political theorist. The stage for this had now passed.

How can we evaluate Duoc as province chief? His own views on his term of office are strangely contradictory. On the one hand, he pointed to numerous governmental failings while he was in Long An—corrupt and abusive officials, inadequate propaganda programs, insufficient and often inappropriate assistance programs. Yet he judged that in the end the decisive government failure was insufficient military force. He denied any serious alienation from the government, emphasizing instead that "when I left the people still had confidence in the government." The local government authorities were not weak; they simply lacked adequate protection.

In my opinion the National Liberation Front would be nothing but an empty political name like Pathet Lao if the Hanoi communists had not sent their army into the South. . . . The reason they have a strong army in the South is that Hanoi sent its troops down, in addition to a number of agents who were regrouped to the North in 1954, to stir up the people here. . . . I completely deny the view that the communists are strong here because they have gotten the support of the people. If I am not mistaken, the people are simply forced to follow the communists because of the threat of terror.[18]

It was because Duoc viewed the trouble in Long An as an outside problem that he argued the need for, and ability of, troops to settle the issue.

At one point in his account, Duoc noted that he had employed the Cong An to track down the local communist agents, but that it was a very difficult task, because a village would only be "swept clean" for a few months until new agents began propagandizing, distributing pamphlets, and so forth. This ease with which people were recruited into the movement would seem to contradict Duoc's contention that the problem was one of "outside agitators" and suggests instead the presence of continuing grievances. This again is an example of Duoc's subjectiveness and inconsistency.

Duoc was basically an honest and energetic administrator with conventional and traditional Vietnamese views on the relation between ruler and ruled. His prescription for Long An was an honest and paternalistic government. He believed that "clean government," without radical change, would keep the peasants happy. His own improvements centered largely on anticorruption and on streamlining administration, with little emphasis on social reform. In retrospect he believed that there was much support for the government when he left Long An, and in this he may be correct. Yet such support is not inconsistent with the presence of a core of bitter opposition.

Some Dissenting Views

Whenever Major Duoc visited our village, he didn't come like a province chief or even the president—he came like a king. He would be driven up to the crossroads in his American car, then stop and have the Vietnamese flag flown from the fender. From there he would be escorted back to the market, where all

18. It should be pointed out that the first reported presence of northern army units in Long An was in December 1967, six years after Duoc left the province. The reinfiltration of regrouped cadres into Long An began in very small numbers in 1960.

the people and local officials in their best clothes would have been waiting for him for hours. He organized it that way so that the government would think people liked him, but it was just a sham.

A village chief from Thu Thua district

The opinions of several individuals—principally hamlet- and village-level officials—on some of the same issues that Duoc raised may illustrate how differently things looked to many people under him. The several individuals quoted below represent substantial bodies of opinion in Long An. All were or are connected with the government in some way, and all are lifelong residents of the province. Thus their views reflect the perspective held by many participants in the government.

The above quotation is typical of the memories many have of Mai Ngoc Duoc: despite his aspirations to appear democratic, and his belief that he was close to the people, he was viewed as behaving like a "king" with his emphasis on the rank and status of his office. A schoolteacher from Can Duoc district, a candidate in the 1967 National Assembly elections, did not recall most of the province chiefs, but he remembered Duoc: "He was very powerful. He would come here with a military escort and a siren on his car. When he arrived there would be a big reception. . . . [Could you say he was democratic?] Hardly, everyone called him 'mandarin.' " A local official said:

Mai Ngoc Duoc was the one who built the agroville. . . . He was a good talker . . . spoke about politics all the time, how the people should work hard, and the government officials would help them. [Could you go up and talk to him?] Heavens no, wouldn't dare do that. Somebody might notice, and then who knows what would happen after he left?

A hamlet chief from Thu Thua discussed the meetings Duoc called when he visited, and the problems of presenting grievances at them:

Imagine how many problems the province chief had to worry about. How could he possibly know what was going on out in the country? He just relied on the reports that his people submitted to him—we never saw him out here in the rural areas. . . . Sometimes he would come up to the market for a big meeting. But suppose a Cong An agent forced you to give him 10,000 piasters. Then there would be the big meeting called by the province chief. The village council and hamlet chiefs would order all the people to come, like herding ducks to market. When you got there, would you stand up and denounce the Cong An? Of course not, nobody dared to say anything—you figure you can always make another 10,000 piasters, but once you're dead, you're dead for good. Instead they would just drag out some halfway presentable old man with a long beard to make a speech. But rather than talk about how the Cong An had stolen your money, he would just say: the whole country supports President Diem for helping the people to have a secure life, etc.—just the reverse of the truth. So everyone just felt, all right, let them do what they want, as long as I don't have to get involved.

Duoc's chief supporter, Le Tai Hoa, also recalled speaking to Duoc about the impression he made.

Mai Ngoc Duoc was an honest and industrious person who was able to accomplish much for Long An because of his influence in Saigon. His biggest problem was that, being born in Hue, he just did not know how to deal with Southerners. He would drive around the province in his American car, flying the national flag, which the people found very offensive. I tried to talk Duoc out of this, but he insisted that he was the personal representative of the president and must uphold the government's prestige. That kind of thing is fine on state occasions, but not when dealing with the peasants in Long An. Southerners just don't like all that formality and rank.

With this kind of attitude, it is hardly surprising that Duoc did not learn more about popular feelings in his province. In talking to residents of Long An ten years later, one gets the impression that the situation was much worse than Duoc imagined. Popular grievances against the government (as expressed by people *in* the government) fell into four categories: theft of government funds and commodities; extortion and theft from private individuals by government officials (principally Cong An and soldiers), torture, and faked elections. The majority seemed to agree with Duoc that the Cong An was the worst offender. The Thu Thua hamlet chief quoted above commented:

After the cease-fire, a lot of Vietminh came back to live under the government. The Cong An was in charge of keeping an eye on these people. A minority of the Cong An agents were honest and tried to do a good job. The majority were just out to have a good time and get money out of people. By the tenth of the month their salary would be gone and they would ask to "borrow" some money from one of the people who had come back. If he didn't "lend" it, he would be arrested. [Why didn't the district chief prevent this?] During Diem's time we had both honest

and dishonest district chiefs. A good district chief would not know what
was going on out here—he wouldn't go from house to house asking
what was bothering people. So the only way he would know about the
"borrowing" was when it got so bad that people could not stand it any
more. Even then only a person with relatives in the government would
dare to denounce the Cong An. And of course a lot of times the district
chief was getting his share of the money from the Cong An, so a complaint would get as far as the district chief's wastebasket.

A village chief from Thu Thua described his own role in the corrupt
practices:

During the Diem period the people here saw that the government
was no good at all. That is why maybe 80 percent of them followed the
VC. I was village chief then, but I just had to do what the government
told me. If not, the secret police[19] would have picked me up and tortured me to death. Thus I was the very one who rigged the elections here.
. . . But even if you had offered me a million piasters, I would not have
said a word, because in those days if you opened your mouth you were
put in jail immediately. But believe me, I'm telling the truth—I know
because I did it myself. Everyone was appointed, so we had to do it.

In Can Duoc, on the other side of the province, the situation was
similar. The National Assembly candidate quoted above was in
charge of ballot counting. He recalled:

The 1959 election was very dishonest. Information and Civic Action
cadres went around at noon when everyone was home napping and
stuffed the ballot boxes. If the results still didn't come out right they
were adjusted at district headquarters. . . . [Didn't anyone complain?]
Everyone was terrified of the government. For example the principal of
the local school failed to campaign "actively" for the government candidate. He was reprimanded severely and transferred somewhere else,
and his family got in a lot of trouble too. [Was there torture?] Of course
there was. The Cong An beat people and used the "water treatment."[20]
But there was nothing anyone could do. Everyone was too terrified.

There were numerous schemes affecting each person's pocket-
book—perhaps an even more sensitive point than the rigged elections. Duoc himself mentioned that one of the schemes his deputy

---

19. An organization separate from the Cong An, working directly for the
province chief.
20. The "water treatment" consisted of forcing water down a person's
throat or else holding his head under water.

was involved in was the forced sale of anticommunist signs to each family. Others alleged that membership in the Republican Youth, which was mandatory, involved the purchase of a uniform of a certain type. Whether true or not, many in Long An were convinced that the profits from importing this material all went to Diem's family.

One consequence of the corruption within the government and of the government's failure to communicate with the people was that a suspicion of wrongdoing fell on everyone. Thus, although the evidence indicates that Duoc himself attempted to reduce the level of corruption and ultimately fell victim to it, he is still widely believed to have been one of its principal perpetrators. People typically re-marked, "Imagine how much money he has now," or "We don't see Duoc here any more—he doesn't dare show his face in Long An because of all the rotten things he did."

Another consequence of the abuses was to reinforce popular feeling against involvement with the government. On the one hand this just meant avoiding contact with authority. For example, once security began to decline a dispensary about a mile from the center of town had to be moved to a more secure location to prevent further thefts of medicine. The only public building available was where the village council met. The chief of the dispensary remarked that he wanted to get help in returning to his old building. He explained: "Before we used to treat more than twenty people a day. Now we are right in the center of town, but we only treat three or four. People don't like to come here to be treated now, since we are in the same building as the village office."

A more damaging aspect of this problem was that the vitality of local government was reduced because qualified people did not wish to hold such posts, as it involved rigging elections and protecting criminal elements within the government. There were other factors as well to dissuade people from seeking local government posts. The hamlet chief from Thu Thua described it well:

> There were many qualified people who would have worked on the village council if they had seen any opportunity to accomplish anything. But they saw that the village council had no real authority. It was just a tool of the district. They also saw the killing going on, this clique rubbing out that clique and so on, and they didn't want to get involved.

Although village council members were now paid (they had not been under the French), the pay was token, and frequently not received at all.[21] Furthermore, appointment was viewed as a misfortune to be borne rather than as an honor to be enjoyed, except of course by those who took advantage of their positions to extort money. Thus it is easy to understand the widespread complaints about village government being slow, inert, and interested only in completing tasks superficially. One individual from Long Huu Island in Can Duoc district remarked that it usually took several days to get the simplest paperwork done, and that the Dan Ve soldiers just had a passive attitude of "leave me alone and I'll leave you alone" toward the guerrillas. He himself had the misfortune to be appointed village information cadre for several months until he succeeded in resigning, but "I just pasted up any posters that came down from district, or called the hamlet chiefs in to paste them up in the hamlet information booths. I myself never left the market." His own grievance was that he was forced to join the National Revolutionary Movement and contribute money, two-thirds of which was sent back to province headquarters, "where Madame Nhu stole it—we never saw any good come of it at all."

This individual's views on government assistance are fairly typical. They reveal that such aid programs as existed had little positive psychological impact, and some actually did much harm. The agroville in Duc Hue, of which Duoc was so proud as a "civilizing" influence, is a good example. It will be remembered that the agroville was a community development project in which each able-bodied male from the entire province was required to put in a week of labor. As a measure of flexibility, individuals were also permitted to pay 200 piasters (about a week's wages) and thus be exempted from labor. From Duoc's viewpoint, this was a successful project, to which each citizen in Long An contributed labor after being "educated" to his civic responsibilities. On the other hand, many in Long An who were affected directly by this project looked on their week spent working on the agroville for someone else's benefit simply as forced labor; the alternative of paying 200 piasters was regarded as just another form of tax—an unjust one at that, because rich and poor paid the same amount.

To the question, "What kind of government aid programs were

---

21. Duoc claimed that this was owing to inadequate village financial resources, such as rented communal lands, which were the source of village salaries. He remarked that he was aware of this problem and had provided for a provincial subsidy for village budgets, but "it took a long time to be approved in Saigon."

there here?" one local official replied, "What do you mean aid? The government took from us instead of giving us aid!" Yet contradictorily, he admitted the existence of numerous aid programs—visits by mobile health teams, an agricultural cooperative, construction of a school, etc. When questioned about this, he resolved the apparent contradiction by remarking on the inadequacy of the programs in relation to needs—the health teams "gave a few shots and went away"; the cooperative sold fertilizer at less than the market price, but, "if you didn't happen to be at the market the day the fertilizer was sold, you didn't get any"; agricultural loans were available "to those who had friends in the cooperative." The school was not viewed as assistance but merely as the fulfillment of the government's duty to provide education.

This same official's reply to a question on the land-reform program is also worthy of note:

Oh, yes there was a government program which was supposed to divide up the land, but the Vietcong had divided it up already. A while ago the new district chief came down here and asked me whether we should give out land. I told him that the VC had already divided it up fairly, so there was no point in disturbing things. He said, "All right, if anyone complains we'll get him some land, but otherwise just leave everything as it is."

In saying "the Vietcong have divided it up fairly," this man, it should be pointed out, was the chairman of the government-organized village farmers' association.

This official felt that the biggest shortcoming in government assistance was "talking a lot but not doing anything," a complaint echoed by countless other people in Long An. He remembered the numerous times Duoc visited Can Duoc, and even one time when President Diem himself came; they all "spoke real fine, but we didn't see anything accomplished." His comment on this deserves serious reflection: "The result was that the people did not trust the government . . . they even didn't trust the Americans. After all, if the Americans really wanted to help the people, really wanted the people to benefit, why would they give all the money to the corrupt officials to be stolen?"

A striking conclusion emerges from talking to the local officials: how much more accurately they understood the actual situation, both in outlook and specific facts, than did district or province chiefs assigned from Saigon. Duoc, for example, acknowledged that "corruption and injustice are the best fertilizer for the communists," but his overall evaluation of the situation in Long An suggested that these problems were under control, even if not perfectly so, and that "most of the people followed the government." Thus there was no legitimate reason to oppose the government, and those who did were just "stirred up" or "deceived." As he said, "I completely deny that the communists are strong here because they have gotten the support of the people. If I am not mistaken, the people are simply forced to follow the communists because of the threat of terror." Local people, on the other hand, perceived the situation in a different way. Hamlet and village officials frequently had friends or even relatives on the other side; for them the fact that these people had abandoned the government was not a question of being "stirred up," "deceived," or "terrorized." Contrast Duoc's view with the comments of one of his Dan Ve commanders.

Q: Why didn't the people follow the government here?
A: We didn't have enough soldiers.
Q: Why didn't you recruit more soldiers?
A: It was very difficult to recruit. Very, very few people wanted to go into the Dan Ve. Here most of the youths didn't follow the Vietcong, but they didn't follow the government either. They just wanted to stand aside and make a living.
Q: Why didn't they follow the Vietcong or the government?
A: They had no faith in either side. They saw how harsh the Vietcong were, but they didn't see the government doing anything for them either.

Others, such as the village chief from Thu Thua, painted a darker picture of their own area:

Before Diem's overthrow in 1963, a great many people here went over to the Vietcong because the government was appointed, not elected. In those days the government lorded it over the people, it did not help them a bit. No matter if you put in a request for something, you would get no help. Even worse, the officials found a lot of ways to make money off the people, so the people hated the government. For example, if I were village chief and I didn't like you, I would put some documents in your house and then call the Cong An. They would pick you up and then torture you until you had to confess. So a lot of people went over to the Vietcong, even though they didn't like them, because they had no choice. If they had stayed, they would have been arrested.

Some emphasized the impact of the national draft in pushing people into the hands of the opposition.[22]

The Vietcong were operating here in 1957, but very weakly. Then because of the draft a lot of people went with them—not so much because they followed the Vietcong as to evade the draft. Nobody wanted to go into the army. They had heard all the propaganda about going into the army and getting killed, etc., so whenever the soldiers came down here, the youths would run off and the Vietcong would protect them. But then their papers would expire, and, if they were caught by the soldiers, they were considered Vietcong and tortured. In those days the soldiers were "heaven and earth." If you had a gun, you could call anyone a Vietcong you felt like.

Cong An files reveal that by 1959 one-fifth of those called for the draft failed to appear.[23] This figure bears more meaning than it betrays at first glance. Clearly, it shows that many people did not like the idea of entering the army, even for eighteen months. Yet this statement could probably be made in any country. The real significance of this figure is that one-fifth of the youths in Long An preferred illegality to military service away from home, *and considered the influence of the government so weak that they could get away with it*. This figure might have been a warning how serious the situation in Long An was at that time—an alarm that 20 percent of the families in Long An (for under Vietnamese custom the sons could not have done this without the parents' agreement) looked

22. Decree 183/QP of May 2, 1957, provided for universal military service of one year in the regular army. In January 1959, this was extended to eighteen months.
23. Monthly draft calls and absences for induction into the regular army, as shown in Cong An files in Long An were:

	Called	Appeared	Absent	Percentage absent
February 1959	170	141	29	18
April 1959	240	199	41	17
July 1959	149	126	23	16
December 1959	274	168	106	35
February 1960	176	137	39	22

The unusually high rate of absence in December is probably explained by the fact that the Vietnamese New Year, a solemn family occasion, fell in January in 1960, meaning that those inducted in December would have missed spending it with their families.

upon the government as so bad or so impotent, or both, that they were willing to accept an illegal status in its eyes.[24]

It seems appropriate to conclude this section with a quotation from a hamlet chief, in which he described the situation in his village in 1959. This quotation lends substance to the figures cited above, and gives some idea of the perseverance and sophistication of the movement the government faced.

The Vietcong were very smart. If they knew that Binh's family had been ill-treated by the government, they would work on that weak point. Perhaps Binh had had money extorted by an official—in his heart he had to feel resentment. So they would come by from time to time and say, "You see how bad the government is, it calls itself nationalist, but in the end it steals your money. . . . Are you just going to do nothing?" So, like fanning a flame, Binh's resentment would grow to anger, and his anger to hatred, and his hatred to revolt. Or maybe Xoai would be building a house. The Vietcong would come by and help him put it up, meanwhile talking about their life—no pay, living in the swamps, being shot at all the time. Naturally, Xoai would take pity on them, so the next time they came by and asked for a meal, he would invite them in. But when they took a meal it was not like our soldiers' way: burst in, demand food, sit around while it was being fixed, eat, and finally grab a couple of chickens and run off. Instead, the VC would go into the kitchen, clean the rice, and while they were waiting for it to cook, they would sweep the house, wash the dishes, and set the table. When the meal was over, they would clean up, and then thank everyone politely. So the owner of the house would think, "The soldiers come in here as if they owned the place, but this other fellow is very polite and helps me out." Naturally, he let the Vietcong eat at his house all the time. That is how the Vietcong gained the people's support. They simply built on the opportunity we gave them.

The Party View

The job of a Party member is to make revolution. No Party, no revolution.

A high-ranking communist defector

As noted in Chapter One, events were not going well for the Party in 1956. Rather than collapsing as expected, the Diem gov-

---

24. Some of the opposition to entering the regular army was based on the deep-seated Vietnamese desire to remain in one's native village. Police reports show several cases of Dan Ve members deserting when drafted into the national army—the Dan Ve served only within its own village, while army recruits seldom returned even to their own province.

ernment was apparently successfully consolidating its position. It had purged itself of unreliable elements such as General Hinh, removed Bao Dai, defeated the sects, and was now beginning to re-establish its authority in the rural areas of Vietminh strength through the installation of village and hamlet authorities, interfamily groups, police, and local military forces. It had declined to hold general elections, or even talks, as stipulated in the Geneva Accords. Moreover, after serious losses, the Party apparatus in the South was under increasing pressure, made possible by the extension of the government apparatus to new areas. All these factors had a serious impact on Party membership, leading to a loss of faith in the Party and to widespread defections. One high-ranking defector described this period in the following way:

After the failure to hold the general elections, the Party continued to agitate, but at the same time serious divisions appeared within it. When the Geneva Accords were signed, there was already much ill will against the Central Committee and Ho Chi Minh, because people felt that the South was always to be treated as a sacrificial animal when it came to reunification. Now the Southerners were called upon to sit by and tolerate more sacrifices. They felt that the Party and Ho Chi Minh had turned out to be more stupid than the French, the Americans, or even Diem himself. As a consequence, a great many Party members abandoned their Party work and surrendered to the government. Moreover, among the population there was also a serious impact. People had sacrificed heavily in the Resistance and had been told by the Party that the Geneva Accords would be carried out. Now they saw that the Geneva Accords were ignored. Thus they ceased paying attention to the Party and occupied themselves with their own affairs. Beyond this, many of those who surrendered, no longer having any faith in the Party, became government officials intent on destroying the surviving forces of the Party.

Thus from 1954 to 1956, and especially at the end of 1956, when talk of reunification by the Geneva Accords ceased, the Party entered a very dark period, "dark" because of a lack of faith in the future and in the Party's judgment, which had proved completely wrong. During that period the Diem government was growing stronger, and so the Party's prospects were very bleak.[25]

---

25. From an interview with a former Party member who will be called Le van Chan. Unlike the other former Party members quoted, Chan did not surrender voluntarily but was captured in a military operation in 1962. At the time of his capture, Chan was deputy secretary of the Interprovince Committee for Western Nam Bo, and had been a Party member since 1947. He is thus the second highest ranking Party political cadre to come into

In this situation there was an urgent need for a clear policy to restore faith among those members who saw the Party as drifting, on the defensive, with no plan and no hope for the future. This need was fulfilled by a long document titled, "The Path of the Revolution in the South," prepared by the Central Committee and given wide circulation among Party members in the South in the closing months of 1956.[26] On the basis of its evaluation of the internal and international situation it described a new long-range strategy to achieve national reunification, to replace the "two-year" strategy which had postulated reunification either through general elections (improbably), or through the Party's superior military and political organization in the event of the collapse of the Diem government.

The introductory passage to "The Path of the Revolution in the South" ascribed failure to reunify the country under the Geneva Accords to "the American imperialist invaders and the feudalist dictator Ngo dinh Diem, who have employed every means to sabotage the execution of the Geneva Accords in the hopes of prolonging

government hands, the highest being a member of the Nam Bo Regional Committee captured in 1959. After a period, Chan was given an amnesty and in 1968 was working with an American civilian government organization. As of 1968 no record could be found in government files of the location of the captured Regional Committee member. It is possible that he did not survive the Diem period.

For clearer understanding and for the sake of uniformity, changes have been made in the following quotations from Chan. In Vietnamese, one's terminology is determined by where one stands in the current conflict. Thus from constant association with government officials, Chan referred to the Party as "the enemy," while An, who did not work with the government, used the terms "Party" and "American imperialism," which came naturally after twenty years in Party ranks. Wherever the meaning of Chan's statements, has seemed unclear, the terminology has been altered to conform to that used up to now. Quotations from all interviews have also been purged of extraneous remarks, repetitions, digressions, etc. In many cases transitional words have also been inserted to convert into narrative form what was originally a dialogue.

26. This document (in Vietnamese *Duong Loi Cach Mang Mien Nam*) was the foundation of Party policy in the South from 1956 to 1959, and is constantly referred to by Party cadres in their discussions of this period. The original document was captured in the Tan Buu area of Long An province in 1957; a copy was located by the author in the Cong An archives in Long An. It is number 1002 in the collection of materials deposited with the Center for Research Libraries (hereafter cited as Race Document, followed by the number).

Working Paper Document 301, a captured notebook of an unidentified high-ranking political cadre, indicates that "The Path of the Revolution in the South" was actually written by Le Duan, at that time secretary of the Nam Bo Regional Committee and a member of the Central Committee.

the division of our country and turning the South into a colony and military base of the imperialists in order to renew the war and take over our country." It then went on with a forceful reaffirmation of the mission remaining to the movement:

> The Vietnamese people, having defeated the French imperialists and American interventionists after nine years of heroic resistance and having forced the imperialist powers to recognize our national independence and territorial integrity at the Geneva Conference, are determined not to permit the feudalist-imperialists to rekindle war, are determined not to allow them to prolong the division of our country and to prolong the existence of their vicious feudalist-imperialist regime in our beloved South.

> To cope with the situation created by the Americans and the Diem regime, to complete the task of national liberation, and to liberate the people of the South from the yoke of the feudalist-imperialists, the Central Committee has put forth three principal goals as the general line for the overall revolutionary effort of the entire country at the present time.

> These three goals are: (1) firmly consolidate the North; (2) strongly push the revolutionary movement in the South; (3) win the sympathy and support of the democratic, nationalist, and peace-loving peoples of the world.

The first was necessary because "the North must be developed into a firm base of support for the revolutionary movement to liberate the South." The second was an integral part of the task of total national liberation. The third was required because "in this way we gain additional strength, the enemy is isolated and weakened, and additional favorable conditions are created for the defeat of the enemy and the complete liberation of our people."

After thus describing the general goals for the whole country, the remainder of the document (some fifteen pages) went on to expand on the second objective, the development of the revolutionary movement in the South by the southern branch of the Party, to whom the document was directed. The document perceived three principal contradictions between the Diem regime and the population of the South, which might be developed in Party activity:

1. the desire for peace, independence, and national reunification;
2. The ardent desire of the people for freedom and democracy in order to protect their lives and property and to assure their material and spiritual needs; and

3. the common desire of the people of the South for adequate employment, sufficient pay for the laboring classes, the prevention of seizure of the peasants' land, the reduction of land rents and taxes, a reduction in the cost of living, and the protection and expansion of various branches of national industries.

These contradictions, usually referred to in Party literature as "peace and reunification," "freedom and democracy," and "popular livelihood," were to become the three principal themes of Party political activity in the coming years.

At this point the document recounted the favorable international situation, owing to the growth of the socialist bloc and to its having surpassed the capitalist bloc in economic production and weaponry. Yet once it had discussed the favorable international situation, the brutal nature of the Diem regime, and the urgency for its overthrow, the document then drew a conclusion which nevertheless proved to be a great disappointment to large numbers of cadres in the South. It abandoned the option of armed activity, which had been maintained as a potential alternative up until that time, and directed that the conflict was to be carried on by means of political activity, for reasons which it went on to develop.

Based on the general world situation, the Twentieth Congress of the Soviet Communist Party brought forth two important judgments:

1. All current international conflicts can be resolved by means of peaceful negotiations.
2. The revolutionary movement in various countries can develop peacefully. Naturally, in those countries in which the ruling class employs a strong police and military apparatus and a fascist policy to suppress the [revolutionary] movement, the concerned revolutionary party must clearly perceive the concrete situation in order to use appropriate methods of struggle.

Based on the general situation and these judgments, our conclusion is that, if all international conflicts can be resolved by negotiation, then peace may be maintained. . . .

If international peace can be maintained through a shift in the balance of forces in favor of the peaceful and democratic bloc, then the [world] revolutionary movement can develop peacefully, and the revolutionary movement in the South can also develop according to a peaceful line.

First of all, we must understand the meaning of "a revolutionary movement struggling according to a peaceful line." "A revolutionary movement struggling according to a peaceful line" means that the movement bases itself on the political forces of the people, and not on their armed forces, in its struggle with the authorities to gain its revolutionary goals. "A revolutionary movement struggling according to a peaceful line" is different from a reformist movement in that the latter relies on the law and the constitution to struggle, while a revolutionary movement relies on the revolutionary political forces of the masses. They also differ in that a revolutionary movement struggles for revolutionary goals, while a reformist movement struggles to attain reforms.

But in the face of the fascist, dictatorial, feudalist-imperialist regime of the Americans and Diem, can the peaceful political struggle line succeed?

The document answered this question in the affirmative:

We must recognize that everything in a country is accomplished by the people. That is a fixed law which cannot be otherwise. Consequently, for the revolutionary movement to succeed, it must follow the direction and the hopes of the people.

The ardent desire of the people of the South is for peace and re-unification. We must clearly perceive that desire for peace. The southern revolutionary movement itself may develop and gain success by seizing the flag of peace, in accord with the feelings of the people. On the other hand, the Americans and the Diem regime are employing a fascist policy of violence to create war in opposition to the wishes of the people. Thus they are certain to meet with failure.

Yet, with their clumsy fascist policy of violence, can the Americans and Diem create a powerful force to suppress the revolutionary movement?

Assuredly not, because their regime is not founded on any significant political force. On the contrary, almost all segments of the population are opposed to them. For this reason the regime of the Americans and Diem is not strong. Rather, it is just a cruel and cowardly regime, which not only has no foundation in the masses but is also being isolated internationally. Its vicious nature certainly cannot shake the revolutionary movement, and certainly it cannot long survive.

Yet, given the favorable international situation, the fundamental weakness of the Diem regime, and the asserted revolutionary enthusiasm of the people in the South, why not move directly to the overthrow of the Diem regime? Here the document finally touched on the heart of the matter: the actual forces of the revolution *within the South* had been seriously weakened. This was attributed to two factors: first, an "objective law," according to which "every revolutionary movement has its periods of ascendancy and its periods of decline," and second, the failure of "a number of cadres to understand the Party's political struggle line . . . which has seriously affected the capability of the movement to develop." Thus in justifying the abandonment of armed activity, the Party referred to what it considered to be one of the principal historical lessons of its existence:

Without an internal force, it is impossible to take advantage of the international situation.

Not only does our national liberation revolution have the character of liberating the nation as a whole: it also has the character of liberating the working people in a small colonial country. For such a revolutionary movement, success is difficult without a favorable international situation.

In the history of the Vietnamese revolution, what has been the most favorable international situation? The most favorable situation occurred when the forces of the socialist powers—the Soviet Red Army and its allies—defeated the fascist imperialist powers; that is to say, the democratic socialist forces were in a victorious position, and the imperialist powers, speaking generally, were weakened.

Since our Party and the revolutionary movement seized this opportunity, the revolution [of August 1945] succeeded comparatively easily.

Yet if the external opportunity had existed but there had been no revolutionary forces within the country, or if they had been weak, then the external opportunity would have passed without bringing success to the revolution. Thus, first and foremost is the existence of an actual revolutionary force within the country. Only then can the external opportunity be exploited successfully.

That is a lesson from our experience.

At the present time a number of comrades in the South . . . look only at the international situation and see only international solutions. These comrades make a serious mistake by failing to understand the course of revolutionary development. As a consequence, the revolutionary movement has not only failed to develop but has moved into passivism.

Without an internal force, it is impossible to achieve the goals of the revolution, regardless of a favorable external situation.

Thus the question is, how to develop an internal force to exploit a favorable external situation.

In answer to this question the document set forth four principles, which were to become the four specific goals for the revolutionary movement in the South:

1. The revolution must be led by a revolutionary party based on a class viewpoint, representing the workers and laboring classes according to the doctrine of Marxism-Leninism [thus the goal: to develop the Party and consolidate its leadership role].
2. A broad and firm worker–peasant alliance must be developed.
3. Develop, consolidate, and expand the nationalist front.
4. Exploit the enemy's internal contradictions to make him weaker and to isolate him, and to introduce our own forces directly into his ranks.

How long the period of political activity might last or what it might lead to were not specified, except that "we are determined to follow explicitly the Party line until the development of the situation permits us to act." Ultimately, victory was certain:

Under the brilliant leadership of the Central Committee and Chairman Ho, and with the determined fighting spirit of the entire Party, we are certain to fulfill our glorious duty as communists, to bring peace, reunification, independence, and democracy to our beloved fatherland.

What conclusions can we draw from this document? Superficially, "The Path of the Revolution in the South" was an exercise in double–think. It acknowledged the cruel and oppressive nature of the government in the South—which did not hesitate to use force to suppress the movement—but then it went on to declare that the matter might be resolved "peacefully." It should be clear that although much remained unsaid within the body of the document itself, it did convey a realistic assessment of the situation at that time. It forthrightly acknowledged the war weariness of the Southerners (which it called their desire for peace) as well as the severe weakening of the Party's forces in the South, owing to the regroupment to the North under the Geneva Accords, defections, and suppression activities by the Diem authorities. To have used a military policy in such a situation would have been a serious strategic error—a manifestation of "infantilism," in communist terminology—for the movement would have been totally destroyed. Hence the document declared that what was in any case an immediate necessity was in accord with the world strategic revolutionary line as set forth at the Twentieth Congress of the Soviet Communist Party. Also clear, but not explicitly stated, is that the Party expected a period of political activity in which it could rebuild its forces toward the day when they would be ready for either a protracted war or a coup d'etat. The previous success of this strategy was mentioned in one passage:

From 1930 to 1945 our Party carried out a prolonged back-and-forth movement of revolutionary political struggle, at times moderate, at times fierce, at times secret, at times overt. Sometimes the struggle was carried on through parliamentary means and in the newspapers, combined with struggle in city streets and in the countryside; sometimes there were limited armed uprisings. As a result, in August 1945, the appropriate opportunity arrived in the high tide of the revolution, because of the political forces among the great majority of the people, who rose up from North to South to smash the feudalist-imperialist, fascist dictatorial regime, reestablishing national independence.

The success of the August Revolution was no coincidence. It was the natural outcome of the history of revolutionary efforts of our entire people and our entire Party.

What was not mentioned explicitly within this document, however, was talked of openly within the higher councils of the Party. Chan and An, for example, said that in Party discussions at province level and above during this period it was taken for granted that armed uprising would be employed in the future, but this was not communicated to lower levels for fear of causing "confusion."

Armed Activity, 1957–1959

The year 1957 was a transitional period for the Party's armed forces in the South. They had been maintained until 1956 because the Party retained the option of armed overthrow through that time. However, with the appearance of the document, "The Path of the Revolution in the South," armed overthrow of the Diem government ceased to be an immediate alternative. Armed units were maintained even after this time, as An mentioned in the previous chapter, but contact with government forces was avoided and became less and less frequent. The Party forces themselves decreased through desertion, disease, and pursuit by government units.

We can gather some idea of the status of Party military forces in the Long An area from a document captured in September 1957 in My Tho (now Dinh Tuong) province near the Plain of Reeds, a few miles from Long An. Titled "Military Supply and Finance for 1957,"[27] the document itself is transitional in nature. It employs many

---

27. *Tai Lieu Quan Nhu Tai Chanh Nam 1957*, Race Document 1006.

Vietminh organizational and administrative terms and refers to the continued existence of the "village government," i.e., the remnants of the Vietminh administration, which were about to be crushed by the Diem government even in such Party strongholds as the Plain of Reeds. Moreover, the document is in the form of a neatly typed and numbered instruction, obviously part of a well-developed administrative system, a method later abandoned in favor of scribbled individual messages as the Party apparatus continued to collapse under government pressure. On the other hand, the document is headed, "Vietnamese People's Liberation Movement, Liberation Army Headquarters," names the Party employed for its public activities in 1956 and later.

The first part of the document discusses the need for a "strong armed force," then details the sources of support for the "Liberation Army." The second part of the document discusses rules for disbursements and cites the difficulties encountered in the support of the armed units:

> At the present time our finances are extremely limited. Aside from the direct support of [district] military units, collections must be sent up [to higher headquarters] for supporting main force battalions and other units directly subordinate to zone [a military term parallel to the inter-province level] and to resolve miscellaneous matters. . . . Thus district should not retain more than 5,000 piasters.
>
> Local units are to be supported according to regulation, but if collections continue to be poor and insufficient to support the local unit, then only one-half of the collections is to be supplied to the local unit, while the remaining half is to be sent upward to support units subordinate to higher headquarters.
>
> Thus we apply the principle: allocate the initial collections [between local and higher headquarters]; large collections, distribute completely; small collections, distribute partially; emphasize self-sufficiency.

At the same time that the possibility of armed activity by Party military units was disappearing, another type of armed activity was on the rise, which the Party called *tru gian*, "the extermination of traitors." Although the period after the circulation of "The Path of the Revolution in the South" was supposedly one of purely political activity, "extermination" activities were considered essential to the survival of the Party's apparatus. They were carried on in absolute secrecy, however, not even being acknowledged within the Party itself below province level. An described the tru gian policy in this way:

Beginning in 1957, 1958, and 1959, but especially in 1958 and 1959 as government terrorist activities increased, there was a natural reaction, although this was not generally discussed. Province level and above had various organizations for "the extermination of traitors," and, according to whether government suppression activity was fierce or not, the Party reacted strongly or weakly.

The principal purpose of "the extermination of traitors" movement was to protect the very existence of the Party. Without exterminating the [government] hard-core elements, the Party apparatus could not have survived. A second purpose was to aid in the development of the Party by creating fear in the enemy ranks and by creating faith among the masses in the skilled leadership of the revolution. Extermination activities had an enormous psychological impact, because the masses saw that the government hard-core elements were being eliminated.

An explained the definition of "traitors," or hard-core elements:

Speaking generally, anyone who worked for the government at that time was considered a traitor, just as in the time of the Vietminh anyone who worked for the French was a traitor. However, the word "traitor" must be understood according to the political outlook of the Party for the purpose of preserving its existence. For example, in a village all the hamlet chiefs are considered to be traitors. Among them, however, there is perhaps one who is particularly honest, with a clear understanding of politics, and who is intent on destroying the communist apparatus in his area, while the others just take bribes and, generally speaking, are only concerned with their personal affairs. In this situation the communists will publicly denounce the government as corrupt and demand that it be overthrown, but actually they will support and encourage the corrupt hamlet chiefs. On the other hand, the honest hamlet chief who has done much for the people and who has a clear understanding of the Party is classified by the Party as a "traitor of major importance." He is eliminated. . . .

The same is true of teachers. Why were there assassinations of teachers, many of whom did not even work for the government? Because they were people with a profound understanding about politics, people who were pure nationalists, who might be able to assume anticommunist leadership in their area. Such people are very dangerous and hence are classed as traitors. Besides these, the most effective members of the Cong An and its sympathizers were classed as "hard-core" and marked for elimination. For the Party to survive, it was absolutely necessary to carry out such extermination activities.[28]

In carrying out "the extermination of traitors," special arrangements were made to conceal the role of the Party, usually—if possible—employing Party agents within the Saigon regime to cast suspicion on the "hard-core" elements, who would then be eliminated by the government itself. This was doubly useful: it protected the integrity of the Party line that only political activity was to be employed, and it created suspicion in one agency about another within the Saigon regime.

Political Activity, 1957–1959

Party political activity during this period followed the four specific goals for the South laid down in "The Path of the Revolution in the South," to develop the Party, to consolidate the worker-peasant alliance, to expand the nationalist front, and to infiltrate and create divisions within the enemy ranks. Of these four, the first was considered the most important, because it was the essential condition for accomplishing the remaining three. Typical of this renewed emphasis on developing organization is the following document, dated September 1957, apparently from the province committee to one of its agents.[29] It described the importance of reestablishing agent networks along the Cambodian border and in certain base areas in Cambodia immediately adjacent to the Plain of Reeds in Long An.

During the Resistance, in order to maintain good relations between the Vietnamese and Cambodian peoples and to consolidate and enlarge our bases, we paid much attention to border activities, and thus the border situation was well organized. However, from the time peace was reestablished until now, this task has been neglected. At present it is very important, and we must make efforts to repair the situation.

The mission and the requirement, as well as the importance, of border activities have been disseminated directly by 21 [a code word, probably standing for province committee] to all K [a subordinate level]. A number of specific tasks have also been discussed by 21. This is to remind you of the following points:

---

28. In this passage An emphasizes extermination activities designed to ensure what the Party calls its "monopoly of leadership" (*doc quyen lanh dao*) of the revolution. Extermination activities were also directed at the *most* corrupt elements in the government if that was judged of benefit to the Party's public standing.

29. Race Document 1008.

It is necessary to instruct fully each E [apparently the village chi bo] along the border on the importance of this task and the joining of the task of developing their own mass apparatus with the task of developing a spirit of Vietnamese–Cambodian unity, and the task of creating an apparatus along the border. Each village E should appoint a representative to meet the comrade from the Cambodian organization in order to resolve all problems and to work together to develop a revolutionary organization on both sides. . . .

It is necessary to win over the progressive armed units of the sects along the border in order to establish a favorable situation for us in every respect.[30]

Thus you must arrange for a number of A's and B's [types of cadre] along each segment to be responsible according to the order of 21. A and B cadres can establish a relationship with Cambodian civil and military officials in order to work together against the plots of the Americans and the Diem regime. . . . Experience has shown that in those areas where a relationship has been established with Cambodian officials many useful matters can be resolved. . . .

At the present time each K along the border has an area in Cambodia with relatively sympathetic Vietnamese inhabitants. As a result, a number of former Resistance cadres, as well as those who are sick, who have fled from the government, or who have relatives, have moved there— now there are several hundred. This situation is very disorganized and has caused considerable harm to border activities as well as to our organization in Cambodia. . . . Therefore cadres must arrange to organize these people, educate them . . . so as not to prolong this situation. . . .

During this period in the Long An area, much of the Party's political activity in "developing contradictions" was carried on under the name of "The Vietnamese People's Liberation Movement," which appeared in 1956.[31] The movement was described in a proc-

---

30. At this time in the Plain of Reeds some sect units still existed independent of Party control.

31. In Vietnamese, *Phong Trao Giai Phong Nhan Dan Viet Nam*. A thorough search of the Cong An archives in Long An province failed to reveal any reference to the National Liberation Front (*Mat Tran Dan Toc Giai Phong Mien Nam Viet Nam*) prior to its formation in 1960, either in captured internal documents or public proclamations, or in official Cong An reports. Where Gerald Hickey refers by name to the "National Front for the Liberation of South Vietnam" as operating in Long An in 1958, he may have been loosely translating *Phong Trao Giai Phong Nhan Dan Viet Nam* as National Liberation Front, which had of course officially appeared under the longer name by the time Hickey wrote his book. See Hickey, *Village in Vietnam*, p. 10.

lamation" dated July 22, 1956 (the final month fixed for general elections to bring about reunification):

> In the present perilous situation for our country, every citizen has the responsibility of aiding in the struggle to smash the rebel authorities, in order to set up a real democratic regime in the South, to restore law and order, and especially to find a peaceful means for bringing about national reunification.
>
> For this purpose the Vietnamese People's Liberation Movement was established. It brings together all national and international opposition political and military forces, supports the just nationalist cause, and is determined to defeat the rebel authorities in order to restore order and peace to our country and freedom and prosperity for our people.[32]

The Party's basic approach in developing contradictions may be expressed simply as, "Exploit everything exploitable," but its activities followed the three principal themes or "contradictions" analyzed in "The Path of the Revolution in the South": "peace and reunification," "freedom and democracy," and "popular livelihood."

The Party's first propaganda theme of "peace and reunification" (*hoa binh thong nhut*) was one of strong appeal to the Vietnamese, who have a particularly deep sense of national culture, perhaps partly as a result of more than a thousand years of struggle against China and almost a century of occupation by the French. Moreover, as the document "The Path of the Revolution in the South" had accurately noted, there was widespread war weariness and a desire to return to the tasks of reconstruction after the nine devastating years of the Resistance.

In Party propaganda, government military efforts were depicted not as a means of self-defense but rather as a means of internal repression or as preparations for the invasion of the North.[33] A 1957 appeal for funds from "Company 12, Liberation Army, Vietnamese People's Liberation Movement" emphasized this theme:

---

32. Race Document 1001.
33. Certainly correctly depicted in regard to the latter. Citing revelations by General Nguyen Cao Ky at a news conference, George Kahin and John Lewis observed, "South Vietnamese commandos had been conducting [air, sea, and land sabotage] operations against the North since 1957 and particularly since 1961." George McTurnan Kahin and John W. Lewis, *The United States in Vietnam* (New York: Delta, 1967), p. 156 [citing *The New York Times* of January 1, 1962, July 23 and 26, 1964; and *Le Monde* of August 7, 1964].

During ten [sic] years of the Resistance, thanks to the unity between the army and the people, the revolutionary army and our people defeated the American and French country-stealers and brought peace back to our land. Today, according to the spirit of the Geneva Accords, our country should be independent and reunited, and our people prosperous. But this did not happen because the Americans and Diem and their stubborn lackeys have sabotaged the Geneva Accords, and blatantly oppress, massacre, imprison, or exile patriots who demand peace and reunification, make trouble for our compatriots in every way, raise taxes, demand forced labor, and force youths into the army in order to rekindle war and bring misery and sadness once again to our people. In the face of such dictatorial, fascist, warlike policies, the Liberation Army has been established, comprising all patriotic individuals who desire peace and reunification, without regard to sect or religion, in order to suppress the stubborn tyrants and support our compatriots in their struggle, and to work together with the people to overthrow the American–Diem regime, and to establish a coalition government in order to bring about reunification with the North by peaceful means.[34]

In propagandizing against government military programs, youths were encouraged to avoid the draft and were promised protection by the movement. For example, a police report from Duc Hoa district dated June 11, 1958, detailed the activities of ten armed men propagandizing against the draft. "They argued that youths should not submit to the draft but should cross to Giong Ket or Ba Thu [adjacent to Duc Hoa in Cambodia] where the 'Liberation Army' would protect and support them."

The Party also devoted much effort to proving that the Saigon authorities were solely responsible for blocking the peaceful reunification of the country. Typical of this propaganda was a widely circulated copy of an official message from Prime Minister Pham van Dong to President Diem, calling for talks leading toward reunification.[35]

On March 7, 1958, the government of the Democratic Republic of Vietnam sent to the government of the Republic of Vietnam an official message suggesting an early meeting between the authorities representing

---

34. Race Document 1009.
35. *Cong Ham Cua Thu Tuong Chanh Phu Nuoc Viet Nam Dan Chu Cong Hoa Goi Tong Thong Cong Hoa Viet Nam* [Official Message from the Prime Minister of the Democratic Republic of Vietnam to the President of the Republic of Vietnam], Race Document 1013.

the two regions, in order to discuss the mutual reduction of military forces and the establishment of commercial relations, with a view to creating conditions for closer relations leading to ultimate peaceful national reunification.

This suggestion accorded with the interests and hopes of all our compatriots from the North to the South, and thus was supported by public opinion nationally and throughout the world. But up until this time that message, like all previous messages, has gone unanswered by the southern authorities.

The message continued for five pages detailing the "unavoidable consequences of American imperialist intervention," such as inflation, instability, bankruptcy, unemployment, as well as social ills such as murder, robbery, prostitution, suicide, and the like. It then proposed four points to be agreed upon in the suggested discussions: the reduction of military preparations and the elimination of foreign military personnel; commercial relations; a ban on divisive and prowar propaganda; and the establishment of postal relations, freedom of travel for minors, and the interchange of cultural, scientific, economic, and athletic groups. The message then reemphasized the responsibility of the southern government for the failure to reach agreement.

The government of the Democratic Republic of Vietnam has always believed that the matter of national reunification, as well as other matters of common interest, can be resolved by means of discussions between Vietnamese, without foreign intervention of any type. Thus the government of the Democratic Republic of Vietnam has many times suggested meetings and discussions between the two regions, but up to this time the southern authorities have never shown a constructive attitude in keeping with the fervent wishes of the people of the entire country.[36]

Under the second theme of freedom and democracy (*tu do dan chu*), the Party emphasized in its propaganda the daily nuisance caused to the people by government restrictions on travel, the expense and bother of identification cards and family books, fraudulent elections, appointed local authorities, and the absence of popular

---

36. The Party of course did not mention in its public pronouncements one important reason why the Diem government refused to agree to measures for economic and cultural interchange, freedom of movement, etc., namely, its fear that the Party would exploit such measures to subvert the regime in the South. For a candid statement of the Party's intentions, see the document quoted below, pp. 108–109.

recourse against criminal behavior by government officials. All these areas were fertile grounds for Party propaganda. Villagers were required, for example, to obtain written permission from the hamlet or village chief to leave the village. This was a particularly annoying requirement given the tendency of local authorities to take their time in furnishing papers as well as the not infrequent demand for "tea money."

Government behavior in elections also lent credibility to Party propaganda. Police records indicate, for example, the following results in the 1959 National Assembly election from Duc Hue district, a communist stronghold.

Village	Mme Ngo dinh Nhu	Opposition Candidate
My Qui	2,330	8
My Thanh Dong	3,600	58
Binh Hoa	2,672	0

The police records also give some idea of the reasons, aside from stuffed ballot boxes, why opposition candidates in Long An did not fare well. Following is a report from one district Cong An chief on the arrest of three individuals during the campaign.

[The three named individuals] have been released, because, after three days' investigation, it was learned that the parties concerned were former members of the Vietminh who were traveling around the rural areas electioneering for Mr. Nguyen Duy Dai [a candidate from one of the districts in Long An] and were not Vietcong attempting to sabotage the upcoming elections. The three have been turned over to their canton chief to be taken back to their home area for reeducation and study.

One Party propaganda periodical[37] denounced abuses by government officials. One article described the torture of four children by two policemen to obtain a confession; another article reported the attempted rape of a girl by an army sergeant on a military operation; a third mentioned a successful confrontation with the police by villagers protesting illegal searches; a fourth described a successful struggle to remove a village chief who "had used the power of his office to seize for himself twenty-five hectares of land" which had been granted to the peasants by the Vietminh during the Resistance.

---

37. *Hoa Binh Thong Nhut* [Peace and Unification], Number 39–40, dated December 31, 1958, Race Document 1014. This periodical began publication in Long An around 1955.

The point of these last two articles was not that the government was good or could be made good, but rather that only by struggle could popular rights be defended. Whether the incidents described actually occurred cannot now be verified. What is certain is that similar incidents were so common in Long An that their exploitation by the Party could not fail to evoke a strong emotional response.

To exploit the third theme of "popular livelihood" (*dan sinh*), the Party's approach was to rely on what it called "the immediate practical interests of the masses" to develop sympathy for the movement and opposition to the government. Depending on the audience it was addressing, the Party emphasized different economic issues. Among workers it spoke of the lack of jobs, industrial bankruptcy, inflation, and similar issues, all of which were attributed to the unjust workings of a capitalist economy and to the dependence of the Vietnamese economy on the United States, which had to flood Vietnam with American goods to support its own economy.

In rural Vietnam, however, the economic issue of overwhelming significance in Party activities was land. Party propaganda constantly referred to the fact that land was distributed to the peasants during the Resistance but was reoccupied by the Diem-sponsored landlords after the Geneva Accords. For example a leaflet headed, "The Thirtieth Anniversary of the Founding of the Party," said that "during its leadership of the Resistance, the Party led in the resolution of the problem of a happy and prosperous life for the people, in particular, the distribution of land and the policy of rent and interest reduction. . . . The entire southern people, under Party leadership, headed by the workers and peasants, have been and are struggling against the Americans and Diem to protect the successes of the revolution, to protect the peasants' land, and to demand peace and national reunification."[38]

It is worthwhile to examine the Party's views on the government's own land-reform program. Because the Party considered land

---

38. Race Document 1034. In this period, before a series of sharp policy changes at the end of 1959, the Party publicly—indeed, with pride—emphasized the sole leadership of the revolution in the South by the Vietnamese Workers' Party, headed by Ho Chi Minh. The pamphlet just quoted, dated January 6, 1960, is a good example. Topped by the Party hammer-and-sickle flag in red, it urged:
  Preserve the unyielding tradition of determined struggle and victory under the glorious flag of the Vietnamese Workers' Party!
  Long live the Vietnamese Workers' Party!
  Long live the Party Central Committee and Chairman Ho!

of such significance in developing the revolutionary movement, it directed that efforts should be made to sabotage the government land-reform efforts, even though it did not view these efforts as a real threat. On the contrary, in the Party's estimation the land-reform policy of the Diem government would create more enemies than friends because first, it would arouse the bitter opposition of the landlords, and second, it would require those few peasants who received land under the program to pay for what they had already been granted at no cost during the Resistance. Moreover, under what was euphemistically referred to as a "rent limitation program" under Ordinance 2, all peasants throughout the country had been required to sign written contracts with their landlords, thereby formally acknowledging that the land they had been granted by the Vietminh still belonged legally to the landlords. As noted in earlier pages, Ordinance 2 had an almost universal impact. In Long An alone over 28,000 such contracts were drawn up. The government's own redistribution program under Ordinance 57 did virtually nothing to counteract the enormously regressive impact of Ordinance 2.

These points are frequently mentioned by Party members in accounting for the sympathy that they were able to develop. They are confirmed by the following policy document, apparently from the Nam Bo Regional Committee, captured in Long An in mid-1957.

Land Policy

I. The Party's view and means for dealing with Ordinances 2 and 57.

The landlords: A number of landlords have temporarily entrusted land to others, or are themselves renting it out to tenants. If we propose discussions with them according to our own policy [of direct purchase by the tenants on favorable terms], they will resolutely oppose Diem. Another group of landlords have had their land confiscated during the Resistance and are now living in the cities. They would prefer to sell their land to the peasants rather than to Diem (if they sell to the peasants, they get money; if they sell to Diem they are robbed [because they received only 10 percent in cash]).

The peasants: The peasants have faith in the revolution and in the Party's land policy.

The peasants are anxious about maintaining current occupation rights [keeping the land granted by the Vietminh] because according to the enemy the problem of land is a political one, not an economic one. As a consequence of this anxiety, divisions have appeared in the peasantry's outlook.

A number of peasants are determined to fight to the death to maintain their land, while a number will do whatever they must [according to Diem] to maintain their occupancy.

A number of old-category middle peasants and rich peasants wish to buy additional land when the landlords are forced to sell.[39]

As a consequence of the actual situation the Regional Committee concludes that Diem can carry out his land policy, but slowly. . . .

II. *Special characteristics of the situation.*

Our view of the land policy:

Temporarily set aside the slogan [used during the Resistance] that the peasantry has permanently achieved ownership of the land. Instead, pay attention to the principle of maintaining the current occupants on their land.

This is a general policy for the entire South, but take care not to abandon the old policy all at once, but rather to rely on the local balance

---

39. In Vietnam the Party developed a five-class analysis of rural society:

1. Landlord (*dia chu*): one who has considerable holdings, perhaps from twenty-five hectares on up in the South. Landlords are also distinguished as a class from others who own land by the fact that they do not personally operate their land but rent it out. Frequently they live in the cities rather than on their holdings. The landlord class corresponds to the industrial capitalist class.

2. Rich peasant (*phu nong*): one who has more than sufficient land to support his family, as well as agricultural tools and animals to operate his land. He will thus hire additional labor, although he may himself work in the fields. He may even rent land from others to operate in addition to his own. His income derives from letting agricultural animals or implements for a fee, from lending money at interest, and from operating his own land and additional rented land, in contrast to the landlord, whose income is derived from land rent.

3. Middle peasant (*trung nong*): one who owns sufficient land to support his family, and who is likely to own some farm animals and tools as well. In communist usage he corresponds to the urban petty bourgeois. "Old-category middle peasants" are those who belonged to the middle peasant class before the Resistance. "New-category middle peasants" are those poor or landless peasants who were granted land by the Vietminh and have since moved into the middle peasant ranks. The latter are considered more revolutionary than the former.

4. Poor peasant (*ban nong*): one who has insufficient land to support his family, and who owns no farm animals or tools. To survive, he must rent additional land and farm animals, and borrow money. During the nonplanting season he may work as a laborer or engage in a cottage industry.

5. Landless peasant (*co nong*): the "rural proletariat," living from day to day, either as tenant or laborer.

These categories employed by the Party in Vietnam are clearly related to the categories employed by the Party in China. For example, see William Hinton, *Fanshen* (New York: Randon House, 1966), Appendix C. I did not find evidence in Long An of the tortured definition and redefinition of classes that Hinton depicts in *Fanshen*.

of forces to determine whether to continue emphasizing ownership or to abandon it temporarily.

To carry out this policy, it is necessary to perform the following specific missions:

Educate the peasants to understand clearly that the revolutionary goal has not changed. We are simply moving back one step in conformity with the balance of forces within the South. Thus the Party proposes that the peasants purchase land not as a permanent step backward but to create the conditions for a subsequent step forward. In this way the peasants will be able to keep their land and will not be impoverished, the landlords will be won over to the peasant ranks to struggle against the common enemy, Diem will not be able to make a profit on the purchase and resale of the land, the landlord forces will be detached from the Diem regime, and the regime's land policy will be sabotaged and thus unable to exploit the people.[40]

At this point the document continues with a discussion of methods for delaying and sabotaging the Diem program, concluding that, when all tactics are exhausted, the peasants should be permitted to purchase the land, although only as a last resort, since this would be "to fall into Diem's trap."

Another document, dated January 3, 1959, was a directive from the Long An province committee to district and province committee members on the conduct of a struggle campaign against the bidding system employed by the government to let public ricelands.

The struggle movement on land:

According to many reports, the Diem regime plans to put up for bid public ricelands for a term of three years, beginning in 1959. It has not been established whether the successful bidder must pay all at once or over a period of time, but it is certain that the authorities will make a robber's profit, while the peasants operating the land will suffer a loss. This year also, the landlords will rely on the sections of Ordinance 2 relating to "expiration of contract" and "termination of contract" to take back their land and seek new tenants, with the goal of increasing land rents.

These schemes of the Diem regime and the landlords are aimed at robbing the peasants of their rights to the land, raising rents, upsetting occupancy, and creating divisions within the peasantry. Certainly, in carrying out this plan to put public ricelands up for bid, the Diem regime will bribe and seduce its lackeys within the government and the army, as well as other scheming elements, to bid, so that the peasants who are now

---

40. Race Document 1005.

working the public lands will suffer a double increase in rents (once when the lands are put up for bid, a second time when the successful bidder rents them out to the peasants at an exploitative rent). . . .

We must use to the utmost every secret, overt, and semiovert capability to educate the peasantry to see this black scheme of the Diem regime and the landlords, in order to create a broad movement of discussion, hatred, and opposition among the population. Guide the peasantry to develop a common determination not to take part in the bidding, producing in them a fervent class outlook, "Poor like each other, who would take away another's rice bowl?" Investigate carefully the village councils and other dishonest elements to discover who is about to bid, then use the force of public opinion to win them over. As for those who are greedy, who have been bribed, or who are unaware, guide people to visit them repeatedly, to appeal to their national feeling, to win them over gently. On the other hand [if necessary], employ the threat of violence to educate and win them over. When dealing with stubborn and tyrannical elements who cannot be won over, expose them, isolate them, and employ the threat of violence to warn them.

Slogans for the struggle movement against bidding on public lands:
Retain the same operators as last year. Take back some land from those who are cultivating much, to divide up among those who have no land, so they will be able to make a living. No middlemen: the operators are to make direct payments to the government, or to elect a representative for each plot of land. No increase in rents. Instead, reduce rents where they are high. . . .[41]

The document further described methods to oppose the bidding system and the termination of contracts on privately owned lands. The most important point of the struggle movement, it said, was: "to make the peasants understand clearly that basically the Diem regime supports the landlords and exploits the peasants."

Propaganda activities under the three themes just described were directed at all audiences: peasant, urban laborer, middle class, intellectual, even landlords and government officials. One audience, however, deserves special attention, because it was considered so significant by the Party: the government army itself. Propaganda activities directed toward soldiers were called *binh van* or troop proselytizing, and were considered one of the major strategic tasks of the Party.

To undermine the government army from within was obviously desirable from the Party's viewpoint. But what factors led the Party

---

41. Race Document 1016.

to believe that troop proselytizing could be effective? Here we come to one of the fundamental differences in outlook between the Party on the one hand and government officials on the other. In the latter's view, the government army was a formidable force, daily becoming more so, because of the extensive training and equipment provided under the American Military Assistance Program. From the Party's viewpoint, the government army could not possibly be a strong force, because the troops were overwhelmingly of peasant or worker origin and thus were fighting against their own interests. The common accusation in Party propaganda, "The government army is just a mercenary army fighting for its wages," was uniformly dismissed by government officials as just another communist slander. Yet the accuracy of the Party's judgment was to be proved over and over again in Long An after 1960, as outpost after outpost surrendered without firing a shot. In the Party's view a man will not risk his life only for the sake of his pay, or because he has been drafted. He will only do so for clearly perceived *interests* involving himself, his family, or his own idea of country. In the Party's words:

In any class society, the ruling authorities have a class character. The army is the principal instrument of state power. Thus the army also has a class character in every class society.

The army in a capitalist state functions to protect the monopoly capitalists and serves to oppress the working class as well as to carry out schemes of invasion and subjugation of other peoples. . . .

In the past five years, the American imperialists and their Diemist lackeys have worked to develop, consolidate, and gain firm control of the army in the South, with the purpose of making it the principal instrument in their plot to turn the South into a colony and a military base. . . . Thus we conclude definitely that the army is the enemy of the revolution and the principal support for the American-Diemist ruling class. . . .

BUT THE GREAT MAJORITY OF THE TROOPS ARE WORKERS AND PEASANTS, WITH WHOM THE REVOLUTION MUST CARRY OUT THE WORKER-PEASANT-SOLDIER ALLIANCE.

On the one hand, the army is the enemy of the revolution. But on the other hand, we must understand that, despite the selection of officers from the reactionary classes, the overwhelming majority of the troops are of peasant and worker origin. . . .

The revolutionary struggle to liberate the southern people, which is actually a class struggle between the workers and peasants on the one hand and the imperialists, feudalists, and comprador capitalists on the other, is destined to become more bitter day by day. . . . Thus we must arouse a class and nationalist outlook in the enemy troops, so they will perceive that serving the imperialists and feudalists is a disgrace, that it means to be fooled and exploited, to go contrary to the interests of one's class, one's family, one's country, and one's very self. . . . If we arouse this spirit, we will develop a strong revolutionary movement among the troops and bring about a worker-peasant-soldier alliance. This will fulfill the requirement of disintegrating the enemy army in thought and organization, thus weakening the principal support of the enemy, until finally the opportunity arrives for the troops, together with the entire people, to rise up and overthrow the enemy.[42]

Troop proselytizing usually emphasized appeals to nationalist feeling as well as to self-interest, as shown in a typical leaflet:

Dear Friends,

Ngo dinh Diem is turning the South into a furnace of war, carrying out a general mobilization plan under the name of "military obligation" in order to bring upon the Vietnamese people a war of mutual slaughter. Ngo dinh Diem is the servant of the imperialists and the representative of the reactionary feudalists now plotting to sell Vietnam into slavery to foreigners. His government has no concern for you and thus cannot possibly represent your interests.

All of you are poor peasants, or workers, or small shopkeepers. In order to protect your own interests, you must fight back against those who have stolen your sweat and tears, stolen the land from you and your families to give it back to the reactionary landlords, who have impoverished our people.

Dear Friends in the Civil Guard and Regular Army,

The powerful forces of the Liberation Army have appeared in order to fight for the ideals of independence, democracy, reunification, and peace. The glorious and lofty mission of the Liberation Army is to exterminate the vicious traitor, Ngo dinh Diem, and a small number of his stubborn lackeys, who have brought you here to fight against the Liberation Army, because of the forced draft, because you have had no choice but to enter the army in order to survive from day to day, or perhaps because you have been fooled by their demagogic "just cause" or their fake "nationalist republic." Clearly understanding your situation, and with a deep feeling for our nation and our race, we have no desire to fight with you, because that would just spill Vietnamese blood, while Diem and the foreigners sit by and harvest their profits.

---

42. From the article *Quan Doi My Diem* [The American-Diemist Army] in Race Document 1038. Here, as throughout the text, italics and capitalization are as in the original document.

Thus we urge you to join with us in fighting against the common enemy of our people, the traitor Ngo dinh Diem.[43]

"The Darkest Days in Party History"

The results of three years of political activity by the Party were contradictory. On the one hand, opposition to the Diem regime in the rural areas was becoming much deeper, and sympathy for the Party's cause was increasing. Yet on the other hand, after a period of recovery in 1957 and 1958, the Party apparatus began another serious and apparently terminal decline in 1959 or late 1958, depending on the area. This in turn brought about a bitter conflict within the Party organization.

What factors led to the Party's recovery in 1957 and 1958, and to the increasing sympathy it obtained in rural areas? Defectors assert that this recovery and sympathy were not principally due to the Party, but rather to a series of "not very intelligent" actions and policies by the Diem government, which were cleverly exploited by the Party. Le van Chan, the former deputy secretary of the Interprovince Committee for Western Nam Bo, analyzed the situation this way:

We can say with absolute certainty that by 1956 the Party was weakened. Yet from the Party viewpoint this was an opportunity to get rid of the passive, undependable elements, and to consolidate the reliable elements. Thus the Party considered that it lost in quantity but gained in quality. In 1957 the Party began to recover, because of a number of not very intelligent actions and policies on the part of the government, which the Party exploited. Among these actions and policies the most deserving of attention were Ordinances 2 and 57 of the land-reform program, which automatically restored to the landlords who had followed the French all the lands granted to the peasants during the Resistance. . . .

This land-reform program had a great impact in the countryside, making the majority of the peasantry angry at the government. The peasants felt that they had spilled their blood to drive the French from the country, while the landlords sided with the French and fought against the peasants. Thus at the very least the peasants' rights to the land should have been confirmed. Instead, they were forced to buy the land, and thus they felt they were being victimized by the government.[44] At the same time the Party apparatus took advantage of this situation to propagandize

---

43. Race Document 1003.
44. As noted previously, almost all the new owners lost their land in Long An, i.e., because they were required to sign tenancy contracts, but very few subsequently found an opportunity to buy their land back.

on how bad the government was, how it was the government of the land-lords, stealing the land from the peasants. Added to this were the issues of corruption and abuses by officials. These things all made the people agree with the Party's propaganda on the land issue. After all, the peas-ants are 90 percent of the population of Vietnam, and land is their life-blood. If Diem took their land away, how could they be free, no matter how else he helped them? Thus in 1957 and 1958 the Party relied on this to recover and redevelop its forces in the South.

Chan went on to discuss the southern peasant mentality and how the Party was able to exploit it:

The peasants in the rural areas have a very limited outlook. Some have never in their lives left their village to visit Saigon or even their own provincial capital. They live close to the land and are concerned with nothing else. While the country is in the middle of a war, while there is industrial progress and some are even using tractors, mechanical pumps, etc., they do not have enough water buffalo to plow the land, and they still use a simple plow. Thus they do not have the time or the concern for large matters like the future of communism—such matters are of no concern to them. In the same way, they do not concern them-selves with the government land-reform plan—how it will expropriate in a certain way, or how it will make small landowners of them. To the peasants, there is no point in thinking about these matters. Their con-cern is to see that their immediate interests are protected, and that they are treated reasonably and fairly.

In this situation, the communists are extremely clever. They never propagandize communism, which teaches that the land must be col-lectivized. If they did, how would the peasantry ever listen to them? In-stead, they say: the peasants are the main force of the revolution; if they follow the Party, they will become masters of the countryside and owners of their land, and that scratches the peasants right where they itch. But if the Party were to say: in the future you will be a laborer, your land will be collectivized, you will no longer own any farm animals or build-ings, but will become a tenant farmer for the Party or the socialist state—if the Party were to say that, the peasants would not heed them. Thus the peasants never think of the distant future of communism. Indeed, Party cadres are instructed never to mention these things, because, according to the teaching of Lenin, the peasant is the greatest bourgeois of all: he thinks only of himself. Say one word about collectivism, and he already is against you. This is a truth the Party has studied and learned to exploit.

Despite the increasing popular disaffection with the Diem re-gime, we must explain the serious decline in Party strength after its temporary recovery during 1957–1958. Chan's lengthy review of this period is useful:

> During 1957 and 1958 the Party apparatus was able to recover, but at the same time the government began to stabilize itself after resolving the conflicts with the sects such as the Binh Xuyen, the Hoa Hao, and the Cao Dai. Besides, there were numerous military campaigns in the rural areas, and the government began to install its village and hamlet apparatus in remote rural areas where the French never dared set foot. When the government local apparatus was established, this naturally limited the Party's activities, but after some time our men were bound to be exposed. Because of this we lost a great number of cadres imprisoned or shot.
>
> Thus the years 1954–1956 were a period of faith in the general elections, but toward the end of 1956 the communists were most pessimistic. Then there was a second period from 1957 to 1958, during which the Party recovered and was comparatively well off. Finally, there was this third period toward the end of 1959, the darkest period for the Party in the South, when if you did not have a gun you could not keep your head on your shoulders. This period was the darkest because of Law 10/59, because of the various political organizations such as the National Revolutionary Movement and the rural youth organizations, and because of the constant military campaigns. There was no place where Party members could find rest and security. Almost all were imprisoned or shot. A number were forced to surrender. Some village chapters, which had had four or five hundred members during the Resistance and one or two hundred members in 1954, were now reduced to ten members, and even those ten could not remain among the people but had to flee into the jungle to survive.
>
> In the face of such fierce activity by the Diem government, the demand for armed activity by Party members increased daily, particularly in the West [Western Nam Bo] and particularly after the proclamation of Law 10/59. Party members felt that it was no longer possible to talk of political struggle while looking down the gun barrels of the government. Yet, despite the bitterness within the Party and their anger at the Central Committee, the Regional Committee, the zone committee, the province committee, the district committee, and the village committee, Party members were unable to break away from the organization that was killing them. There never were clear factions or groups within the Party demanding armed activity, which might have broken off from the Party organization in the South or from the Central Committee in Hanoi —that could never happen. Nevertheless, there were individuals—say, draft-age youths—who became so angry that they took weapons the Party had hidden and came out of the jungle to kill the officials who were

making trouble for them or their families. They did this, not because the Party had condemned these officials, but to preserve their own lives or to defend their families. Sometimes these individuals were so angry at the Party that they purposely allowed themselves to be captured afterwards —just to spite the Party.

Chan's comments on this period are confirmed by a document captured in July 1959 titled, "Situation and Missions for 1959," prepared by the Nam Bo Regional Committee.[45] After analyzing the favorable international situation and the progress of the Party in the North, the document went on to discuss the developments in the South:

The enemy has been determined to consolidate his oppressive war apparatus by increasing its strength and its reactionary character in a number of villages, and to use it to attack the Party while the people's movement under the Party's leadership is not yet strong enough to stay the enemy's bloody hand. Thus in the recent period, generally speaking, *the enemy has created greater losses for the Party and for the popular movement than in previous years*, and has been able to carry out a relatively greater number of plots, particularly those of an oppressive and a thieving nature, *although the people's struggle movement against the enemy has also progressed, compared to previous years. . . . Basically, the movement is in a defensive position in the face of the daily increasing strength of the enemy's attacks. . . .*

By analyzing the enemy's past activities and plots, we see that the American-Diem regime has become temporarily more stabilized, and that it has been able to gain hold of and employ in some degree the village authorities. As a result, it has been *relatively successful* in its attacks on our struggle movement and on our Party organization, and in carrying out its policies of war, oppression, theft, and the prolonged division of our country. Nevertheless, the mass movement has also advanced. . . .

In the past year the enemy has fiercely attacked the movement and our Party organization, creating considerable losses, although the enemy's plot to destroy the mass movement and our Party has basically failed.[46]

---

45. Race Document 1025.

46. Such expressions as "considerable losses" and "relatively successful in its attacks on the struggle movement" are very strong language for a communist document, even an internal document. Even "The Path of the Revolution in the South" did not use such language, though it was developed in similar circumstances. Thus we may be sure that the situation was actually very grave.

The reader should note that this document places the start of the Party's decline in 1958, rather than in 1959, as Chan noted. This difference is prob-

Despite this sober assessment of the past year, the document was optimistic about the future because of the "daily increasing hatred of all classes of people for the American-Diem regime, and the daily more bitter contradictions." The document prescribed a continuation of the political struggle along the lines previously laid out.

Documents captured in the Long An area indicate that the Party's general situation was if anything more serious there than elsewhere throughout the South: in Long An the Party apparatus was close to collapse by the end of 1959. Police records show that in 1959 an average of twenty-six persons a month were being arrested for involvement with or membership in the Party, and an additional nine a month surrendered or were killed or captured. As a result, recruiting was difficult, the population was becoming more afraid of becoming involved, especially after the proclamation of Law 10/59, and Party cadres could not safely move in populated areas. A captured letter dated January 1, 1959, from a province committee member to a local cadre, gives some idea of the situation at the beginning of the year.

I had promised to meet you on the 28th of December, but the situation suddenly changed. The Cong An were everywhere. On the 23rd Ong Bay [another cadre] was seriously wounded and captured, and an armed cell of three men were killed.

With the situation constantly threatened by the enemy, it was impossible to meet you. You must have waited a long time for me. Let's meet again on the 10th at the same time and place as before.

I am not clear about the situation in your area, but, based on the general situation, I would like to make the following suggestions:

1. Always be on the lookout for the enemy's plots against us. After a military operation they will pretend to withdraw, but actually they will send in their secret agents to follow us. Once they find us, they will pounce.

Our working habits and methods (illegal) have a number of shortcomings: impetuousness in carrying out tasks; subjectivism; lack of watchfulness after seeing the enemy withdraw at the end of a military operation. If we are not careful, we will be exposed, and they will be able to capture us.

2. I suggest that in the present difficult situation you should proceed carefully. Do not rush out after you see the enemy withdraw at the

---

ably because Chan was from Ca Mau, a communist stronghold during the Resistance and chronologically the last area in which the government reestablished its local apparatus in the years after the signing of the Geneva Accords.

end of an operation. Pay attention to protecting against spies, and stick close to your sympathizers in finding a place to stay. Your living place must be secret, and you must arrange for a person to go ahead and lead you carefully wherever you go. . . .

3. You and Chinh Dat should not meet directly but should establish a contact point. You must stay four or five kilometers away. In the present complex situation we must rigorously carry out the practice of separation. Only in this way will we be able to preserve the existence of our organization.[47]

A circular from the province committee dated November 1959 shows how far the situation had deteriorated by that time.

Right now, as a consequence of our old working methods, the majority of our apparatus has been exposed, including Party members, Labor Youth, activists, and propaganda chains. . . .

In the process of developing a new force, you must enlarge the struggle movement of the masses. Avoid working on the old people who have been seen with us constantly and who have thus been exposed. . . .

At the present time surrender and confession continue to occur, causing damage to the movement and reducing the prestige of the Party. In the face of the enemy's policy of increased terrorism and of the proclamation of Law 10/59, demoralization and pessimism have appeared among the cadres and Party members. There are even places (Duc Hoa) where two members requested to leave the Party. A number of cadres no longer dare to operate, and in villages A and B56, when the enemy propagandized Law 10/59, a number of Labor Youth members asked to resign.

You must educate, consolidate, and mobilize in the cadres, Party members, and the masses an absolutely revolutionary outlook, so that they will prefer death to surrender.[48]

Government records confirm this severe decline. One important indicator is the rate of collection of land taxes. Land-tax rolls are kept at village level, and the rate of collection is an important sign of the vitality, or even the existence, of village government and the extent of the opposition it is meeting in carrying out its activities. It is thus significant that the percentage of assessed land taxes collected in Long An increased from 5.8 percent in 1955 to 81.6 per-

---

47. Race Document 1015.
48. Race Document 1028.

cent in 1959, as the government progressively reestablished its local organs in more remote areas of the province.[49]

A second significant indicator of the relative strengths of the two sides is the rate of surrenders to the government. For the last seven months of 1958 a total of 81 individuals surrendered, while for all of 1959 the total was 79.[50] The figures for these two years alone might be inconclusive, yet in view of the testimony of captured documents and former Party members, and particularly in view of the direction these figures were subsequently to take, one interpretation is the most persuasive: that the apparent decline in surrenders in 1959 represented literally the end of the movement in Long An.

As the situation took on an increasingly hopeless appearance for the Party in late 1958 and in 1959, the latent internal opposition to the Party's political struggle line became more apparent. The southern branch of the Party had never been content with the political line. Thus "The Path of the Revolution in the South" had to devote so many pages to justifying it. From conversations with individuals who were in the movement at this time, it becomes clear that southern Party members had found armed activity congenial and effective during the Resistance, and were now anxious to resolve their difficulties in the same way. But Party documents from this period are full of exhortations to have faith in the political struggle and to cease demands for an "armed solution." The document on land struggle quoted above noted, "It is necessary to overcome the attitude that slights or lacks confidence in the mass political struggle against terrorism and emphasizes armed methods." Similarly the document, "Situation and Missions for 1959," considered this first among the Party's shortcomings:

A not inconsiderable number of Party members have not yet understood and developed confidence in the Party's political struggle line, and have not yet grasped the Party motto: "The long hard struggle is certain to be victorious." They do not yet have confidence in the force of the masses, do not enthusiastically concern themselves with the live-

---

49. The assessed land taxes collected from 1955 through 1959 were: 1955, 5.8 percent; 1956, 16.2 percent; 1957, 59.2 percent; 1958, 68.9 percent; and 1959, 81.6 percent. Figures for the years 1955 and 1956 were obtained from the archives of the Directorate General of the Treasury in Saigon. Figures for succeeding years were obtained from the province treasury office in Tan An.

50. See Appendix II for a complete presentation of these figures.

lihood, the hopes, and the desires of the masses, do not rely on the masses, and do not lead the masses in struggle against the enemy.

The principal, most widespread and erroneous attitude in the Party is: rightist passivism, due to overestimating the enemy and underestimating ourselves, and due to a less than totally prepared viewpoint. This erroneous attitude appears in the daily struggle movement in the shape of a tendency toward reformism, a fear of arousing the masses to struggle, or else a reliance on individual assassinations and careless extermination of traitors, a passive waiting for the armed uprising, or a lack of urgency in attacking the enemy and a lack of determination to overcome difficulties and hardships.

Ironically, the very Party committees that were exhorting the rank-and-file Party members to have faith in the political struggle line were at the same time vigorously protesting through Party channels to the Central Committee that the political struggle line was no longer workable. Although there were some breaches of Party discipline by individuals, the great majority carried out the political struggle line faithfully, "no matter what the losses," in An's words, "for otherwise they would no longer have been communists." Yet by 1959 it was becoming clear that, despite words of encouragement, the choices were, as the November circular stated, surrender or death . . . or a new policy.[51]

---

51. There has been considerable debate over the so-called "last gasp" interpretation of this period favored by American military leaders. Critics of this interpretation are fond of citing the testimony of then Major General Samuel L. Myers before the Senate Foreign Relations Committee on April 17, 1959, to the effect that "The Viet Minh guerrillas . . . were gradually nibbled away until they ceased to be a major menace to the Government," to demonstrate the self-delusion of American military leaders about Vietnam. Nevertheless, General Myers only echoed what the Party leadership itself was saying about the Party during this period, and no doubt his testimony relied on the very documents cited in the previous pages, few of which have previously been available to the public. In the critics' view, the revolutionary movement was not in decline but on the upswing during these years, and to support this interpretation they cite numerous examples, some spurious, as will be shown in the following pages. Thus the critics' views on the upswing in the revolutionary movement are not correct, although they are correct in their assessment that the revolutionary *potential* was increasing. This was also the assessment of the Party leadership itself, and, as we have seen, a point of much bitterness within the Party.

What permitted this anomaly to exist—that is, the revolutionary organization being ground down while the revolutionary potential was increasing—was of course the Central Committee's decision that, except in limited circumstances, violence would not be used, even in self-defense, against the increasing repressiveness of the government.

CHAPTER THREE

War Comes
to Long An

> The enemy has been defeated politically. His isolation and weakness
> are increasing daily. If we have faith and determinedly attack him, then
> we will be victorious, and if we are victorious at this point the
> situation will cross to a new stage.
>
> Instruction from Long An Province Committee, November 1959[1]

The Fifteenth Conference of the Party Central Committee, meeting in Hanoi in May 1959, set forth a new line for the revolution in the South. No copy of the decision of the Fifteenth Conference is available, but from interviews with defectors and from subsequent instructions to lower echelons we can gain a clear idea of its contents. We can also tell from the tone of subsequent Party commentaries that the new policy must have been born of a sharp conflict within the Central Committee, in which the proponents of change overcame the backers of the political struggle line just reconfirmed in the Regional Committee's annual strategy document for 1959. For example, the Regional Committee's 1961 annual strategy document noted: "From 1954 to 1959, because of our rightist tendency for the peaceful maintenance of our doctrine, our enemies seemed to be strong enough. In consequence, after we corrected our rightist mistakes and mixed the political struggle with the armed one, the situation was quickly changed."[2] Another document from 1960 asserted: "If we do not educate the people to rise up and smash the government, then we will fall into legalistic reformism, as we did before."[3]

In substance, the new policy called for the limited formation throughout the South of armed units, according to the slogan "po-

1. Race Document 1028.
2. Document 241 of the series gathered by Douglas Pike for *Viet Cong* (Cambridge: MIT Press, 1966). This source will hereafter be cited as Pike.
3. This quotation and those on the following pages are from *Hoc Tap*, Nos. 1, 2, and 3 (January, May, August 1960), Binh Duong province, Race Document 1038.

litical struggle mixed to the right degree with armed struggle." This approach had three principal purposes: the preserve the physical existence of the Party, to support the political struggle, and to partially cripple the government apparatus at the lowest levels in the rural areas. The quotations in the previous chapter showed the tremendous difficulties the government hamlet and village apparatus had created for the Party. The crippling of the government apparatus in turn would thus have the dual advantage of establishing large "secure areas" without which the revolutionary movement could not move forward, and at the same time of denying the material and human resources in these areas to the government.

If the system of village and hamlet councils, Dan Ve, spies, and Cong An is paralyzed, then our secure base areas will be enlarged, the government will no longer be able to recruit troops and obtain forced labor, nor will it be able to attack our organization effectively and use the local population to strike back against the revolution. Destruction of the government's local apparatus is the first step in bringing about the rapid collapse of the government. It will enforce a high degree of isolation on the central government and bring about the loss of its most effective means of carrying out its dark plots.

During 1959, when the fundamental decisions on strategy were being made by the Central Committee, the expectation was that the development of the situation in the South would lead to a gradual weakening of the Diem regime, culminating in an uprising and seizure of power such as the Party employed against the Japanese authorities at the conclusion of World War II. The Party apparently did not expect the conflict to develop into the type of three-stage war of resistance employed against the French, because of the inherent weakness of the Diem regime—a weakness which had been saved exposure by the Party's restraint in using violence until that time. The Party discounted the likelihood of American intervention. On the other hand, it acknowledged that the "insane imperialists" might become openly involved. However, this would only prolong and complicate the conflict, not alter its outcome.[4]

That the Party did not cringe at the prospect of American intervention is established by its successful attack on the headquarters of the 32nd Regiment at Trang Sup, Tay Ninh province, on January

4. See, for example, the article *Muc Tieu Phan Dau Cua Toan Dang va Toan Dan Ta Hien Nay* [The Current Struggle Objective of Our Entire Party and Our Entire People], *op. cit.*

25, 1960. As a member of the Tay Ninh province committee, Vo van An had attended the planning session for this attack approximately a month earlier. He noted that cadres from the Regional Committee explained that the purpose of the attack was to launch the new phase of the conflict with a resounding victory and to show that the military defeat of government forces was easy, not difficult. Regional Committee cadres acknowledged that the attack (which was to receive considerable attention) would "arouse the watchfulness of American imperialism," but that the threat to the final success of the revolution, even if America intervened, had already been considered by the Party and discounted.[5]

---

5. It was this attack which Philippe Devillers inexplicably placed a year too soon in his frequently cited article, "The Struggle for the Unification of Vietnam" (*China Quarterly*, No. 9, January-March 1962). When he wrote, "In the course of that December and the following January armed bands sprang into being almost everywhere," the year was 1959, not 1958, as indicated in the text. The armed bands did not spring into existence spontaneously because of the Phu Loi incident in December of 1958, as he suggests, but instead on orders from the Central Committee, which reached to district and village level in the South only in November 1959, because of the Party practice of requiring a complete discussion of a new policy at each committee level before the decision is passed to the next subordinate echelon. Devillers is correct in his subsequent statement that "the initiative [for armed action] did not originate in Hanoi." This fact does not, however, cast doubt on "the point of view of most foreign governments, in the West especially . . . that the fighting going on in South Vietnam is simply a subversive campaign directed from Hanoi." While it is obviously erroneous to say that it was *simply* "a subversive campaign directed from Hanoi," because the grievances on which the campaign was founded lay in the South, nevertheless the major strategic decisions were made by the Central Committee in Hanoi.

In this context Devillers' emphasis on the March 1960 "Declaration of the Veterans of the Resistance" as proving that the southern Party organization began acting independently is mistaken, because the armed line had already been approved and had begun to be carried out, as the Trang Sup attack demonstrates. In fact, the Declaration, according to defectors' statements, was simply the product of a meeting called in accord with Central Committee policy, with the dual purpose of arousing internal support for the new phase of the revolution and of misleading public opinion about the true leadership of the revolution.

The view that a coordinated policy of armed activity was initiated in the South by a militant group outside the Party, or by a militant southern faction breaking with the national leadership, is not supported by historical evidence —except that planted by the Party—and it is vigorously denied by defectors. For example, both Chan and An, who did not know each other, found very amusing several quotations from Western publications espousing this view. They both commented humorously that the Party had apparently been more successful than was expected in concealing its role.

Several other prominent works, such as *La fin d'une guerre* by Jean La-

The Party described its own view of the situation at that time as follows:

The Vietnamese people must build socialism in the North and smash the American–Diem regime in the South. Only in this way can peace and reunification be brought about by peaceful means. . . .

To carry out these goals, what road must the Vietnamese people as a whole and the southern people in particular move on? The path of revolutionary progress in the South at the present time is the path of uprising and seizure of power. The path of uprising and seizure of power is the sole correct path, most appropriate to the present situation. . . .

The immediate mission for the entire Party and the entire people is to prepare actively in every way for the uprising and seizure of power. . . . But the uprising and seizure of power is a course requiring long preparation, the accumulation of forces and their preservation, consolidation, and development, a favorable opportunity for action, and a determination not to be impetuous, not to rely on others, and not to be passive.

What is the correct concept of uprising and seizure of power?

Uprising and seizure of power is a path of political struggle combined with armed struggle. Neither purely political activity nor purely military activity can reach the goal of uprising and seizure of power. Thus political struggle must be combined with armed struggle, and both must proceed together. But political struggle is still the fundamental and principal form. The purpose of armed struggle to to support the political struggle. . . .

In the course of preparing for the uprising and seizure of power, what possibilities may develop which we should be aware of in order to exploit or defend against them?

First: a peaceful possibility may develop. Although this possibility is remote, the Party does not reject it but must know how to exploit it. Through the pressure of our people's struggle, the American–Diem authorities may be obliged to carry out a number of proposals set forth in the official message of our government, such as economic relations, cultural exchanges, freedom of mail, travel, etc. We must know how to

---

couture and Philippe Devillers, and *The United States in Vietnam* by George McT. Kahin and John W. Lewis, tend to the same conclusion regarding the independence of the southern revolutionary movement from Hanoi as expressed in Devillers' article. All these writers correctly emphasize the effect of the increasing repressiveness of the Diem regime in generating pressure for armed action in the South. However, by relying on the incomplete—and sometimes planted—data available at the time they wrote, they reached conclusions regarding the independence of the southern movement which do not seem justified on the basis of subsequent evidence.

exploit this possibility to weaken the enemy further. But at the same time that we exploit it we must not allow the masses to lose sight of the goal of uprising and seizure of power.

Second: a situation of prolonged armed struggle may also develop. If in our leadership we overstress the armed aspect and remain passive in the base areas, if we fail to build up the political struggle movement in the cities and the countryside and fail to develop a political force among the workers, the urban poor, the peasantry, and the other classes, then we will not have a powerful political force to weaken the enemy decisively when the moment arrives for the uprising and seizure of power.

On the other hand, the possibility of prolonged armed struggle may also develop because of the warlike and insane nature of American imperialism. Should the Americans directly intervene militarily, then the armed situation would develop into a prolonged conflict between our people and the imperialists. Nevertheless, the final victory would be ours. At the same time we must judge correctly and see that the possibility of American intervention is extremely limited at the present time.

Another section of this text clarified the role of armed activity and differentiated it from armed activity in the period of the Resistance:

At the present time armed struggle proceeds in the direction of an uprising and seizure of power, and not, as in the Resistance, according to the concept of seizing the rural areas in order to surround and finally to liberate the cities. At the present time the armed struggle is not guerrilla warfare, nor is it continuous prolonged conflict, liberating large areas and establishing a government as during the Resistance.

At the present time the armed struggle consists of arming the entire people for self-defense and propaganda. To accomplish this it is necessary to build upon the organized political forces of the masses. The people must arm themselves, both for self-defense and also to strike back against and to destroy the village and hamlet officials, Dan Ve, Cong An, informers, landlords, and other cruel hard-core elements, to defend their own interests, to protect their lands, and to preserve their country. The people must not sit passively and wait for others: they must rise up and liberate themselves. On the other hand, the people must also have various armed units to exterminate the cruel hard-core elements in the government and army and to work with the people to collapse the government and army in morale and organization.

The purpose of armed self-defense activity is to serve the political struggle. On the other hand, the political struggle also has the function of preserving and strengthening the armed struggle. But the principal purpose of armed struggle is to support the political struggle in creating and developing political forces among the workers, peasants, and other classes. . . .

To a certain degree and in a certain area, our armed forces will also have to resist the enemy's terrorist sweeps, and when necessary strike deep into the enemy's area, creating a psychological impact to strengthen the political struggle movement of the masses in the rural areas and the cities, creating favorable conditions for a further advance in the creation and organization of the mass political forces.

The attack on Trang Sup was just the first of many such "strike[s] deep into the enemy's area, creating a psychological impact."

Why did the Party approve this sharp change in policy? In retrospect it seems clear that it had no choice: it was then or never. As Le van Chan noted at one point, "The Central Committee kept calling for political struggle. If they had kept that up, where were they going to find the cadres to carry it out?" He went on:

During 1957 and 1958 the Party was able to recover its apparatus and its mass organizations, and it counted on contradictions within the government to produce a coup. Thus it emphasized troop proselytizing activities with the hope that in the event of a coup it could seize power. Because the Party judged that it had a sufficient chance to seize power in a coup through its mass organizations and its apparatus, it did not allow the armed forces it was still maintaining in the South to appear.

However, by 1959 the situation in the South had passed into a stage the communists considered the darkest in their lives: almost all their apparatus had been smashed, the population no longer dared to provide support, families no longer dared to communicate with their relatives in the movement, and village chapters which previously had had one or two hundred members were now reduced to five or ten who had to flee into the jungle. Because of this situation Party members were angry at the Central Committee, and demanded armed action. The southern branch of the Party demanded of the Central Committee a reasonable policy in dealing with the southern regime, in order to preserve its own existence. If not, it would be completely destroyed.

In the face of this situation the Central Committee saw that it was no longer possible to seize power in the South by means of a peaceful struggle line, since the southern regime, with American assistance, was becoming stronger and not collapsing as had been predicted. Not only had the southern regime not been destroyed, it was instead destroying the Party. Thus it was necessary to have an appropriate line to salvage the situation; if not, then it would lead to a situation which would not be salvageable. As a result, the Fifteenth Conference of the Central Committee developed a decision permitting the southern organization, that is, the Nam Bo Regional Committee and Interzone 5 [a portion of central Vietnam lying below the 17th parallel] to develop armed forces with the mission of supporting the political struggle line. These forces were not to fight a conventional war, nor were they intended merely for a guerrilla conflict. Their mission was to sap the strength of the government's village and hamlet forces, or what they called the "tyrannical elements." They were only to attack such units as entered their own base areas, in order to preserve the existence of the apparatus and to develop forces for a new line which the Central Committee would develop. Only in November of 1959 did this policy reach the village level, and it was from this decision that the guerrilla movement and the current armed forces in the South sprang into existence.

On the other hand, we might well ask why the Central Committee had waited so long before moving into the armed phase of the revolution in the South. This is a subject of considerable debate in the West. Some believe that the North was occupied with its own problems, while others emphasize that the Central Committee must have been under pressure from the Soviet Union not to begin an adventure in the South that would create difficulties for the then-current line of "peaceful coexistence." Evidence exists to support both these viewpoints, and it is likely that both factors entered into the Party's deliberations.

It is significant, however, that southern cadres interviewed by this author mentioned neither of these factors in accounting for Hanoi's desire to postpone the armed phase. Rather, they noted that the Central Committee felt that the political situation in the South was not yet "ripe." They looked on the disagreement between the southern branch and the Central Committee as a natural conflict between those making sacrifices at the front and those making policy decisions in the rear, much like the discontent of American field commanders in Vietnam over restrictions imposed by Washington. An discussed the subject in this way:

> The general situation, as I know from my own area, and as cadres from other areas told me, was that the cadres and the people were terribly anxious to cross to the armed phase, but that the Central Committee sought every means to prolong the political phase according to its concept of the "ripe situation." What is a "ripe situation?" It is one in which the masses have been brought to a point where, if not a majority, then at least a certain number must follow the path laid out by the Party: they must see no other escape from their predicament.

How does one create a "ripe situation?" That is the purpose of political struggle. During that period Diem's terrorist policy was becoming more blatant day by day, and the alienation of the people from the government was becoming greater and greater. Thus the Party pushed the struggle movement, which increased the terrorism. But the more the people were terrorized, the more they reacted in opposition, yet the more they reacted, the more violently they were terrorized. Continue this until the situation is truly ripe, and it will explode, according to a saying of Mao Tse-tung: "A firefly can set a whole field ablaze." Yet for a firefly to set a whole field ablaze the field must be extremely dry. "To make the field dry" in this situation meant that we had to make the people suffer, suffer until they could no longer endure it. Only then would they carry out the Party's armed policy. That is why the Party waited until it did.[6]

---

6. An interpretation with a slightly different emphasis but leading to the same conclusion is contained in *Working Paper* Document 301, the captured notebook of an unidentified but apparently high-ranking political cadre. Commenting on this period the notebok read:

Immediately after the reestablishment of peace the responsibility of South Vietnam was to use the political struggle to demand the implementation of the Geneva Accords. The responsibilities and procedures for struggle were appropriate to the situation at that time, and they corresponded with the desires of the great majority of the masses who wished for peace after nearly ten years of difficult resistance. At that time, although the American-Diemists used cruel force to oppose the people and the revolution, and the masses struggled decisively against this repression in many places and at many times, the contradictions had not yet developed to a point where the use of armed struggle could become an essential and popular tactic. . . .

From 1957 to 1958 the situation gradually changed. The enemy persistently sabotaged the implementation of the Geneva Accords, actively consolidated and strengthened the army, security service, and administrative apparatus from the central to the hamlet level, crudely assassinated the people, and truly and efficiently destroyed our Party. By relying on force, the American-Diemist regime was temporarily able to stabilize the situation and increase the strength of the counterrevolutionaries. At this time the political struggle movement of the masses, although not defeated, was encountering increasing difficulty and increasing weakness; the Party bases, although not completely destroyed, were significantly weakened and in some areas quite seriously; the strength of the masses and of the revolution was lessened. But in reality the years during which the enemy increased his terrorism were also the years in which the enemy suffered major political losses and the social contradictions which existed became increasingly evident. . . .

Since the end of 1958, particularly after the Phu Loi massacre, the situation truly ripened for an armed movement against the enemy. But the leadership of the Nam Bo Regional Committee at that time still

village chiefs, youth leaders, Cong An, etc. Some were simply shot, while others died more agonizing deaths. Moreover, the Party had planned a great many more than twenty-six executions, but after a few days the police reports typically began to read: "five armed men surrounded the home of the hamlet chief, but he had already fled the hamlet several days before." The Party's goal of paralyzing the government was well on its way to fulfillment.

While the government as a whole did not collapse, the great majority of local officials who lived alone among the people—hamlet and village chiefs, police agents, information cadres— either stopped working or fled to market towns where outposts were located. This occurred first and most completely in areas closest to the traditional centers of antigovernment activity, the Rung Sat in the east and the Plain of Reeds in the west.[9] For example, the deputy district chief of Can Duoc reported that by Tet, 90 of 117 hamlet chiefs had already resigned, and by the end of 1960 only six chiefs of the hamlets closest to the district headquarters still remained at their posts. Thereafter, he went on, officials seldom left the areas immediately surrounding village outposts—perhaps only once or twice a month to collect taxes, induct draftees, or provide birth and death certificates —and then only when escorted by a squad of troops.[10]

By loosening the restraints on the use of violence, the Party eliminated the previous asymmetry between government and Party agents in the rural areas. Formerly government agents could move

---

9. The assassinations of January and February were concentrated near these two areas. Thus of twenty-six assassinations in January, thirteen occurred in Duc Hoa and Duc Hue districts, adjacent to Cambodia and the Plain of Reeds; four occurred in Can Giuoc and five in Can Duoc, adjacent to the Rung Sat. Four assassinations occurred in Ben Luc, and none in the districts of Binh Phuoc, Tan Tru, and Thu Thua. Of six assassinations in February, one occurred in Duc Hoa, two in Can Duoc, two in Ben Luc, and one in Binh Phuoc.

10. This deputy district chief was one of the rare people who could work in his home area as a central government official. Having spent most of his life in Can Duoc, he was well acquainted with the local situation and the local people—indeed, he had gone to school with the current commander of the communist district company. He was the only district official who had been in Can Duoc more than two years, and thus he was frequently consulted by the recent appointees, including the district chief himself. This situation arose, however, not by design but because Can Duoc was outside the "national priority area" and so the government was forced to use a local person. As of 1968 he was scheduled to be replaced by a graduate of the National Institute of Administration as soon as one became available.

with relative impunity while Party agents operated under the constant threat of capture or death. Suddenly the threat was equalized for both sides, and rather than meet this challenge the government apparatus largely withdrew into outposts and relied on conventional military units for security, thus conceding freedom of movement in the rural areas to the Party. Thus the Party actually became the ruler in considerable areas of the province as early as 1960, gradually expanding and consolidating its grip in the following years.

After Tet of 1960 a vastly larger number of people moved into the Party and Party-controlled groups, because the threat of exposure and capture had been greatly reduced by the elimination of the government's "eyes and ears." Although Party losses increased compared to 1959, the Party's very existence was no longer threatened as it had been before, because the movement's adherents multiplied must faster than the movement's losses.

This rapid equalization of power is reflected in the same factors which illustrated the increase in the government's strength in earlier years. As we saw in the last chapter, the government had managed to increase land tax collections to 81.6 percent of assessments by 1959, but the following years reversed the trend: 1960, 74.4 percent; 1961, 50.6 percent; 1962, 47.0 percent; 1963, 40.3 percent; and 1964, 20.9 percent. Surrenders to the government, 79 during 1959, dropped almost to the vanishing point: 19 during 1960, and 14 during 1961.[11]

In many other provinces of the South events followed a similar course, as we can see from the following captured document, "Message from the Regional Committee to All Comrades at the Village Level," dated March 1960, which was an urgent evaluation of the accomplishments and the mistakes of the new policy of armed activity. It was considered so important by the Party that the accompanying instructions read: "You must not wait for each echelon to discuss this message before passing down. Instead, copy immediately and send to the village level in order to ensure timely guidance."[12]

Dear Comrades,
    At the present time a number of very favorable developments have

---

11. For a complete presentation of these figures, refer to Appendix II.
12. Pike Document 182. *Working Paper* Document 34 is an English translation.

taken place in the general situation in the South. This has occurred since we have successfully carried out the policy of "pushing the political struggle, mixed to the right degree with armed propaganda activities." In this message the Regional Committee wishes to discuss the past and present situations and the direction and procedures for developing our successes and correcting our errors, so that the movement may advance yet another step.

Our preliminary moves have recently produced a number of accomplishments. Compared with the previous period, the mass struggle movement for the various "popular livelihood" and "democratic rights" slogans, such as "oppose forced labor," "oppose oppressive exactions," "oppose agrovilles," "oppose land theft," "oppose terrorism" and "oppose forced membership in reactionary organizations" in the last two months of 1959 and the first month of 1960 has developed strongly in a number of areas.[13] In many places in the countryside the masses have smashed the enemy's oppressive machinery and achieved definite victories for freedom and democracy and for practical economic interests. . . . In the capital and in the rubber plantation areas the movement is also beginning to increase, particularly the student movement in Saigon and the labor movement on the rubber plantations in the East.

These initial accomplishments have been brought about since we correctly carried out the decision and instructions of the Central Committee and the decision of the Fourth Regional Conference (October 1959). At the same time these accomplishments were made possible by the enthusiasm, determination, and unceasing efforts of all our comrades. Since we began to study the decision of the Fourth Regional Conference, a new enthusiasm has appeared in the Party, which has manifested itself in initiatives that have enabled our comrades to resolve a number of difficulties from the previous period and to carry out successfully the Party's policy. Although these accomplishments are only the first step, nevertheless they are a favorable foundation for the future advance of the southern branch to complete its responsibilities to the Party and to the people.

The most outstanding feature of the recent period is that we have vigorously employed armed activities together with the political struggle. Thanks to extermination activities directed against the hard-core elements and to appropriately defined antiterrorist efforts directed against the correct targets, the masses in many areas have had the opportunity to

---

13. Table 1 shows that the kidnappings in Long An began in November 1959. It is likely that the three assassinations in February, October, and November of that year either were cases of personal revenge or else were authorized by the province committee under the long-standing "extermination of traitors" policy.

rise up and struggle with the enemy. This fact proves that the Party's present policy of "pushing the political struggle, coordinated closely and to the right degree with armed activity" is completely correct. . . .

We see that the local apparatus of the southern authorities is very weak and frail, which encourages us to believe that if we provide proper guidance, then the mass movement can destroy the enemy's administrative machine and can block and repel the enemy's plots. . . .

In summary, the people's struggle movement in the South has resolved and overcome a number of earlier difficulties, and is now advancing in a new climate. After an overall evaluation of the recent developments, the Regional Committee is unanimous in its opinion that the movement will develop on firm foundations and in the exact direction laid out by the Central Committee.

Nevertheless, in carrying out the new policy, according to the Regional Committee, many local organizations had been overenthusiastic and premature in their actions, believing that the time for the overthrow of the Diem regime had already arrived. The Regional Committee went on to point out that after a long period of attrition of Party forces, the balance of forces was still not sufficiently favorable. Thus a further period of political activity, of "aggravating contradictions," lay ahead in order to develop new forces among the masses.

Alongside the initial accomplishments just mentioned, a number of Party organizations have committed errors, in some cases very serious errors.

From the point of view of execution, the most serious error has been that in a number of areas the armed self-defense forces have not properly carried out the Party's instructions. Instead, they have overstepped the guidelines and attacked a number of targets which are not yet appropriate, punishing a number of elements which it is not yet necessary to punish, warning and threatening village and hamlet officials and spies in a haphazard manner.

In a number of areas the local leadership has committed rash and adventurist acts, such as breaking up the government apparatus, instructing the people to tear up their identity cards, urging the people to commit provocative acts like seizing outposts, burning village offices, blocking roads . . . in short, destroying the legal position of the masses. On the other hand, there are areas where vehicles have been forbidden to circulate, rice mills belonging to the capitalists have been closed and the people forced to mill the rice themselves . . . creating difficulties for the people's livelihood. . . .

There are now many areas which have deviated into developing armed self-defense organizations and guiding armed activity, while slighting the development and leadership of the political struggle movement among the masses. . . .

These errors have occurred for the following reasons:

1. Principally because a number of comrades have failed to understand the present balance of forces. . . . Although the Party and Group apparatus has recovered and developed in a number of areas, nevertheless in general the Party and Group development has proceeded slowly. In many areas the revolutionary apparatus is still suffering losses or is in the stage of reconstruction.

Moreover, the enemy, although weak and afraid, has not yet reached the stage of collapse. He still has the capability of concentrating forces and employing his oppressive apparatus to strike heavy and bitter blows against the movement, creating difficulties and obstacles for us. Thus we defeat the enemy in one area, but he can still cause us losses in another.

At the present time we are still in an indecisive, back-and-forth period, and have not yet reached the direct revolutionary stage of destroying the government and placing political power in the hands of the people. In this back-and-forth period we must accumulate and preserve our forces and develop our apparatus. Speaking generally, we must preserve the legal status of the masses, not eliminating the government apparatus but just crippling it. At the present time we are pushing the struggle movement in order to pass from the indecisive period to the stage of direct revolution.

To ignore the balance of forces and rashly call for a general uprising is to commit the error of speculative adventurism, leading to premature violence and forcing us into a very dangerous defensive position.

2. A second reason is that a number of comrades have not yet grasped the path of the revolution's advance in the South. Our struggle movement is headed toward an armed uprising and seizure of power. To succeed, we must rely on a seething mass political struggle movement, progressing from lower to higher forms, from limited to widespread, from scattered to conventional, extremely vigorous and strong.

Armed activities only fulfill a supporting role for the political struggle movement. It is impossible to substitute armed forces and armed struggle for political forces and political struggle. Formerly we erred in slighting the role of armed activity. Today we must push armed activity to the right degree, but at the same time we must not abuse or rely excessively on armed activity.

The Regional Committee then enumerated five immediate tasks that the Party organization would have to carry out in the coming period:

1. Push the mass political struggle movement to obtain and defend democratic rights and popular livelihood for all classes of people.
2. Develop a widespread public-opinion campaign against the government's terrorist policy in the countryside.
3. Actively push armed propaganda activity.
4. Push propaganda efforts, particularly among government troops and officials.
5. Take urgent action to consolidate and develop the Party and the system of activists and hard-core supporters.

Finally, the Regional Committee reemphasized that present policy only called for "crippling" the government apparatus so that it would "be ineffective in carrying out the enemy's policies," and concluded:

The current internal situation presents many advantages, yet there remain many difficulties. We believe that if we grasp and determinedly carry out the Party's decisions, then assuredly the revolutionary movement in the South will move forward, each day gaining new victories. This will shorten the indecisive stage and advance the southern revolution to a new period, the period of directly smashing the enemy and bringing complete victory to the nationalist democratic revolution.

Under the glorious leadership of the Central Executive Committee and Chairman Ho, let us all heroically march forward.

"A New Line Which the Central Committee Would Develop"

The preliminary measures approved at the Fifteenth Conference of the Central Committee in May 1959 were apparently only stopgap moves intended to catch up with events which had in fact overtaken the Party in the South. On the one hand the Central Committee had approved certain new policies of violence described above to preserve the physical existence of the Party organization in the South; on the other hand it had approved certain other measures to prepare a proper foundation of public opinion for other actions it was about to take. Typical of these measures relating to public opinion was a meeting described by An:

What was the purpose of the meeting of former Resistance members in March 1960? And why was it held under the name of "former Resistance members?" The first purpose of the meeting was to mobilize the very many former members of the Resistance themselves. Second, among the masses, it would show that the former Vietminh in the South could no longer endure the Diem regime: that they themselves were rising up in opposition—so everyone could see that the people's liberation movement arose in the South and had not been imported from the North. . . .

Of course the meeting was held on orders of the Party.[14]

The breathing space which the Party obtained by these moves was used to develop a coordinated long-range strategy for the South. Moreover, the decisions involved were so important that they required the approval of a Party Congress—only the third in the history of the Party in Vietnam. It was this Third Party Congress, meeting in September 1960, which definitively approved the new direction of Party policy in the South, including most importantly the shift to armed activity already under way, the formation of a new national front, the alteration of the name of the Party in the South, and the upgrading (for the second time in history) of the Nam Bo Regional Committee into a direct extension of the Central Committee itself.

The need for a national front is one of the lessons which the Party in Vietnam has learned from bloody experience and never forgotten. Party thinking about this subject was decisively influenced by the failure of the Nghe An soviets in the 1930s—a failure that, in the Party's reading of history, was due to "infantilism" and a "left deviationist" strategy of "digging up the old society by its roots" [*dao tan goc, boc tan re*]. By failing in its extremism to recognize the need to form temporary alliances with certain intermediate classes, the peasantry drove those classes into the arms of the counterrevolutionaries, resulting in the bloody suppression of the Nghe An soviets. Consequently the Party now emphasizes the need to neutralize these intermediate classes by means of a broad national front, thus splitting the ranks of the enemy and easing the advance of the Party's core forces: the workers and the peasants. This role of the front has been formalized in communist doctrine in the *tam buu phap*, or "three instruments of revolution" of Mao Tse-tung: the Party, the army, and the front. The Party is the brain, the army the muscle, and the front is the means of fracturing the society in such a way that the army can do its job with least resistance.

Reinforcing this theoretical demand for the creation of a

14. Race Document 1041 is a copy of the "Declaration of the Veterans of the Resistance" which resulted from this meeting.

national front in the South in 1960 was another issue of immediate practical urgency: the now revealed existence of widespread revolutionary military forces, growing stronger day by day. In the words of Chan:

> Why did the National Liberation Front appear in 1960? Was it because the Vietnamese people or the opposition politicians wanted to establish a front? No. It was because of the Party's judgment of the situation: armed forces had to be unleashed, for without fighting there was no way to save the Party. But under what name could these forces fight? We could not keep calling them the Hoa Hao People's Socialist Alliance, for the Hoa Hao would call us liars. We could not call them Binh Xuyen because Bay Vien in France would disavow them. We could not call them Cao Dai for the same reason.
>
> We had to have some name under which to lead these forces which were developing day by day. The situation was urgent, not because of the internal politics of the southern regime and not because of the sects or the politicians in opposition to Diem. . . . The situation was urgent because, where the Central Committee had called for one soldier, ten appeared, forcing us into a passive position. The Central Committee could hardly permit the International Control Commission to say that there was an invasion from the North, so it was necessary to have some name . . . to clothe these forces with some political organization. . . .
>
> Thus the Front had to appear in order to conceal this military activity. At the same time it was necessary to send representatives abroad to show that the Front was not communist, in order to isolate the [Diem] government internationally. . . . Thus both the internal and the international situations forced the appearance of the Front at that time, although it had been planned since 1959.

That the Front would never turn on its creator was ensured by placing both overt and covert Party members in key positions at each echelon, such as chairman of the Front committee and chief of the military affairs section; by establishing no separate vertical chain of command for the Front, in order that each echelon would be a horizontal dependency of its corresponding Party committee; by selecting suitably manipulatable individuals for positions in the Front; and finally by ensuring that the Front never commanded military units except in name. This in turn was guaranteed by the continuing requirement that commanders and political officers of military units be Party members.[15]

---

15. The means by which this control of front organizations is to be exercised by the Party are detailed in such Party instruction manuals as *Bon Bai*

The same realities which dictated the formation of a superficially independent front in the South also dictated the announce-
ment of the superficially independent People's Revolutionary Party.
Although the People's Revolutionary Party was not officially announced until a year after the National Liberation Front, the latter
had been formed in such a hurry that in practice they were both presented together in the rural areas. As for the peasantry, noted An,
they all knew there had been no real change in the Party:

> The formation of the People's Revolutionary Party had no signifi-
> cance to the peasantry. They live in intimate contact with the Party and
> thus were aware that it was still the communists. The People's Revolu-
> tionary Party was useful only in dealing with city people, intellectuals,
> and foreigners.

The decision to upgrade the status of the Nam Bo Regional
Committee was in anticipation of the new and more bitter stage of
the revolution in the South, just as had been done before in 1951.
Said one intelligence report: "During the Lao Dong Party Congress
of 1960, almost a dozen southern or central Vietnamese were made
members of the Central Committee of the Lao Dong Party. This
group of men were subsequently chosen to form the Central Office
for South Vietnam as an extension of the Lao Dong Party in South
Vietnam."[16]

While these developments were occurring at the higher levels
within the Party in the South, in Long An events followed the complex "back-and-forth" pattern predicted in the "Message from the
Regional Committee." The initial impact of the Party's new strategy
of violence was strong in Long An, so that within less than two years,
as already noted, tax collections were down 50 percent, surrenders
to the government had virtually ceased, and the government was in
effect eliminated from all but the urban areas. Duoc's successor as
province chief in October 1961 put the Party on the defensive for
a little over a year, but by mid-1963 the situation was as bad for the
government as it had been before and was growing worse.

For a majority of the rural population the greatest immediate
impact of this transition to Party rule was a significant and remarkably swift change in landowning patterns. A Cong An report from

---

Hoc Ve Cong Tac Dang Cua Huyen Uy [Four Lessons on the Party Tasks of
the District Committee], Race Document 1059–1060.
16. *Working Paper* Document 208.

Can Duoc dated June 13, 1960, contained the first evidence of activity in this area:

Vo van C———, arrested June 12, 1960, on orders of the district chief.
Born: 1903, in Tan Lan village, Can Duoc, Long An
Son of Vo van M——— and Le thi L———, both deceased
Wife: Nguyen thi T———
Children: none
Profession: farmer
Religious or sect affiliation: none
Previous convictions: none
Charge: accepting land distributed by the Vietcong on the night of April 11, 1960.

Thereafter land frequently entered the police reports.[17]

---

17. Examples:

July: Lai van C——— arrested on a charge of following Vietcong agitation in a land dispute.

August: A platoon of armed Vietcong called a meeting of the residents of Binh Loi and Binh Thuan hamlets, Nhut Ninh village. In front of the meeting the Vietcong warned our soldiers, hamlet chiefs, and police that they must cease work immediately under penalty of death. The Vietcong then forced the soldiers, hamlet chiefs, and policemen to stand up one by one and swear in front of the people that they would cease work, and that if they failed to do so they willingly accepted the death penalty. The Vietcong also forbade landowners to recover land from their tenants. In addition, those who had just bought land were forbidden to remove the current tenant or to allow anyone else to work the land.

September: At eight o'clock on the night of September 9, four Vietcong, armed with two submachine guns and two rifles, entered the home of Mr. Vo van T———, Binh Cong hamlet, Vinh Cong village. They ordered Mr. T——— to return a piece of land (which T——— is currently working himself) to Mr. B——— of Binh Chanh hamlet, Hoa Phu village. The province police office is respectfully requested to find some means to cope with these actions of the communist bandits in sabotaging the government land-reform program.

October: Two years ago Mr. Truong van D——— purchased two hectares of land at Long Tri village. Since that time he has farmed the land himself. Many times the Vietcong have come to the home of Mr. D——— demanding that he return the land to the tenant who was operating the land at the time he purchased it. D——— repeatedly refused. For this reason at eight o'clock last night a group of Vietcong armed with three rifles surrounded D———'s house, seized D———, and tied him up. They then called together all the hamlet residents and condemned D——— to death for the crimes of taking the people's land and serving as a spy for the Cong An. After thirty minutes the hamlet residents were dismissed.

The Vietcong then took D——— to a place approximately 300 yards away and shot him.

The strategy on which these actions were based is summed up in the Party's land-reform slogan: "Turn the landless, poor, and middle peasants into one bloc, allied with the rich peasants; fragment or win over the landlords." The goal of land redistribution was to win a large number of adherents, firmly committed to the revolutionary movement, from among the landless and poor peasants, at the cost of only a few enemies among the landlords or those already in the government and thus determined to oppose the revolution in any case. This was achieved by making minimal demands on the middle and rich peasants in the redistribution process. Lower middle peasants might even gain some land (should there be any remaining after satisfying the demands of the landless and poor), particularly if they were active in the revolutionary movement. Typically, the demands on the rich peasants, at least in the initial stage of the process, were only for a reduction in the rates of interest they charged on crop loans, or the rentals they levied for the use of farm animals or implements. However, as Party influence in an area became more complete, rich peasants were generally forbidden to hire agricultural laborers and this, together with certain social pressures, induced many to "donate" land to the revolution. Similarly, landlords who elected to remain in Party-dominated areas and who declined involvement with the government were permitted to retain some of their land, and on the remaining land were permitted to collect rents ranging from 5 to 15 percent of the crop (as opposed to the 25 percent legal maximum in government areas and the 50 percent which was often levied).

The continuing requirements of this policy were spelled out in a document titled, "Status of the Revolutionary Movement in the South," dated September 1962:[18]

Close unity between the poor and middle peasants is a problem of major importance in rural policy. Thus, in settling agrarian problems, while trying to meet the needs of poor peasants, we should absolutely avoid encroaching on the rights of middle peasants by taking their land for distribution to poor peasants. Uncultivated or communal land may be distributed, but the province committee should be consulted. In instances in which rights of middle peasants have been encroached upon, but not very seriously, it is better not to try to readjust the situation, but we should acknowledge the mistake and promise not to encroach on their

---

18. Pike Document 257.

rights again. If their rights have been seriously encroached upon, we should remedy the situation in a very tactful manner to consolidate the unity among the peasantry.

With regard to poor peasants, in addition to temporary distribution or assignment of land to them where feasible, we should also give them guidance to develop their land and to increase production, promote solidarity and mutual assistance between peasants so that they will help one another with funds and seeds, and combat usury. We should give close guidance to middle and poor peasants in order to build up a united bloc in rural areas and to boost production. With regard to rich peasants, we will continue to protect their economic interests, and in our political union with them we will primarily use educative methods to limit their passivity. With regard to landlords who are not wicked agents of the enemy, we will recognize their right to collect rents, but will force them to reduce rents. If they return after escaping when we have intensified the people's movement to weaken enemy pressure, we should give them back their property that we have temporarily administered. With regard to wicked enemy agents who have been condemned, we will confiscate their land for distribution to peasants but will keep some for their wives and children.

With regard to wicked landlords who are also government employees or military officers, policies will also be determined.

Land redistribution was an integral part of the Party takeover in the rural areas of Long An, the promise of land being one of the principal means of obtaining a core of activists in each village to drive out the government authorities. As indicated in the documents cited in the previous chapter, land was one of the major themes of Party propaganda in the years from 1956 through 1959. Now with the disappearance of the local government authorities, meetings would be called by the Party-sponsored Farmers' Association, ordinarily on a hamlet-by-hamlet or village-by-village basis (depending on the remaining government presence), to distribute land without charge, under the guidance of the village chi bo, and usually with a member of the district or province committee in attendance. Usually the Party members would already have researched the local land situation very carefully and established the general shape for the local redistribution, in accordance with Party policy. Available for distribution were French-owned land, the land of government officials and of landlords who had fled, village communal land, and land "donated" by "patriotic landlords." Meetings would be seeded if possible with one or two such individuals in order to spur the generosity of others.

Under the priorities established by the Party, the landless had first call upon available land, followed by poor peasants who had actually contributed to driving out the government, followed by others having some land already, in order of need. Distributions were arranged so that (within the limits of availability) the first two categories always received land, with the choicest lands going to those who had most actively worked with the Party, whether Party members or not. At the meeting the Party leaders (usually under the guise of the Farmers' Association) would suggest the outlines of the redistribution based on their own investigations, and then call for comments or complaints, and especially for "donated" land. Once a consensus had been reached, the results would be publicly announced to avoid subsequent disputes over ownership, with the Party cadres declaring that land ownership would remain thus as long as the government did not return. Nevertheless, it was made clear that these lands were only provisionally entrusted to the new owners, with the understanding that final arrangements would be made after the complete defeat of the government. According to some reports deeds would be given on request, but this almost never happened, since possession of such a deed meant an automatic jail sentence for the possessor if it fell into government hands.

According to the reports of defectors, Party members were obliged to complete land redistribution and rental and interest reduction within three months after the government had been driven out of an area. The results of local redistribution meetings had to be formally approved by the province committee, but this seldom changed what had previously been decided by the villagers themselves.

Another important economic reform which accompanied the Party take-over in Long An was the establishment of a system of progressive taxation. Formerly public and private land rentals had been a fixed percentage of the crop, while the government land tax was a flat amount annually per hectare, proportionate to the grade of the land. The government revenue system also relied heavily on use and consumer taxes and on fixed fees for the issuance of documents and permits. Thus the financial structure existing at the time of the Party take-over was strongly regressive, striking proportionately hardest those least able to pay. In its place the Party instituted a progressive system [luy tien], following a flexible and locally determined formula based on income, size of family, and class affiliation. The initial impact of this progressive system of taxation was in turn reinforced by the fact that financial demands of the Party in Long An were relatively light until 1965.

The defectors interviewed were in substantial agreement that no other Party activities had such an immediate and profound impact on local attitudes. It will be worthwhile to quote Chan at some length on the land issue:

According to Party doctrine, the issue of land is an integral part of people's war. Thus, when the Party seizes an area, it considers that land reform is a strategic task which must be carried out regardless of cost, in order to produce an impact on the peasantry and in order to set the peasantry in opposition to the government and the landlords. At the same time this is a means of making the peasantry accept the need to pay taxes and to send its youth into the army. According to Party doctrine, the national democratic revolution has two missions: anti-imperialism and antifeudalism. The one implies the other, because the landlords have conspired with the imperialists. It can be explained very simply to the peasants: if you want to keep your land, you must fight the imperialists, and if you want to fight the imperialists, your son must go into the army and you must pay taxes. That is the strategic line of the Party.

The Party's present land-reform program is basically the same as during the Resistance: to reduce land rents, to reduce interest, to reduce rental payments for farm tools and animals, and to confiscate the land of absentee landlords. The ownership of land and the right to collect rents of religious organizations is recognized, as well as that of landlords who remain in Party areas. Thus the land situation in the South is not the same as in the North, particularly in regard to denunciation meetings. This is for two reasons. First, in the South making a living is much easier since there is so much land. Second, the Party does not dare push the land issue so strongly as in the North, because from the time of the Resistance so many of the Party members in the South have belonged to the landowning elements, the petty bourgeoisie, and the intelligentsia. Now the Party has reduced the numbers of such people, but it still does not dare push the land issue strongly because of the need to win over landed and religious elements in the present stage of the national liberation movement.

Party policy is to distribute land to the lowest elements in the countryside, that is, the landless and poor peasants and certain middle peasants. As for landlords, they are to be overthrown, just as are the rich peasants, although this depends on the stage of the revolution. At present the Party distinguishes various types of landlords: those to be destroyed are the ones who participate in the government; fence-sitters are temporarily permitted to retain their own land, while patriotic landlords are permitted to collect land rents up to a certain level and on a certain amount of land. With rich peasants the Party tries to educate them and persuade them to reduce the rates they charge for interest and for rental of farm tools and animals. During this period the Party never touches their land in the South, but if they have much land and cannot work it themselves, the Party persuades them to let it out at a very low rental.

Once it starts distributing land, what does the Party say to the people? It never says that the land is theirs permanently—only that it is theirs for ten years, fifteen years, perhaps their whole life, but still only provisionally. This is a lesson drawn from the Resistance, when the peasants got the impression the land was theirs permanently. In the North after the war was over the government needed various areas for industry, etc., but the peasants refused to return the land, demanding compensation and making difficulties. Thus since 1960 when land redistribution began again, the Party has always said that the land is only provisionally distributed, not permanently, because it plans after seizing the South to establish collective farms, industrial areas, etc. Despite what the Party says, the peasants feel that the land is permanently theirs, and should the Party succeed in taking over the South, it will meet with no small opposition thereafter.

Nevertheless, once the peasants received land, their living standard increased tremendously. Formerly they had to pay rent to the landlord and interest to the moneylender. Now for the first few years they could keep the entire harvest, and thus their living was comparatively easy, just as it had been in the Resistance. But as the pace of the war increased, those who received land had to pay for the war, for whenever the Party mentioned land it also mentioned politics: the peasants now own the land, but the peasants are also the main forces of the revolution. Only by sending their sons into the army and paying taxes could the war be won, and only by winning the war could they keep their land. Thus land is a life and death issue, inextricably tied to their own interests. Although sometimes their taxes to the Party are five or seven times those to the government, they nevertheless pay them: in the time of the French, when their parents had no land, their life was extremely harsh. Now they have land, and they are willing to pay and to send their sons into the army to preserve it.

Chan also spoke of the extent to which assistance to the revolutionary movement was "forced" as opposed to "voluntary."

This is a subtle point. One cannot say that support is voluntary, and one cannot say it is not voluntary. Previously the peasantry felt that it was the most despised class, with no standing at all, particularly the landless and the poor peasants. For example, at a celebration they could just stand in a corner and look, not sit at the table like the village notables.

Now the communists have returned and the peasants have power. The land has been taken from the landlords and turned over to the peasants, just as have all the local offices. Now the peasants can open their eyes and look up to the sky: they have prestige and social position. The landlords and other classes must fear them because they have power: most of the cadres are peasants, most of the Party members are peasants, most of the military commanders are peasants. Only now do the peasants feel that they have proper rights: materially they have land and are no longer oppressed by the landlords; spiritually they have a position in society, ruling the landlords instead of being ruled by them. This the peasants like. But if the communists were to go and the government to come back, the peasants would return to their former status as slaves. Consequently they must fight to preserve their interests and their lives, as well as their political power.

On the other hand, there are some, particularly the middle and rich peasants, who do not like the communists, because the communists hurt their interests: they are not permitted to charge interest and rentals as before, and if they want to hire laborers they are accused of exploitation. Thus they don't like the communists, but they don't dare oppose them, because, if they oppose the communists, they must go to live in a government area. But do they have enough money to go and live in Saigon? Probably not, and so they must be content to remain.

Thus there are those who willingly and voluntarily support the Party, and those who are forced, and to say that everyone is forced is mistaken. One must make distinctions between classes of people in order to understand the situation.

The success of the Party with these methods can be judged from the testimony of Duoc's successor as province chief, Major Nguyen Viet Thanh. On coming to Long An in October 1961, Thanh recalled, he could not drive more than two kilometers in any direction from the province capital, except along Route 4, without coming under enemy fire or meeting a roadblock; moreover, road-blocks removed in the morning would be replaced by afternoon. In Thanh's judgment Duoc was removed because of this drastic decline in security: Duoc was basically an administrator (and a good one, Thanh said), but he had neglected military operations. Thus when he took over as province chief, Thanh began a vigorous counter-attack which for a time paid dividends.

Thanh had certain advantages over his predecessors in dealing with the situation in Long An, for he himself had been born in Binh Phuoc district of Long An in 1931, the son of a member of the Forestry Service. After receiving the *tu tai* from Chasseloup-Laubat

School in Saigon, Thanh attended the military academy at Dalat, graduating with the rank of second lieutenant in 1951. He then fought against the Vietminh for one year in the South and two years in the North. After the Geneva Accords, he traveled with the rank of captain of the United States and spent eighteen months at the Army Infantry School.

It is not inaccurate to say that Thanh is the most fondly remembered of the province chiefs of Long An. Those who worked with him are full of anecdotes to illustrate his popularity and sincere concern for the people of Long An: how he created bad feelings among some officials by forbidding the use of public vehicles for private purposes, how he broke off with his father over the latter's attempt to influence an appointment, how he was always at the scene of an incident, no matter what the hour of the day or night, how the chief of public works cried because Thanh kept waking him in the middle of the night to repair blown culverts. It is interesting to note that in numerous previous interviews, government officials emphasized the need for a policy of nonlocal service for administrative officials and military officers in order to prevent corruption. Thus it is indeed ironical that Thanh, certainly the most dedicated province chief of Long An, and the one upholding the highest standards of personal integrity, was also the first native of the province to become province chief. Nevertheless, just as Duoc's administrative skills did not save the situation, so Thanh's military skills and transparent honesty were insufficient in Long An. In particular, it was Thanh's unfortunate fate to inherit responsibility for the strategic hamlet program, just getting under way in Long An at the moment of Thanh's arrival.

In Thanh's view the basic reason for the serious position of the government on his arrival in Long An was that the government had failed to take sufficient measures against the Party's stay-behind apparatus in the South after the regroupment to the North. In Thanh's own words:

Our mistake before was in not eliminating the Vietcong still hiding in the South. During the regroupment to the North the Vietcong left many hard-core Party members in the South. Like germs in our blood, they could act up at any time. Our mistake was in being too honest, not deceitful like the communists. Perhaps at that time the government was forced by financ⁻ᵃˡ considerations to reduce the size of the army—I don't remember the numbers exactly. Thus when the enemy became active again, we did not develop forces to react in time. That was our failure.

In saying this Thanh was clearly unaware that the government had actually been devastatingly effective in rooting out the Party's apparatus in the South, and that this effectiveness had been founded principally on the police, not on government military forces. Nevertheless, because of this reading of history, and presumably influenced by his military training, Thanh responded to the situation with an intensive series of military actions, relying partly on forces organic to the province and partly on forces belonging to the Seventh Division stationed in My Tho. It is likely that his judgment in this was also influenced by the increasingly serious nature of the engagements occurring in Long An. The first attack on a government outpost had occurred in Binh Phuoc district in August 1960. According to the police report:

> At 5:00 P.M. a platoon of Vietcong consisting of approximately thirty armed men attacked the Dan Ve outpost at An Vinh Ngai village, killing two policemen and three Dan Ve. One submachine gun and five rifles were lost. Two of the enemy were killed but were carried off by their comrades.

By the time of Thanh's arrival the engagements were much larger, typified by one in mid-1961 in western Thu Thua district. There a marine battalion from the Capital Military Zone had come upon an unidentified enemy force in prepared positions and had suffered significant losses before withdrawing.

The second prong of Thanh's counterattack in Long An was the strategic hamlet program. In retrospect, Thanh believed that the program was sound in concept, but that its execution was crippled by the desire to go too fast and the lack of sufficient cadres to organize the people. The pressure on Thanh to "go fast," however, was irresistible, and he remembered with some bitterness that he had to make a monthly trip to Saigon to report on progress in the strategic hamlet program, only to be reprimanded each time by Ngo dinh Nhu for his failure to push the program fast enough. Of the forty-two provinces under Saigon's jurisdiction at the time, Long An stood third from the bottom in the execution of the program, which Thanh attributed to the difficulty of forcing the relatively scattered population of Long An to move into the new hamlets.[19]

---

19. According to information supplied by Earl Young, approximately 90,000 people were involved in the construction of the strategic hamlets in

It is clear from talking to former residents of the strategic hamlets that those completed were done in form only, with few defensive weapons or obstacles, and with the occupants themselves often forced to buy barbed wire and pickets.

Despite the shortcomings of the strategic hamlet program, this two-pronged counterattack succeeded in stabilizing the situation for a time.[20] This is apparent in the temporary slowing in the rate of decline of land-tax collections, as well as the sharp rise in the number of surrenders after Thanh's arrival: from 14 in 1961 to 109 in 1962 and 332 in 1963. Nevertheless, Thanh was aware that by mid-1963 the situation was again beginning to deteriorate, and he attributed this to the lack of sufficient troops "to defeat the Vietcong decisively." During that period Thanh had under his command only eight companies of Bao An (one for each district) and a limited number of Dan Ve in certain villages. More could not be recruited, Thanh noted, because of financial limits imposed from Saigon. Thanh did not remain to see the denouement of the situation in Long An, however. In June 1963 history repeated itself as Thanh was relieved for failing to agree to fix the upcoming National Assembly elections.[21] Events thereafter moved rapidly downhill, and in the chaos

Long An, or roughly a quarter of the population of the province. At the time Young was USOM representative in Long An.

20. Evidence from numerous captured documents indicates that the Party initially underestimated the strategic hamlet program. For example, see Pike Documents 35, page 2, and 257, page 13.

21. The strange ways of history are illustrated by the subsequent careers of those involved in Long An at this time. Thanh's successor as province chief duly fixed the election as Thanh had refused to do, but was swept out of office in the days following the November coup. He was one of the six Vietnamese officers killed in the accidental firing of rockets by an American helicopter in Cholon during the attacks of Tet, 1968. His three immediate successors lasted only a few months each. The winner of the rigged election, a female dentist and a refugee from the North, fled to Paris during the early days of November, returning to Saigon only in 1967.

On the other hand one of the defeated candidates, Le Tai Hoa, became a prominent member of the National Assembly. Thanh himself, at the time these interviews were conducted in 1968, had been promoted to brigadier general, commanding the Seventh Division. He was widely viewed as the most competent and incorruptible of the ten Vietnamese division commanders. Confirmation of this judgment occurred a short time after Tran van Huong became prime minister. He promoted Thanh to the rank of major general and appointed him commanding general of the Fourth Corps Tactical Zone, comprising all of the vital provinces of the Mekong Delta south of Long An. Thanh was killed in a helicopter crash on May 2, 1970, while observing a military operation in Cambodia.

following the fall of President Diem, the last of the strategic hamlets was destroyed in Long An.[22]

The Government's Last Days in Long An

Arriving to take over as province chief in May 1964, Lieutenant Colonel Pham Anh found the situation "not very good." Anh had been born in Hue in central Vietnam, but he had spent much time in the South and was familiar with Long An from having conducted military operations there as an ARVN regimental commander. Anh described the events that took place just before his appointment:

> A month before I arrived, the Vietcong were operating extremely strongly in Long An, in order to prepare a springboard for their march on Saigon. First they attacked the Dan Ve-Bao An Training Center at Go Den and held it for a night, and then they attacked the Chieu Hoi Center near the province capital and kidnapped a number of returnees. The goal of the first of these attacks was to make it impossible to recruit soldiers and to make the Bao An and Dan Ve fearful and put them on the defensive. The seizure of the Training Center destroyed their morale, and people no longer dared to enter the Bao An or the Dan Ve. The goal of the second attack was to put an end to the Chieu Hoi program.
>
> These two attacks were extremely effective politically. After the attack on the Training Center the trainees fled in disorder back to their home districts, and morale collapsed. Returnees stopped coming in because we could not protect them. New-life hamlets and bridges were destroyed, and district towns like Tan Tru were cut off and had to be supplied by helicopter. At that time we controlled only the province capital and the district towns.

Anh offered many of the same judgments as his predecessors to account for this situation. For example, he agreed with Thanh that the government had failed to react sufficiently in the years after the Geneva Accords, although, as noted above, this widely accepted view of events is seriously mistaken. Anh also agreed with Thanh that one decisive difference between the two sides which put the government at a disadvantage was that the opposition could use terror, at any time and place of its own choosing, while the government could not.

---

22. For some indications of how desperate the situation was for the Saigon administration in Long An even as early as January 1964, see "Survey of Secondary School Opinion" included in the materials deposited with the Center for Research Libraries. It reports the findings of two United States Information Service studies of rural attitudes and security conditions in Long An during December 1963 and January 1964.

Students saluting Nguyen Ngoc Tho, vice president of the Republic of Vietnam, and Mai Ngoc Duoc, then a district chief in Quang Ngai (p. 45). 1956 photo courtesy Vietnam Information Service.

Mai Ngoc Duoc distributing gifts to representatives of the poor in Long An. He prided himself on his close rapport with the people (p. 50). 1960 photo courtesy Vietnam Information Service.

Mai Ngoc Duoc, in mandarin dress, speaking at the National Day celebration on October 26, 1960. Banderoles at the left applaud the agroville program (p. 53). Photo courtesy Vietnam Information Service.

President Diem (right) addressing the people of Long An. Mai Ngoc Duoc, whose legal authority as province chief was reinforced by his relation with Diem, is shown at center. The man in national dress at left is a representative of the local notables (p. 54). 1960 photo courtesy Vietnam Information Service.

The Duc Hue agroville in 1968: an American Special Forces camp used for the surveillance of the Cambodian border (p. 55). "H" at lower left is a helipad. Photo by author.

Major (later Major General) Nguyen Viet Thanh, at the microphone, during change of command ceremonies in 1961. Seated at the table are Mai Ngoc Duoc, ʿoutgoing province chief (left), and Minister Nguyen van Vang (p. 130). Photo courtesy Vietnam Information Service.

The official caption of this photo reads: "Residents are enthusiastically constructing the perimeter of their strategic hamlet." Memories of residents, as revealed in contemporary interviews, differ appreciably (p. 132). 1963 photo courtesy Vietnam Information Service.

Strategic hamlet protective fence and pointed bamboo stakes in Can Giuoc district, Long An province, September 1963 (p. 133). Photo courtesy Earl Young.

The fence and moat erected by villagers for protection of a strategic hamlet in Ben Luc district, Long An province, mid-1963 (p. 133). Photo courtesy Earl Young.

A destroyed strategic hamlet fence, about six miles southeast of Tan An in Long An province, August 1963 (p. 134). Photo courtesy Earl Young.

A strategic hamlet defender. Said the photographer, "This shot is my favorite of all the thousands I took in Vietnam: the grim determination, cynicism, and pure desire to survive are all displayed in his face. His only complaint: he wanted more ammunition." Photo courtesy Earl Young.

A destroyed strategic hamlet, with roofs removed to prevent the return of the occupants (p. 134). Photo courtesy Earl Young.

Remains of the government military training center in Long An after the attack of April 1964 (p. 134). Photo courtesy Earl Young.

Protagonists of two social orders meet on the battlefield: a fallen guerrilla and his captor. Man on right is a member of the Long An Provincial Reconnaissance Unit, paid and directed by the Central Intelligence Agency (p. 213). 1968 photo courtesy Vietnam Information Service.

President Nguyen van Thieu bestowing land titles in Long An, under the decade-old Ordinance 57 program. Colonel Nguyen van Nguu, province chief, at left. 1968 photo courtesy Vietnam Information Service.

The bridge on Route 4 over the eastern branch of the Vam Co River at Ben Luc, showing the replacement of a section destroyed by a floating charge in 1968. Photo courtesy Vietnam Information Service.

Comrades-in-arms: Colonel Nguyen van Nguu, province chief, and Colonel James A. Herbert, province senior advisor, at a school opening. 1969 photo courtesy Vietnam Information Service.

"The democratic process." 1969 photo courtesy Vietnam Information Service.

The fertile rice land of Long An. The name of the province, from literary Sino-Vietnamese, means "prosperous and peaceful." Photo courtesy U.S. Army.

**MAI VÀNG NỞ
KHẮP THÔN TRANG,
NẾU KHÔNG GIẶC
CỘNG XÓM LÀNG
YÊN VUI.**

The joys of rural life, as seen in an anticommunist poster depicting Tet,
the Lunar New Year. Says the message:

> *The countryside is filled with cherry blossoms;*
> *Without the communist rebels,*
> *Life in the village would be peaceful and happy.*

The Vietcong use terrorism to instill fear. In a hamlet they will pick out a couple of people who they say cooperate with the Americans, and shoot them, to set an example. From the Vietcong viewpoint this is legal, and if they make a few mistakes, nevertheless the person who does it is not punished. But after they kill a few people, the whole hamlet is afraid and the Vietcong can force them to cooperate, while we have not enough strength to protect the hamlet at night.

On the other hand, the government is democratic and could never approve arresting and shooting someone. Even though I am sector commander, I do not have that right. Thus legality is our strength but also our weakness—our weakness because the people do not fear us. The Vietcong can kill one person and terrorize a whole village. Thus their soldiers must follow them, because if they don't, they will be killed.

But we cannot stay with the people all the time. We come and go with operations by day, but we do not have enough strength to protect the people by night. I have yet to figure out how to protect a hamlet with thirty people. From a purely military viewpoint how can it be done? The Vietcong wait and wait, perhaps six months before they attack. We can build for two years, but they can destroy in one night.

The person who finds the key to that puzzle has solved the problem.

Anh's attempt to deal with the situation involved several measures. One of these was the establishment of a "free strike zone" in the northwestern part of the province. The need for this Anh reasoned as follows:

If we examine the geography of Long An we see that there are two clearly defined regions. The first, in the northern part of Thu Thua, consists entirely of swamps with little population. There the Vietcong could easily hide, turning it into a base to strike out against Hau Nghia and Saigon, or south toward My Tho and Go Cong. On the other hand, the area along the highway is the heavily populated and economically important one. After surveying the situation, I concluded that to enlarge the area under our control we must prevent the enemy from concentrating his forces into battalion or regimental size and using this base to strike our areas. If we left him free to operate in that area, we were dead. Thus at the very least we had to establish a free strike zone and tell the inhabitants that we would bomb at will. In this way the enemy would have no sanctuary and would constantly have to be on the move. He would thus not have enough strength to attack us according to his plan.

As a consequence, between ten and fifteen thousand residents were moved from this area into other parts of the province in late 1964.

At the same time a coordinated plan called *hop tac* (cooperation) was adopted to pacify the provinces immediately surrounding

Saigon. The plan was envisaged first to secure the main lines of communication and then gradually to expand these pacified zones, like a "spreading oil spot." This was to come about by replacing main force units with locally recruited forces and then moving the main force units onto a wider perimeter. As part of this plan two ARVN regiments were transferred to Long An from central Vietnam: the 50th Regiment was to secure Route 4 leading from Saigon to the Delta, and the 46th Regiment was to secure Route 5 leading from Saigon to Go Cong.

Meanwhile, the Party had not been inactive. Ideally, according to defectors, the Party would have called for its general uprising and final wave of attacks during the coup of November 1963. It had not done so, however, because of an insufficient development of its military forces. As a result, it called for a "general mobilization" on July 20, 1964, the tenth anniversary of the signing of the Geneva Accords. According to the terms of the order for mobilization, every male from eighteen to thirty was required to serve, but several defectors from Long An report that there was widespread evasion: perhaps only one-third of those eligible were actually inducted into military units. Another third fled to government areas, and the remaining third agreed only to dig up roads or to transport supplies, but not to carry weapons. Defectors report that at that time they had no authority to arrest those who declined service.

Nevertheless, in Long An the size of the Party's forces continued to rise, as did their combat capabilities (see Table 2). By late 1964 Long An's own battalion, the 506th, had become so large that it was split into two units. These, moreover, were considered so good that they were singled out for special praise by General Nguyen Chi Thanh, commander of all communist forces in southern Vietnam until his death in 1967. "The Long An battalion is the best one in

TABLE 2: ESTIMATED REVOLUTIONARY MILITARY STRENGTH, 1962-1965 [a]

	1962	1963	1964	1965
Village guerrillas	800	950	1,100	1,150
District companies	. . . [b]	400	480	600
Province battalion	. . . [b]	200	500	450
Total	. . . [b]	1,550	2,080	2,200

NOTES: [a] For comparison purposes, figures contained in *Ban Tran Liet Viet Cong* indicate that total revolutionary military strength in Long An in the last six months of 1959 was approximately 400.
[b] Not available.
SOURCE: Long An sector J-2 intelligence estimates.

the entire region," he said. "The Duc Hoa battalion is good, too."[23]
By early 1965 these forces were masters of the situation in Long An,
moving at will and defeating government units superior in size
wherever they chose to engage them. One American advisor who
served with the 50th Regiment at that time has since written his view
of the situation. His conclusion, like that of many others on the
scene, was that, in the face of mounting revolutionary strength, the
arrival of ARVN forces did little to enhance the government presence. And by 1965 that presence was very slim indeed.

As a part of this intensified effort [the *hop tac* plan], the 25th ARVN
Infantry Division, initially located in Quang Ngai, about 240 kilometers
south of Hue, was ordered to move south and assume responsibility for
the area south and west of Saigon. The first element of the Division to
move, the 50th ARVN Infantry Regiment, was dispatched by air early
in September, 1964, and immediately moved into the pacification zone in
Long An province. Within a week the Regiment assumed full responsibility for Zone A, an area about 26 kilometers long and 5 kilometers wide,
astride the important Saigon-My Tho Highway (National Highway 4)
and extending through the depth of Long An.
[After recounting the difficulties in attempting pacification, the
author then explained that it was decided to focus efforts in the vicinity of
Tan Buu village, which could serve as a base of operations against the
506th Battalion.]
Although substantial progress had been made [in the Tan Buu area]
by the beginning of the 1965 New Year, the area had not attained the
desired six-point criteria, but there was optimism that complete pacification would soon be accomplished. These hopes proved to be short-
lived, for on the night of 8–9 January a Viet Cong battalion attacked
our positions and succeeded in overrunning the company command post
and weapons platoon. Even though the loss of life was not high, it was
by any standard a major defeat for the ARVN Regiment, and one from
which it had not fully recovered by June, 1965. Consequently the pacification activities of the unit slowly ground to a halt.

---

23. In a speech at the Fourth COSVN Congress in April 1966; this remark
is at page 14 of the English translation released by JUSPAO on March 30,
1967. The Duc Hoa battalion apparently refers to this offshoot of the 506th
Battalion, since according to Party military and administrative boundaries,
Duc Hoa was still part of Long An. Under government organization Duc Hoa
and Duc Hue districts had been split off from Long An in 1963 to become
part of the new province of Hau Nghia.
The apparent anomaly of the modestly rising number of surrenders to the
government during this period is probably explained by the communist force
buildup just described.

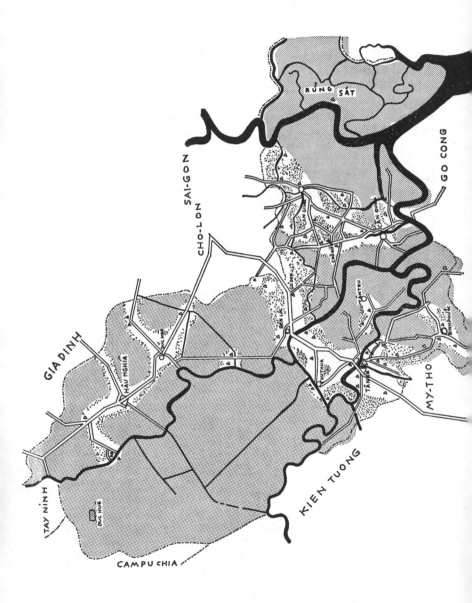

BẢN ĐỒ TỈNH LONG-AN GIẢI PHÓNG

MAP OF LIBERATED LONG AN PROVINCE

CHÚ THÍCH
Legend

Vùng giải phóng – Liberated areas

Vùng tranh chấp – Contested areas

Địch tạm chiếm – Temporarily occupied by enemy

Thị trấn giải phóng – Liberated city

O   Thị trấn – City

△   Bót – Post

=   Lộ – Road

⌒   Sông – River

(Kinh – Canal

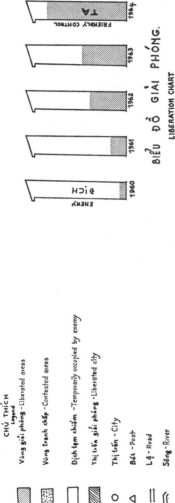

ĐỊCH
ENEMY

TA
FRIENDLY CONTROL

1960   1961   1962   1963   1964

BIỂU ĐỒ GIẢI PHÓNG.
LIBERATION CHART

This map, redrawn by a USOM artist in early 1965 from one in the possession of a captured Party member, depicts the security situation in Long An province in late 1964, as seen by the communist leadership. Lieutenant Colonel David E. Shepherd, then USOM province representative, observed that "At the time most all who saw it, both U.S. and Vietnamese, agreed that it was most accurate."

The map follows communist administrative boundaries, still including Duc Hoa and Duc Hue districts and the Rung Sat, which under government organization had been removed from the jurisdiction of Long An in earlier years. Similarly in the legend "enemy" refers to the Saigon government.

The reader should compare this map with the one shown on the rear endsheet, depicting the security situation, as seen by government officials, in late 1968.

The inertia that set in as a result of this episode was increased by the failure of the high command to recognize that Zone A had not been secured and pacified. Despite evidence to the contrary, Zone A was declared secure and the second phase of the operation, the conduct of pacification in the Zone, was initiated. . . .

By the beginning of summer, 1965, the situation had deteriorated so much that our position had regressed to what it had been when the pacification plan was initiated. . . .

The foundation on which the VC activity in Long An province rested was the hardcore 506th VC battalion. Deprived of this base the local VC were little more than bandits and capable of being managed, in time, by the forces available to the province. Unfortunately the VC battalion proved itself to be an extremely effective combat unit which on three separate occasions succeeded in tactically defeating much larger government forces in the field. The ARVN did not conduct a ruthless campaign to hunt down and destroy this organization, thus dooming any real hope for the pacification of Long An province.[24]

By early 1965 revolutionary forces had gained victory in virtually all the rural areas of Long An, and they had the ability, based on the balance of forces within the province, to seize and hold the only remaining islands of government authority: the province capital and the six district towns. They held back because, to be successful, the attacks would have had to be simultaneous throughout the country to prevent a reinforcement of any one area, and elsewhere the Party had not quite yet achieved the victorious position it had already gained in Long An.

---

24. Lieutenant Colonel Edwin W. Chamberlain, "Pacification," *Infantry*, LVIII:6 (November-December 1968), 32–39.

CHAPTER FOUR

Lessons from Long An

Correct thinking leads to correct actions; incorrect thinking leads to incorrect actions.

Communist training manual

This chapter will explore the differences between the approaches of the communist leadership and the government leadership that allowed the revolutionary movement, with such sparse human and material resources, to accomplish what the government failed to accomplish with such a comparative wealth of resources. These differences are of three kinds: strategic, organizational, and policy. Any one alone might have ensured the defeat of the government in Long An. In fact, however, they are inseparable; the second and third are logical and necessary complements of the first. Let us therefore consider first the strategic differences.

The Strategy of Victory versus the Strategy of Defeat[1]

If a single factor could explain the victory of the revolutionary movement in Long An, it could be stated as the communist leadership's *comprehensive view of revolution as a stage-by-stage social process.* The sophistication of communist strategic thought was never matched on the government side. Instead, the government's one-dimensional conception of a multidimensional process ensured its defeat, regardless of its resources. Its strategy—to the extent it can be said to have had one—was simply a strategy of defeat. The communist strategy was a strategy of victory.

What were the elements of this communist strategy of victory? To comprehend this it is first necessary to understand several concepts which are fundamental in communist revolutionary thought. These are: the concept of social class, the concept of contradiction,

---

1. Regrettably the term strategy as generally employed has a specifically military meaning, as in Clausewitz' classic definition: "The theory of the use of combats for the object of war" (as opposed to tactics: "The theory of the use of military forces in combat"). In this discussion strategy refers not to the matching of military means to military ends, but to an overall plan of action to achieve one's goals.

the concept of force, the concept of the balance of forces, the concept of security, and the concept of victory.

The Concept of Social Class

The foundation of communist social analysis is a theory of society and social development that depicts society as composed of different classes of people, defined by their relationship to the productive system of the particular period. As noted in Chapter Two, the Party divides rural Vietnamese society into five classes: the landless peasant, the poor peasant, the middle peasant, the rich peasant, and the landlord.

The Concept of Contradiction

While other analytic schemes are hospitable to the class analysis of society, in communist thought there is the additional element of contradiction—that is, the mutual opposition of parts—derived from the dialectical nature of Marxist philosophy. Thus a second distinguishing feature of Marxist social analysis is its view that social classes represent different and potentially hostile interests which are manifested in class struggle, or what a noncommunist observer might describe as conflicts of interest. Yet while noncommunist analysts depict numerous types of conflict—religious, racial, economic, political—in communist thought these are all viewed as manifestations of the social organization of the particular period. Thus they all appear as social contradictions.[2]

Moreover, in communist thought some apparent conflicts are not considered to be true contradictions existing "objectively." The apparent conflict between the working classes of two hostile countries exemplifies a contradiction which exists only subjectively in the minds of the participants, because they simply do not understand their "true" interests.

The Concept of Force

This concept, while never explicitly defined in Party literature, is implicit in every communist discussion of revolution or of social change in general. The term is employed in two senses. In the first and more general sense it denotes a particular, though not neces-

---

2. Throughout this discussion the term social is used in this sense, to embrace several aspects of human interrelationships—economic, political, cultural—which are commonly distinguished.

sarily organized, group or constellation of groups, in the sense of their attitude toward the status quo, seen, for example, in the phrase "the progressive forces in society." In the second and more specific sense, the term denotes *a person or group of persons acting in concert so as to determine the actions of others.* All means by which the actions of others may be determined are included: threat (compulsion), personal loyalty (leadership), institutional loyalty (legitimacy), and positive incentives (interests). Force is not exclusively a military concept. On the contrary, military force is just one type of force, one that employs a particular means and is significant at a certain period. It should be emphasized that "force" as used in communist terminology, although it may have a personal or a national context, is fundamentally a term concerning people. A force is only a force to the extent that, and in the ways that, it is an interaction of people.

Inherent in this concept is the fact that a force cannot be created by coercion. To believe otherwise is to be caught in a paradox: who is to coerce the coercers? While it is true that an organized force may exploit some unwilling individuals, these individuals can be only a part—and obviously not the motivating part—of the organization. Because a force cannot arise from coercion, it must arise from motivation.[3] Motivation in turn derives, in communist thought,

3. The approach employed here in comparing government and revolutionary organizations is the "inducement-contribution" theory of organizational behavior outlined by Chester I. Barnard in *The Functions of the Executive* (Cambridge: Harvard University Press, 1956). According to Barnard, successful organization is a product of efficient cooperation, and "successful cooperation in or by formal organizations is the abnormal, not the normal, condition. What are observed from day to day are the successful survivors among innumerable failures" (p. 5). In Barnard's terms the present effort is thus a parallel study of a successful organization (the revolutionary movement), and of a failure (the Saigon government).

The core of Barnard's theory may be summarized in a few words: "The contribution of personal efforts which constitute the energies of organizations are yielded by individuals because of incentives. . . . The individual is always the basic strategic factor in organization. Regardless of his history or his obligations he must be induced to cooperate, or there can be no cooperation. . . . If an organization is unable to afford incentives adequate to the personal contributions it requires it will perish unless it can by persuasion so change the desires of enough men that the incentives it can offer will be adequate" (pp. 139–149).

It is interesting that both the captain of industry, Chester I. Barnard, and the great revolutionary leader, Mao Tse-tung, are in complete agreement on the critical role of the individual as "the basic strategic factor."

from social contradictions. Political activity is the maximizing of one's own forces and the minimizing of the enemy's forces by the manipulation of contradictions.

The Concept of the Balance of Forces

By combining the concepts referred to above, we may visualize a society as composed of numerous contending forces, whose distribution for and against the status quo is referred to in Party doctrinal materials as the "balance of forces." Inherent in this concept is the idea of a *power relationship*, that is, the relative ability of the contending forces to enforce their will on an opponent. In its most primitive formulation this power relationship is determined by sheer numbers on each side. However, there are many factors that directly or indirectly alter the fundamental power relationship established by simple numbers. These are in general:

technological factors such as weaponry and communications;

organizational factors, i.e., the extent to which efforts of many individuals can be concentrated on one object, or to which the efforts of an opponent can be fragmented;

morale factors;

spatial factors;

economic factors; and

external factors, i.e., those affecting the ease of aid or intervention by external forces.

Consequently, the concept of balance of forces is a compound of two distinct and independent concepts: a *force ratio*, or roughly the number of people on each side; and a *power ratio*, or the ratio of effectiveness of each side's operatives after taking into account the impact of power-augmenting factors.

The utility of the concept of balance of forces is that it provides the Party leadership with a unique criterion directly productive of victory or defeat (defined below) by which every effort can be evaluated in commensurate terms: every course of action is judged against every alternative course of action in terms of its impact on the balance of forces.

The usefulness of this concept is also illustrated by its ability to resolve certain puzzling situations which are unexplainable in other conceptual schemes. The most obvious example is that the Party may "control" a hamlet with only one local guerrilla, while the government is unable to do so with continuous battalion sweeps through the hamlet area. By applying this concept of force, we see that the lone guerrilla represents a monopoly of force in his hamlet, except for the few hours a month during which the government battalion is sweeping through. On the other hand, the battalion does not even represent a force as defined, because the only means by which a battalion can determine the actions of others—the threat of violence—is ineffective if the battalion is present only a few hours. In the same sense, artillery and air power, though they represent a considerable expenditure of resources, may not represent a force as defined, or they may represent a much weaker force than a single man on the ground in the right place.

Knowing what factors go into making up a force, the Party can then act to maximize its own forces and to minimize the enemy's. This is done by:

> manipulating contradictions, that is, dissolving those apparent but unreal contradictions which diminish one's forces, and aggravating those contradictions which increase them;
>
> allocating manpower most efficiently among the different types of forces (as the above example shows, one guerrilla may be a more effective force than a battalion of mechanized infantry);
>
> manipulating the various factors which directly or indirectly influence the power relationship between contending forces (yet regardless of the level of these power-augmenting factors, the total magnitude of one's forces is bounded by the breadth of the social forces placed at one's command by the social system—i.e., the force ratio).

The power relationship expressed by the concept of balance of forces serves another important purpose for the Party leadership. Because the goal of the revolution is the overthrow and suppression of the exploiting classes, the question confronting the Party, as it does every revolutionary movement, is, "How do we get from here to there?" It is certain that the ruling classes will employ violence to retain their position, and thus violence will have to be used to combat them. But when? If the revolutionary movement moves too soon ("left-wing adventurism") in an attempt to suppress the opposition, it will end up being suppressed itself. If it moves too late ("rightist legalism"), it may miss an opportunity to seize power.

From the communist viewpoint, the struggle is continuous, shifting from one form to another until the stage of generalized violence and overthrow is reached. The critical issue at every point is the appropriate form of struggle: parliamentary activity, violent or nonviolent agitation, or revolutionary violence. Communist policy is to exploit to the fullest a number of legal, semilegal, and illegal activities. However, the appropriate combination of activities (the Party line) is determined by the distribution of power between the allies and the opponents of the revolution—the balance of forces. Thus this measurement is the principal strategic barometer in communist thinking.

On the basis of this analysis we see that "revolutionary war" can be defined as the stage of the conflict when the balance of forces is sufficiently favorable to the Party that violence is appropriate. The "three stages" of revolutionary war are nothing more than shifts in strategy to ever more decisive forms of military conflict permitted by the continuous shift in the balance of forces. The change from stage to stage marks the progressive narrowing of the material and manpower base of the incumbent power, leading to its eventual collapse as the instruments of violence on which it relied for survival are destroyed.

The Concept of Security

The concept of security as employed in Party doctrine differs markedly from the comparable concept in conventional Western military thought. While this concept is nowhere explicitly defined in Party literature, it is nevertheless absolutely central to the differing results of government and revolutionary efforts in Long An.

In a tactical sense, any terrain, any installation, or any group of people can be secured by a sufficient concentration of military forces. While this foundation of security may be valid for any limited number of pieces of terrain, installations, or groups of people, it obviously cannot be valid when applied to a whole theater or national unit. There is a logical contradiction in "concentrating one's forces everywhere," because concentration means centralizing dispersed forces in a limited number of locations. Thus security as it applies to a theater or national unit must have a different foundation.

The foundation of security in a strategic sense is a *sympathetic environment*, that is, an environment (the population) composed of sympathetic and neutral elements, from which the hostile elements have been removed.[4] It can be seen that a sympathetic environment throughout the theater of operations leads to the same result as would the concentration of forces "everywhere," but at

---

4. Appendix I contains a more rigorous definition.

much lower cost, because the network of sympathizers reveals the location of enemy forces. By doing so it makes possible a flexible use of forces that can disperse to avoid attack or concentrate to defend against, or to conduct, an attack. The ratio of sympathetic to neutral elements depends on the degree of security required as well as the rapidity of communication and mobility of opposing forces. Within reasonable dimensions for all three, the ratio is very low—for example, just one or two agents per hamlet in the Vietnamese context.

Integral to this concept of security is a measure constantly emphasized in Party policy and training documents—*maintaining the legal position of the population.* This means that the population is not asked to undertake actions that would make it the object of attack or reprisal by the government. Then, because the population is not the object of attack or reprisal by the government, it need not be protected. Although the population will be subject to contact by the government, no undesirable consequences will follow, because the population will have been immunized against government appeals by appropriate policies (described below).

The corollary to the legal position of the population is the *illegal position of the Party's apparatus,* that is, its overt forces. This illegal position demands a different life style, that of an "outlaw," with no fixed residence, constantly subject to sudden and perhaps ugly death. The sharp break involved in the transition from a legal to an illegal status demands a much higher level of motivation among those who elect the latter. Thus there is a "threshold" effect in the creation of an illegal apparatus. The potential represented by a diffuse low-level feeling of goodwill among a segment of the population will go unexploited without a highly motivated minority who will risk death to realize that potential.

This definition of security also allows the Party to define precisely the role of military activity. In general terms the role of military activity, as of every other kind of activity, must be to diminish enemy forces and to augment one's own. The relative emphasis between the two, and the means by which they are accomplished, depend on objective conditions as well as on the stage of the conflict. During the early stages the principal role of military activity is a defensive one, to develop forces through protecting the process of political activity. This is accomplished by a highly mobile apparatus, and in practice the individuals who carry out political activity provide their own protection as well. Only to a limited extent, particularly during the latter stages of the revolution, are the traditional means of altering the balance of forces—offensive combat—the principal means.

We can see that, in comparison with the conventional tactical concept of security, this concept and the special role it assigns to military activity during a substantial span of the revolutionary process allows for an enormous economy of manpower: with no need to protect the population, and with no need to concentrate military forces "everywhere," all one's military resources may be devoted to protecting the process of political activity or to an offensive role in attacking the enemy.

The Concept of Victory

The communist concept of victory is an extremely simple one: a decisive superiority in the balance of forces, that is, the unchallengeable ability to determine the actions of all within a specified domain, whether it be a hamlet or a nation. At any point less than a decisive superiority, the relative influence of each side will be in proportion to the balance of forces in the domain in question.

With these concepts in mind, it is possible to outline the successful communist strategy in Long An, yet even here it is necessary to distinguish between social strategy and military strategy. The communist social strategy was an integrated program to *motivate* forces; the communist military strategy was an integrated program to *apply* forces. Logically the former is fundamental to and governs the latter.

The successful military strategy employed by the Party in Long An was derived from Mao Tse-tung's basic prescriptions for warfare in a backward agricultural country: to contest the urban areas and to gain victory in the rural areas through a worker-peasant alliance. Because the countryside is the "heart" which pumps human and material resources into the government, its initial loss by the government will destroy the defensibility of the urban areas which the Party at first may have to concede. Through the Party's seizure of the rural areas initially, the government is forever precluded from developing sufficient forces to achieve victory on a national scale.

In Vietnam, "victory in the rural areas" meant achieving a decisive superiority in the balance of forces at the village and hamlet levels, the only units of social and geographical significance to the rural Vietnamese. Thus the very condition for victory on a national scale was the prior victory in a certain number of the 12,000 hamlets south of the 17th parallel. It is extremely significant that most of these victories were obtained, not during the military phase, but rather during the premilitary phase of intense political activity to establish a favorable balance of social forces (in ordinary language, the winning of popular sympathy for a just cause). Once this had been accomplished, it generally took only the threat of violence to cause the local government apparatus to collapse. As we saw in Long An, only twenty-six individuals were assassinated at the start of the new policy in January 1960, yet this small number, reinforced by a continuing low rate of assassinations afterwards, was sufficient to cripple the government apparatus at the village and hamlet level. Within a comparatively short time, the government's strategic position became hopeless, although the actual translation of the government's political defeat into military defeat took another five years.

Here it is worth remarking that this plan of events was followed, not because of any abhorrence for violence on the part of the Party, but rather because it judged that this was the only feasible approach. In this the Party's reasoning was unassailable: moving the conflict from a nonviolent to a violent phase would only translate the existing balance of social forces into an analogous balance of military forces, for what are effective military forces but social forces with guns? This is the significance of the repeated harsh words in Party documents for those who wished to resort to arms before 1960, or who wished to slight political activity thereafter. Premature violence, in the judgment of the Party leadership, would only have served the government's cause by snuffing out the revolutionary movement before it had had the opportunity to alter the balance of social forces. Instead, by the Party's taking a defensive military posture and undermining the government's local apparatus through political activity, the government's battalions and regiments were subsequently crippled and collapsed through poor morale, defections, lack of intelligence, lack of recruits, and lack of material resources. For the most part they never even confronted their opposition on the battlefield.

The military strategy just elaborated has often been described. Although it was a significant element in the revolutionary victory, it was by no means the distinguishing or even the most important aspect of the communist approach to revolutionary war. The decisive yet least explored factor in the Party's success was its social strategy.

The most useful characterization of the Party's social strategy is that it was strongly *preemptive*. That is, although the Party's natural base of support according to Marxist doctrine lay in the urban proletariat, the Party developed policies to preclude the government from motivating other social classes comprising the great majority of the country's population. By developing policies more congenial to the interests of these classes than were the policies of the government, the Party ensured that when the conflict crossed into the military phase the majority of the population would choose to fight against the government in defense of its own interests, or would at least not choose to fight against the revolution. In practice, the preempted classes in the rural areas were the landless, poor, and middle peasants, who were the objects of "winning over" (*tranh thu*). Vigorous efforts were made not to alienate the rich peasants, although the best that was generally hoped for was their "neutralization." The landlord class, representing only a small percentage of the population, was willingly conceded to the government, although attempts were made to recruit even among the "patriotic" landlords.[5]

The Party's successful preemption of its target classes, through certain policies discussed further on in this chapter, ensured that government efforts to escalate military activity rebounded against the government itself. While the government could effectively motivate the minority of the population in the social classes whose interests would be harmed under the society represented by the revolutionary movement, every attempt to demand counterrevolutionary efforts from the preempted classes simply drove them into the arms of the revolutionary movement. Moreover, the onus for forcing the jump lay upon the government and thus was doubly damaging. It was this escalation of demands on the preempted classes which accounted for the steady and substantial rise in revolu-

---

5. As events were to prove in Long An, it was possible for the government to draft a certain proportion of the preempted classes, train them, and issue them weapons, but it was not possible to make them fight. This accounts for the contrasting performances of government and revolutionary military units in Long An. Several reasons commonly cited for poor performance by government forces—low pay, poor living conditions, inadequate weapons—were all demonstrably of marginal significance, because during the entire period discussed in previous chapters the pay, living conditions, and arms of the revolutionary forces were greatly inferior to those of the government. The other factor frequently cited, poor leadership, is far more relevant, but it cannot be viewed as an independent variable because the differing leadership capabilities of the two sides were direct consequences of their differing social organization and recruitment patterns.

tionary military strength in Long An in every year from 1960 to 1966, at the same time as locally recruited government military strength rose only marginally.

In contrast to the Party's multidimensional view of the situation as one of managed social conflict—manifesting itself at a certain stage in military form—government officials did not possess a consistent theoretical view of the situation confronting them. Their understanding was seriously hampered by their view of the situation as the attempted overthrow of the government, whereas the full dimensions of the process only come into view when it is conceptualized as the attempted overthrow of the existing social system itself. The social system is here used in the sense of a system which, among other things, defines and maintains a particular distribution of values within a human community. By mistaking a part of the process for the whole, government officials overlooked the key operative factors —those personal motivations which lead people to favor one distribution of values over another. Consequently, most of the subjects mentioned above—social class, contradiction, balance of forces, revolution as a stage-by-stage social process—were represented in the minds of government officials by what must be called, for lack of a better term, blank areas of consciousness. While individual officials each had favorite "explanations"—terror, invasion from the North, corruption, inadequate material aid by the government— none had a comprehensive and consistent theoretical interpretation of events, Marxist or otherwise. Perhaps Duoc came closest with his Confucian theory of *an cu lac nghiep*: a paternalistic government providing "peace and prosperity." Yet when pressed, even he could not conceive of any legitimate reason for following the Party: those who did were either "terrorized" or "deceived."

The phenomena which government officials took to define the whole problem—assassinations, threats, kidnappings—were actually just epiphenomena of a social process of which they had no conception, but they represented the sole consistent concern of all the province chiefs of Long An: the overt threat to "physical security" which had to be handled by suppressive means. Moreover, since government officials conceived of security only in the tactical sense common to conventional military doctrine, they fell naturally into treating the problem by the only methods they knew: conventional military and police operations. That is, they took for granted their ability to recruit forces and then proceeded to conduct operations as though they were dealing with a foreign invader. In fact, however, the situation was past the point at which the forces available to the government were sufficient to handle security as a tactical problem. Beyond this point, which will be called the "crossover point," there is simply no suppressive solution.[6] While this formulation as stated is purely definitional, it is important to recognize that there is a point, definable at least conceptually, beyond which *no solution exists* if based on a tactical conception of security, that is, based on suppression. Likewise, once beyond this point, conventional military training is simply not relevant—at least, not until proper preemptive measures are adopted to bring the force relationship back past this crossover point. Beyond this point military activity, depending on how sharply defined is its object, will be either ineffective or counterproductive. In the case of the government, it was highly counterproductive. This reaction by the government had been anticipated by the Party leadership and was indeed one of the critical requirements for the success of the Party's own strategy, because the Party's continued generation of forces depended on the counterproductive effects of the government's own measures.

It may be useful to show by some specific examples how the very terms in which government officials thought about the problem crippled their ability to deal with it appropriately. The most remarkable conclusion from reviewing hundreds of pages of interviews with government officials is that terms such as "class," "conflict," and "contradiction," or their non-Marxist equivalents, never once appear. The meaning of this, of course, is that the overt acts to which government officials gave their attention were simply not viewed as consequences of the organization of the society itself. Rather they were viewed as "criminal acts" without social content, and their perpetrators were often called "bandits."

A similarly narrow interpretation was associated with the word "force," which government officials always used with a military, never a social, content. For the communist term "balance of forces" there simply was no corresponding concept in the government vocabulary. The closest word was "control" (*kiem soat*) by which government officials referred to the domination of an area by superior military forces. Yet "balance of forces" is superior in two important

---

6. This subject is treatment more rigorously in Appendix I. As defined there, the crossover point is the one at which the degree of security available to one side under the existing balance of forces falls below the level needed by its local apparatus.

respects: it focuses directly on the operative process—the tension between conflicting forces, broadly defined—and it is a concept capable of describing a range, while "control" is inherently an absolute term, referring to a final state. As noted previously, government officials were at a loss to explain the apparent paradox of "less than complete control" posed by the single guerrilla versus the mobile battalion, and they drew the erroneous conclusion that the only response was to station heavy military forces in each hamlet.

Similarly, the concept of "security" as employed by government officials carried important consequences. As the term was always used, it meant *the physical prevention of enemy movement in defined areas*, that is, the tactical conception of security mentioned earlier. Moreover, because there was no distinction in government thinking analogous to the communist distinction between "legal" and "illegal" positions, government strategy had to provide for the "protection of the population," although the population was not the object of attack but of contact by revolutionary forces. In communist strategy the problem of contact with the government was resolved by policies intended to immunize against contact, while the government attempted the physical prevention of contact between the people and communist agents. In other words, rather than protecting the relatively few government agents responsible for contact with the people, the government chose to "secure" the entire population among whom these individuals circulated.

The actual strategy the government adopted in its attempts to prevent a revolutionary take-over was only articulated to any appreciable degree in the military domain. It may be summarized as a city-based strategy involving the abandonment of the rural areas and withdrawal into populated centers. These were to be employed as bases for a gradually widening net of operations into rural areas, or the so-called "oil spot" theory. According to this strategy, as revolutionary forces were worn down, the heavier government military units could be moved onto a wider perimeter, their place being taken by police or paramilitary organizations which could maintain sufficient security to reestablish the local organs of government.

It may be seen that the conceptual categories on which this strategy was based—the use of a tactical conception of security for an entire national unit, and the concept of "protecting the population"—created terrific demands for military and police forces, demands impossible to meet once the threat became widespread. In practice, there were only enough troops to protect physical installations, not the population. Thus predictably, as time went on, more people were "deceived," more people turned against the government, and even the physical installations were lost. It should also be apparent that the aspects of government military strategy most often criticized by foreign observers—the endless repetition of fortifications and large troop units in static defensive roles—were consequences of the government's confusion of tactical and strategic conceptions of security. Perhaps even more significant is the fact that government strategists had no inkling that "security" could have any other meaning than the one they imputed to it.

The reason it proved impossible to develop sufficient forces to carry out this military strategy with a greater degree of success is that there simply was nothing in the planning of government thinkers analogous to the Party's social strategy, that is, an explicit and conscious reordering among various social groups to motivate the forces required for whatever military strategy had been decided upon. No such conscious reordering existed in government planning because the existing system was implicitly assumed to be adequate. The only acknowledged failing of the system was its corruption. However the attempt to eliminate corruption was not a reordering but just a repair to make the existing system perform more efficiently.

We can see in Duoc's comments how government officials failed to establish the mental connection between the application and the creation of forces, which would have clearly shown that the existing system could not be defended without significant changes. Duoc, it will be recalled from Chapter Two, reported to the Ministry of the Interior the great increase in violent acts in 1960 and requested several battalions of troops. His retort when he received only two companies of mobile forces was, "How can you pacify a province with two companies?" Thus the *creation* of forces was never a factor in Duoc's calculations—forces were obtained simply by requisitioning them from the Ministry of the Interior. Duoc attributed the refusal of his request to budgetary limitations or perhaps to discrimination against him by his enemies at the ministry. Regrettably, the structure of the government military recruitment system masked the true reason: that adequate military forces could not be recruited. Had Duoc simply been told to recruit within Long An whatever forces he needed for its defense, he would have seen this immediately. Whether he would have drawn the appropriate conclusions is another question.

The best description of the course adopted by the government is that it was a purely *reinforcement* strategy, which might be defined as applied to the government as one which acted only in ways to consolidate and strengthen the existing distribution of values. The government reaction to such acts as assassinations, kidnappings, and armed propaganda meetings was to strengthen its apparatus for their suppression through physical reinforcement (barbed wire and barricades, arming holders of power), numerical reinforcement (military recruitment, compulsory membership in mass organizations), and restrictive measures on the population (curfews, movement controls). It was a reinforcement, and not a reordering, of the existing system.

In conclusion, then, we can see that the fundamental difference between the strategies adopted by the Party and the government was this: the Party adopted a strategy heavily weighted toward preemptive measures, that is, measures that shifted the power relationship between the government and itself by shifting the underlying balance of social forces—the force ratio; in contrast, the government strategy consisted principally of reinforcement measures, measures that would alter this power relationship by manipulating such factors as weaponry, training, etc.—in other words, by shifting the power ratio.

The Dynamics of Preemptive and Reinforcement Strategies

Analyzing situations of social conflict in terms of preemptive and reinforcement measures allows us to make certain predictions about their evolution and also allows us to pinpoint the important factors in that evolution.

Assuming no collapse of will by either side, every conflict situation which begins in a state of low mobilization has an inherent dynamic of escalation, until either one side gains victory or an equilibrium of forces (stalemate) is reached.[7] The level of mobilization at which victory or stalemate will occur will depend on three variables: (1) the depth of the social conflicts which each side is capable of manipulating to generate forces; (2) the effectiveness of the opposing forces; and (3) the conflict-aggravating consequences of mobilization and their relative impacts on each side. If in com-

---

7. "Mobilization" is not used here in the sense described by Karl Deutsch in his article "Social Mobilization and Political Development," *American Political Science Review*, LV (September 1961), 493–514, but rather in its original, more limited sense of formal enlistment into some kind of collective effort, e.g., being drafted into a military organization. It thus might be desired by the person mobilized, or it might not.

bination these three variables are sufficient, then the situation will be one of open-ended escalation, that is, both sides will proceed to full mobilization.

In the situation of a government threatened by revolution, a variety of strategies may be selected by the government, ranging from a purely reinforcement strategy to a purely preemptive strategy, or any combination of the two. For the government, a purely reinforcement strategy would dictate only those measures that strengthened the defenses of the existing system—barbed wire, arming holders of power, incarcerating or killing opponents of the existing system. A purely preemptive strategy would dictate only those measures that reallocated values so as to eliminate the motives for revolution—e.g., admitting new groups to political decision-making, redistributing land, reallocating national income in favor of certain groups. The important process isolated by this analysis is that the more heavily weighted toward reinforcement the selected strategy becomes, the higher the level of mobilization (and potential or actual violence). This is another way of saying that the cost of maintaining the status quo in the face of opposition is a higher level of mobilization (and of potential or actual violence).

A hypothetical example will illustrate this point. Assume a water-scarce situation, say, a desert, in which 10 percent of the population monopolizes all the water wells. If faced with violence by the remaining 90 percent of the population, the 10 percent might devote its resources to a purely reinforcement strategy, e.g., fortifications and military patrols; or it might devote its resources to a purely preemptive strategy by digging more wells and sharing its water with everyone; or it might choose some intermediate course, say, by sharing with an additional 30 percent of the population, and suppressing the remaining 60 percent. Depending on objective conditions, a number of courses might result in an equilibrium, but the more heavily reinforcement was stressed, the higher the level of continuous mobilization which would be required—at least until the excluded portion of the population died of thirst.

In selecting the appropriate strategy, those attempting to put down revolution face a dilemma: they wish neither to dilute the existing distributive arrangement with any additional groups nor to be overthrown, i.e., to lose their privileged position completely. The issue thus resolves itself into the factual question of whether the existing system can be defended at an acceptable level of mobilization, or, indeed, at any level of mobilization at all, given the existing distribution of values it has to offer to those mobilized in its defense. Should it be discovered that, because of the existing distribution, the system is not capable of generating sufficient forces for its own defense, then logically those in command should preempt just the minimum portion of the population necessary to ensure their own survival at an acceptable level of mobilization.

We may just as easily analyze the identical situation from the viewpoint of the revolutionary leadership. In selecting the appropriate strategy to overthrow the government (the defender of the existing system), they, too, are caught in a dilemma: although they do not want to dilute the promised distribution of values which their movement represents with any additional groups, they do want to win, that is, to realize the promised distribution. The issue thus resolves itself into the factual question of whether the existing system can be overthrown by the forces the revolutionary movement can generate through the promised distribution of values. Should the leaders foresee that the existing system cannot be overthrown at an acceptable level of mobilization with their present forces, then, logically, the revolutionary leadership should preempt just the minimum portion of the population necessary to gain victory at an acceptable level of mobilization.

The government leadership in Long An, however, made no careful analysis and took no conscious decision to adopt a purely reinforcement strategy, for it was insensitive to the social bases of the situation it confronted. In this the thinking in Long An completely reflected the thinking in Saigon. On the other hand, the Party leadership had explicitly judged that at the current stage of development of Vietnamese society a purely reinforcement strategy—one based on arming the working class alone—could not possibly succeed.[8] Likewise, it had explicitly judged that the existing system could not be defended, because its distribution of values was too narrow.[9] Thus the Party leadership made the conscious decision to adopt a strongly (though not purely) preemptive strategy, or what it referred to as "the strategy of [temporary] alliances by stage" (*sach luoc dong*

---

8. This judgment was of course not unique to Vietnam, but was one of the major strategic innovations of Mao Tse-tung in communist revolutionary thought. Mao's brilliant departure from Leninist strategy is described in Benjamin Schwartz, *Chinese Communism and the Rise of Mao* (Cambridge: Harvard University Press, 1951), chap. 13.

9. For example, "The Path of the Revolution in the South," quoted at length in Chapter Two.

minh giai doan), of which its front policy is the most outstanding manifestation.[10]

Viewed in these terms, we can see why the Party's preemptive strategy was one of victory, while the government's reinforcement strategy (what Mao Tse-tung scornfully refers to as a "weapons decide everything" strategy) contained a built-in dynamic of defeat. If the assumption is valid that in 1960 the majority of the rural population was preempted by the revolutionaries from voluntary mobilization by the government—and succeeding pages will show why this was so—then no matter to what level the government chose to escalate, it could never achieve sufficient forces for victory. In fact, the forces which the Party employed to overthrow the system were

---

10. An explicit formulation of one aspect of this preemptive strategy is contained in a Regional Committee document dated January 1961, "Instructions to Zones 1, 2, 3 and 4 [eastern, central, and western zones of Nam Bo and the Saigon-Cholon Special Zone]."

Naturally, among these classes [composing the Front] only the working class occupies the vanguard leadership role. The alliance of the workers and peasants is the basic force composing the Front, because these two classes make up the absolute majority of the Front's numbers and moreover have the most resolute and self-sacrificing spirit. However, in the present realistic situation in the South, these two classes do not have the capability of achieving decisive victories for the revolution.

For this reason the Central Committee has developed a front policy and established the National Liberation Front, in order to attract the bourgeoisie and the intellectuals, including the urban students and youths, intellectuals and bourgeoisie, and the middle and rich peasants in the countryside. In their speeches at the Third Party Congress, Comrades Le Duan and Le Duc Tho stated their judgments that these elements in the South, although possessing a [progressive] spirit and political awareness, are easily turned into opponents of the socialist revolution and of Marxism-Leninism and easily develop a passive self-serving attitude. Nevertheless, in the present situation in the South, the Central Committee believes it necessary to do everything possible to attract these elements into the Front. In this the Central Committee is not betraying the class line of the Party and the revolution, nor will the Central Committee entrust important revolutionary responsibilities to these elements. This step is taken only to exploit to the fullest the capabilities and the standing of these elements, in order to advance the revolution and to enhance the standing of the National Liberation Front. This policy is a temporary strategy. When the revolution is victorious, it will be revised, and at that time we will act openly and assume leadership of the revolution.

A photograph of this document is contained in U.S. Department of State, *A Threat to the Peace: North Viet-Nam's Efforts To Conquer South Viet-Nam*, Far Eastern Series 110, Publication 7308 (Washington: U.S. Government Printing Office, 1961), Part II, p. 96.

generated by just those measures that the government took in the mistaken belief that it was defending itself—restrictions on movement, an annoying system of identification cards, compulsory mass organizations, the national draft, the agroville, the strategic hamlets. In this sense it is not strictly correct to say that the government was overthrown by the Party—rather, the Party, by certain explicit policies of provocation such as the struggle movement, maneuvered the government into overthrowing itself. The government's escalation along a reinforcement strategy was the necessary condition for its own defeat. The fact that this defeat occurred at such a low level of mobilization is attributable to the general ineffectiveness of the government forces.

On the other hand, had the government by appropriate policies (i.e., by altering the distribution of values) prevented the Party from preempting the classes it did, then the situation would never have advanced to the level of violence that began in 1960, because communist doctrine permits advance to the stage of generalized violence only when a favorable balance of social forces has been achieved, that is, when the majority of the population has been preempted.

Community-Oriented Organization versus Centrally-Oriented Organization

The strategic differences outlined above manifested themselves in a number of critical organizational differences between the opposing sides in Long An: differing goals, differing numerical strengths at certain levels, and differing loci of authority.

On the revolutionary side the criterion for judging an organization's effectiveness was how well its efforts contributed to the goal of political activity, that is, to the manipulation of contradictions so as to create and support forces. Any specialized functions were clearly and directly subordinated and never allowed to conflict with that supreme goal. On the other hand, the government apparatus in the rural areas was fundamentally an administrative organization. We may recall Duoc's judgment, when he became province chief in 1957, that besides corruption, one of the government's most serious failings was its low level of competence in administration: the handling of tax collections, preparation of accident reports, etc. Consequently he established his professional training course for government officials in Long An. It is interesting to note by contrast that Party training materials specifically warn against allowing the Party apparatus to become "an administrative organization."[11]

This difference in goals was the obvious consequence of the differing tasks each side felt had to be accomplished, on the basis of the differing strategies each adopted. This asymmetry in goals had two important consequences: first, it allowed the Party to concentrate all its human resources on the critical task of altering the balance of forces; second, it obscured for the government the actual impact on the balance of forces of its own administrative activities. Here it will be useful to distinguish two types of functions performed by the government apparatus: "conflict-aggravating," e.g., collecting taxes, conducting the bidding on communal lands, enforcing of land-rent payments, producing a quota of draftees; and "conflict-minimizing," e.g., visiting the sick or providing assistance to the poor. It was in fact the success in carrying out the conflict-aggravating functions and not the conflict-minimizing functions by which the central government evaluated the performance of its local apparatus. Consequently, the more "effective" local government was—from the viewpoint of the central government, not the local community—the more it aided the Party in its goal of altering the balance of forces against the government.

Another remarkable difference in the two organizations was in numerical strength. At the only levels of social significance in rural Vietnam—in hamlet and village—the Party motivated five to ten times the number of workers as the government. We might take as a specific example the village of Phu Ngai Tri in Binh Phuoc district. Before 1960 this village had a five-man village council and five hamlet chiefs—a total of ten people theoretically working full time for the government. After the government was driven out, the village chi bo in a short time grew to fifteen members, that is, fifteen people who were expected to work at least as hard (and in fact worked much harder) than their government predecessors. Moreover, by 1963, when the Front was finally established as a working organization in the village, there were an additional thirty to forty workers in front organizations. These were in addition to the platoon of guerrillas which had been organized by that time. (The government had also had a platoon of Dan Ve in the village before it was driven out.)

---

11. For example, *Bon Bai Hoc Ve Cong Tac Dang Cua Huyen Uy* [Four Lessons on the Party Tasks of the District Committee], Race Document 1059–1060, p. 69.

On the other hand, government manpower was concentrated at the district and province levels, as extensions of the central ministries. The Ministry of Information, for example, had an office in the province capital of Tan An and branch offices in the district capitals, each staffed by three or four people. With these staffs and with the emphasis which existed on office-centered activity, visits by Ministry of Information cadres to each hamlet took place on an average of once a month or less prior to 1960. In their absence the village and hamlet officials were expected to carry the government message to the people. The level of efficiency with which this task was accomplished has been discussed amply in previous chapters.

A third significant factor was the differing loci of authority in the revolutionary and government hierarchies. Within the government hierarchy the province chief and to a lesser extent the district chiefs were the principal decision makers—although frequently extremely minor matters (for example, Duoc's desire to simplify paperwork) were beyond even their competence. The province and district chiefs interviewed were quite explicit in their opinion that hamlet and village officials were just "errand boys" for the district chief, with negligible authority of their own—and, indeed, that it should be no other way. Hamlet and village officials similarly expressed their own view of their role as puppets of the central government (e.g., the comment of the village chief cited in Chapter Two, that "I just had to do what the government told me.").

On the other hand, in Party doctrine and practice the village chi bo was the most important echelon and the one at which the initial and usually the binding decisions were made. For example, in such matters as taxation, justice, military recruitment, and land redistribution, a Party village secretary had as much and often far more authority than a government province chief. Several quotations will serve to illustrate the importance the Party attaches to the chi bo. One, from a training document entitled "Village Party Branch Development," described the chi bo in the following way:

The development of the chi bo is extremely important and in fact is the foremost principle in the development of the Party, for these reasons:

1. The chi bo is the bridge between the Party and the masses, the eyes and ears of the Party among the masses, the brain of the masses, the source of Party plans and policies for the masses, and the leadership organization in the struggle of the masses. Without the chi bo, Party plans and policies could not be transformed into the strength of the mass

struggle. Thus the revolution could not possibly succeed, and the interests of the masses could not possibly be protected.

2. The chi bo is the foundation, the basic organization, of the Party. If the chi bo is strong, the Party is strong.

3. The chi bo is the site of constant direct confrontation with the enemy, the area of direct leadership of the masses in their struggle to drive back and ultimately completely overthrow the enemy.

4. The chi bo is the foundation of the Party's development, the entry point through which the most outstanding elements among the masses are brought into the Party, the place for testing every Party member, and for involving every Party member in the discussion and decision on Party plans and policies.

Every Party member, cadre, and committee member must grasp the importance of the chi bo and understand his own responsibility in developing the chi bo. . . .[12]

In developing the chi bo, the ultimate standard which is set is that of an "autonomously operating" chi bo, i.e., one which continues Party activities, guides the mass struggle, recruits and trains members, even if cut off from higher echelons.

A second example is provided by a policy guidance circulated to Party members in Long An in October 1961. The article explained a number of missions to be carried out among the population in the coming period, such as a step-up in military, political, and troop-proselytizing activities, and the establishment of the National Liberation Front in Long An. Despite encouraging progress in the past, the article stated, the Party apparatus at the village level was still too weak to carry out the assigned missions:

In general almost all the chi bo are still passive. A number of chi bo cease activity in the absence of a district committee member or district cadre. . . . The above situation shows clearly that the chi bo does not yet have sufficient ability to lead the masses in the three areas of political struggle, armed struggle, and troop proselytizing, and to develop forces as the decision of the Party instructed. . . . In order to carry out [the missions described in the Party decision] the immediate requirement is to develop the strength of the Party. . . . In order to develop the strength of the Party, *the primary requirement is to strengthen the chi bo, for only if the chi bo is strong will the Party be strong.* . . .

The Party has put out many decisions to "consolidate and develop the Party, of which the consolidating and developing of the chi bo is

---

12. Pike Document 251.

foremost." In the past, however, we have not firmly resolved to do this, nor have we had a concrete plan to carry it out. As a consequence, at present many chi bo are still small and weak, a number fairly large but not strong, some passive, with insufficient ability to lead the movement. The reason for this is that we have not yet understood: *only if the chi bo is strong* will the Party be strong, that is to say, *the chi bo is the very foundation of the Party.* . . .

The goal of consolidating the chi bo is to raise them to the "autonomously operating" level. . . .

Consolidation of the chi bo is the immediate and most important requirement of our Party organization at the present time, which every one of us must act to carry out.[13]

A specific issue—land—will illustrate the importance of the chi bo and its relatively greater authority than a government village council. Under Party practice land redistribution was essentially a local matter, decided by local people at the village level. Final approval of land redistribution lay technically with the province committee, but this was mere routine and seldom changed what had been decided within the village by members of the village itself. By contrast, the government land redistribution was carried out by cadres of the central government, on the basis of an inflexible law which made no provision for the differing needs of each locality.[14] Final authority, legally and practically, lay with the ministry in Saigon. As noted in previous chapters, the initial benefits of the government land redistribution (insignificant as they were) took two years to arrive in Long An, while the Party's procedures for land redistribution were never reported to have taken more than three months.

Thus under government organization the critical decisions affecting people's lives were made initially at the very lowest level by the district chief, and usually—as in the case of land redistribution —at a much higher level, on the basis of relatively inflexible laws or regulations adopted by the central government. In contrast, the revolutionary organization ensured that critical decisions affecting popular livelihood were made by local people, with relatively more

13. *Hoc Tap* [Study], No. 6, October 1961, an internal publication of the Long An Party Branch (Pike Document 33). A number of provinces in the South began to publish a periodical of this name around the beginning of 1960. It should not be confused with the *Hoc Tap* published in Hanoi.

14. A significant confirmation of this point lies in the fact that in only one province of central Vietnam did any land even fall under the provisions of the government's redistribution law.

flexibility and with some sensitivity to the demands of the particular situation.

Military organization also showed certain significant differences between the two sides which had important consequences for their differing effectiveness and appeal. During the entire period discussed thus far, manpower for the government regular army was obtained through a draft. On induction, draftees were sent to the national training center just outside Saigon for basic training, after which they might be sent to serve anywhere in the country. Only rarely was service in one's home province. Youths could volunteer to serve in the Dan Ve or Bao An (indeed, Duoc had noted that "it was required to volunteer"), but on reaching a certain age they still had to leave home and enter the regular army. Such a system of service far from home goes completely against traditional Vietnamese preferences, and accounts for the cases in which even members of the Dan Ve and Bao An would desert when called for service in the regular army.

With this situation in mind, it is interesting to note that the Party's system of military recruitment was based on an entirely different principle known as *don quan*, which may be translated as "promotion by echelon." Under the don quan system, a man's military service began with his service as a hamlet guerrilla. As the inductee's military proficiency and "political consciousness" developed (and the latter was given attention equal to the former), he was promoted from echelon to echelon, serving progressively farther and farther from home. Rarely, however, would anyone ever have to serve outside his home province. According to interviews with defectors, during most of the period discussed thus far "promotion" in this way was considered a mark of prestige and was eagerly sought, at least by those who did not have family responsibilities. The advantages of this system, both from the standpoint of morale and from the standpoint of familiarity with terrain and population, are obvious.[15]

---

15. In my opinion, few steps the Party could have taken would have been so effective in crippling the morale and effectiveness of the government's military forces as was the government's own decision to adopt a policy of nonlocal service. While this point is frequently emphasized by Party cadres, only one government official interviewed (a retired district chief) raised the issue, and most appeared not even to be aware of this critical organizational difference. This one individual who did mention it felt very strongly that the

We may conclude that on the basis of these important organizational differences alone it was not surprising that the revolutionary movement was able to develop greater forces than the Saigon government in rural Vietnam: the revolutionary movement devoted more manpower and more authority to the critical levels and to the critical kinds of activity. Integral to these organizational differences, however, were differences in the social origin of the decision makers in the revolutionary movement and the policies on which their decisions were based.

Policies of "Looking Down" versus Policies of "Looking Up"

Others have commented on "the organizational weapon" or "the organizational genius" of the Party, as though there were a magic structure capable of overcoming all obstacles, understood only by the Party. Such a view is misleading. The Party's demonstrated organizational superiority in Long An came about through the development of social policies leading to superior motivation. For the Central Committee in Hanoi to calculate that it had to motivate ten times more manpower than the Saigon government at the village level—and to issue orders to that effect—was a simple intellectual and administrative exercise. On the other hand, the actual ability of the Party's agents in the field to carry out these orders was contingent on the existence of the proper policies. Here we come to the crucial difference between the revolutionary and the government efforts in Long An: the differing distributions of values which they represented and the consequent differing elements among the rural population which they attracted.

The policies which made possible the victory of the revolutionary movement, in the judgment of those interviewed who actually took part in bringing it about, can be grouped for ease of discussion in three general categories: policies redistributive of wealth and income, policies redistributive of power and status, and policies of provocation and protection.

Policies Redistributive of Wealth and Income

The economic policies of the revolutionary movement favored groups in rural Vietnam different from those favored under government policies. In rural Vietnam the economic issue of overwhelming

---

government's policy should be changed and had made numerous suggestions to that effect over the years. Thus far, however, he had "received no reply."

significance was land—the principal means of livelihood. The distinction between the revolutionary and the government land policies and the actual beneficiaries of each have been discussed in detail in previous chapters. In its overall impact, the revolutionary land program achieved a far broader distribution of land than did the government program, and without the killing and terror which is associated in the minds of Western readers with communist practices in land reform. The actual process relied far more on social than on physical pressures, and the principal violence was brought about not by the Party but by the government, in its attempts to reinstall the landlords.

In evaluating the importance of the revolutionary land policy, it is probably not correct to say that the land issue was responsible for bringing the greatest number of people into the movement. There were, after all, numerous personal motivations leading to entry into the movement, and the revolutionary land policy was just one of many favoring the poor over the rich, the ill-educated over the well-educated, and the countryside over the city. When defectors are questioned on this point, they tend to account for the uniqueness of the land issue by saying that it had the broadest and most forceful immediate impact on the rural population. It was thus the single most important factor in confirming the good faith of the Party with the people. While much of the society of the future remained a promise, this aspect of the new society had already been brought into being in the present—and here the Party's performance was in stark contrast to that of the government.

The issue of land is clearly one on which government officials were victims of their own propaganda—they simply denied, for the most part, that the Party had given out any land. Duoc, for example, was convinced that communists "take land" from the people by collectivization. When confronted with the actual figures, such officials responded that the Party did not actually "give" land, but rather turned the people into "slaves of the Party," with the Party taking everything but what was necessary to a minimum subsistence living. Again the facts contradict such an interpretation, as the differing tax policies of the Party and the government clearly show. Party policy provided for a progressive tax system, according to ability to pay, while government taxation in Long An was based principally on use and consumption taxes, such as market taxes, sales taxes, fees for issuance of documents, etc. In its actual impact, such a system is regressive, with the heaviest burden proportionately falling on those least able to pay.

The government land tax provides an excellent example of how its tax structure discriminated in favor of the wealthy. Government land taxes are actually very low, for example, eighty-five piasters per hectare on the grade of land which produces one hundred *gia* of paddy per hectare a season. In fact, the low tax rate was a measure beneficial not to the general population but rather to the minority who held the majority of the land in Long An. The hectare of land on which eighty-five piasters of tax was due produced, at the legal rate, twenty-five gia of rent for the landlord, or 1,250 piasters at the prices prevailing during the period discussed thus far. Frequently, of course, the rent was much higher than the legal maximum of 25 percent. Since the tenant was responsible for the maintenance of the land and its irrigation works in their original condition, the landlord's only expense was the eighty-five piaster land tax. In 1962 the communist tax on a family with six children farming two hectares would have been about two gia or one hundred piasters, in contrast to the fifty gia or 2,500 piasters the family would have had to pay the landlord under the government system.

While communist taxes increased significantly from 1965 to 1966 in response to the increased pace of the war, the point had been vividly made for many years to the poor and landless peasants of Long An: they were far better off economically under the policies of the revolutionary movement, because the heavy unearned income which had formerly accrued to the landlord was now retained by the operator.

Policies Redistributive of Power and Status

Let us define power as the ability to influence critical decisions affecting one's own life, and status as the feeling of prestige one acquires by occupying a role approved by one's peers.

As already noted, under government organization critical decisions were made at the lowest level by the district chief, or at higher levels by the province chief, regional delegate, etc., all appointees of the central government. These positions were held initially by civil servants and later by military officers. Advancement to the required civil-service rank of *doc su*, or entry into the officer corps, was conditional on holding the *tu tai* (equivalent to the French *baccalaureat*). Since the *tu tai* was effectively limited to the urban middle and upper classes and the rural landlord and rich peasant classes, the overwhelming majority of the rural population was simply excluded from power over the decisions affecting their own lives. Instead, power was exercised by those social elements who were least capable of empathizing with the rural population, and whose personal interests were in conflict with those they ruled.

In analyzing the composition of the government village and hamlet organizations, two "pure types" can be identified, which in practice shaded into one another. In one case, village and hamlet officials might be drawn from the same social elements as district and province officials. This was the traditional pattern of local government in Vietnam until the appearance of the Vietminh. On the other hand, when it was no longer possible to fill local positions with these people, the central government had to resort to appointing "faithfuls" of lower economic position—perhaps shopkeepers or poor farmers who had served honorably in the army and were considered reliable. The motivation of the latter group was generally very weak. Sometimes they took the job for the extra money, although many village budgets did not provide adequately for the salaries of local officials. Frequently they simply felt obligated to take the job when asked, because no one else would, and viewed their responsibilities as a burden and a distraction from the business of making a living. The comparatively few strongly motivated individuals holding these positions were generally those who had suffered economic loss or the death of a relative at the hands of the Vietminh.

Regardless of who occupied these positions or what their motivations were, they had negligible authority compared with appointees of the central government at district level and above. How true this is can be seen from the establishment of the free strike zone in Thu Thua district in 1964. Almost fifteen thousand people had to leave their homes—village and hamlet officials like everyone else. Once the province chief had made the decision, no village or hamlet official had the authority to contradict it. Yet the province chief's decision was made, not on the basis of what the population of the province desired, but on the basis of instructions from Saigon.

By contrast, the social basis of recruitment and promotion within the Party was entirely different. Class origin was the key criterion, outweighing even technical skills or education in importance. Priority in recruitment and promotion was given to the lowest economic strata, that is, those most excluded from power under the social system maintained by the government.[16] The Party still welcomed the membership of those having an intellectual background, but promotion came slower for them despite other qualifications, and they were usually given staff instead of leadership positions. They might become committee members, but only after much more rigorous and lengthy testing than for a member of worker or peasant origin.

The Party justifies this policy on two grounds. First is the Party's judgment of human motivation: all actions are ultimately determined by interest. Intellectuals are suspect because, when "the chips are down," they can survive as well serving a reactionary movement as a revolutionary one, while workers and peasants have nowhere else to turn. Second, the Party has learned from experience that peasants and workers will accept the leadership of someone of their own class much more easily than from a person of intellectual background, despite the fact that the latter may have greater technical skills or mental ability.

Likewise, Party practice is to employ local people at every echelon, in contrast to the government practice of forbidding service in one's home area for those exercising significant authority (officials at the district level and above). Moreover, it is significant that even these requirements as to class and local origin are not considered sufficient by the Party to ensure that revolutionary organizations are "close to the people." The Party has thus institutionalized close communications between its organizations and their constituencies by such enforced working principles as criticism and self-criticism, "from the masses, to the masses," and "the higher-ups go down."[17] None

---

16. For example, *Bon Bai Hoc Ve Cong Tac Dang Cua Huyen Uy* [Four Lessons on the Party Tasks of the District Committee] criticized some chi bo for admitting too many members not drawn from landless and poor peasant ranks: "At the present time in many chi bo the majority of Party members belong to the middle peasant class. Because of an inadequate education in the revolutionary consciousness of the propertyless class, these Party members have brought into their chi bo the middle peasant way of thinking, which only considers the narrow interest of one's self or one's family, for example in false declarations and concealing property in tax payments, passivism, fear of hardship, family favoritism, or in encouraging others' sons to enter the army but not one's own son. Such narrow, selfish thinking will destroy the propertyless class character of the chi bo and hence their prestige and ability to lead the masses" (p. 70).

17. Each of these principles has received considerable attention in the literature on the Chinese Communist Party and so will not be elaborated here. On criticism and self-criticism see, for example, John Wilson Lewis, *Leadership in Communist China* (Ithaca: Cornell University Press, 1963), pp. 160–

of these working principles had any counterpart in government practice. The best that can be said of government practice is that its underlying attitude—with some notable exceptions—was that the people were objects of distrust (i.e., "simple" and "easily deceived"), to be manipulated at will.

Finally it should be noted that one of the most significant factors in the Party's ability to offer alternative routes to power lay in the continuous promotion system, from the village chi bo to the Central Committee, on which the Party's vertical organization was based. This is one of the major factors accounting for the great difference in performance of revolutionary and government local organizations: no matter how hard a government village chief worked, he could never hope to be more than a village chief, whereas a poor peasant could hope to become the village secretary, the district secretary, or even higher—his lack of education and his inability to speak flawless French would not weigh against him. In fact, they would be in his favor.

Party policy on class origin similarly dictated that Party military forces provided greater upward mobility to power positions for non-elite groups than government organization. The government officer corps was recruited from elite groups because of the educational requirement of the *tu tai*; for enlisted personnel there was no hope of achieving officer rank. In Party military forces, on the other hand, officer-level positions were filled directly by promotion of the best-performing men in the ranks.

162; on "from the masses, to the masses" see chapter 3 *passim*. The Vietnamese practice of "the higher-ups go down" resembles the Chinese practice of *hsia fang* (Lewis, pp. 221ff.) only in the latter's post-1960 form. One of the major purposes of the *hsia fang* movement was what in the West would be called a "reduction in force," hence involving the long-term transfer of cadres to lower levels. In contrast, the principle of "the higher-ups go down" as described in interviews and documentary materials from Vietnam was solely intended as a measure to ensure accurate perception at higher levels. In accordance with this principle, Party committees at various echelons do not actually exist as continuous bodies in one location. Instead, they meet once or twice a month, depending on conditions, for a period of from two to four days, and then disperse to carry policy back to the basic executive levels, where the higher echelon cadres live and work beside lower echelon cadres for two to three weeks at a time. Out of a twelve-member district committee, for example, only two or three members of the current affairs committee would be left at the actual physical location of the district committee to transact routine business in the absence of the full committee. This principle is spelled out in *Bon Bai Hoc Ve Cong Tac Dang Cua Huyen Uy*, Race Document 1059–1060.

In conclusion, we may say that the combination of these factors —emphasis on class and local origin, concentration of authority at low levels, institutionalization of communications through enforced working principles, a continuous promotion chain—demonstrated clearly that political and military organization under the new society conformed to majority local interests, whereas the existing government organization was objectively the pawn of "outsiders"—both in the sense of place of birth and sympathy with the local area, and in the sense of following social life styles and economic interests different from those of the majority of the rural population.

As for status, certainly the government offered numerous positions, such as interfamily group chief, leader of youth and paramilitary organizations, etc. Why were these not status roles? The answer lies in the involuntarism that characterized membership in government organizations. For example, membership in government organizations such as the Republican Youth was universal and compulsory, whereas membership in revolutionary organizations during the entire period discussed thus far was largely voluntary— even, remarkably, after the "general mobilization" of July 20, 1964.

How could the revolutionary movement offer status roles which were voluntarily sought, while the government had to resort to coercion? Here we must return to the definition of status given above: a feeling of prestige obtained by occupying a role approved by one's peers. The comments of defectors that they joined the movement "for adventure," or "since I was tired of being treated like trash because I was poor" are examples of the status roles available to the rural poor through the revolutionary movement but not through the government. Why, after all, did so few people volunteer to join the government army "for adventure" or because they were "tired of being treated like trash?" To occupy roles in the revolutionary movement was perceived by major segments of the local population as defending its interests, while to occupy government roles was seen as being manipulated by outside forces in opposition to local interests —not to mention that it sometimes involved cooperation with and protection of criminal and corrupt elements within the government. Thus government roles were not regarded as giving status.

Policies of Provocation and Protection

As Vo van An noted earlier, it was Party policy to provoke the government into repressive and violent actions such that government repressive acts and demands and government violence would themselves become major conflict issues, superimposed on the existing distributive conflicts within Vietnamese society. The Party was correct in its judgment that government doctrine, based on the use of reinforcement, not preemptive measures, would drive additional segments of the population into opposition, where they would have no alternative but to follow the Party's leadership to obtain protection. Several examples will show how the Party gained strength from its policies of protection.

Chronologically, the first group of individuals who sought the protection of the Party were former members of the Vietminh who were persecuted—either on an official or a personal basis—by agents of the Diem regime. A certain number of former Vietminh who had taken up a legal existence were in fact still active for the Party. An himself was such a case. On the other hand, one gets the impression from talking to Party members who were still active in the South in the days following the regroupment that the majority of those persecuted by the government had actually severed their connection with the revolutionary movement and would have been content to continue that way, had they not been hounded into hiding by extortionate demands for payoffs or by the imminence of death at the hands of the Cong An. In Can Duoc district alone, for example, the deputy district chief estimated that some forty individuals had fled into hiding by the middle of 1955. Having literally no future under the existing system except imprisonment or death, such individuals had a high incentive to work for its overthrow.

A second significant group of individuals who sought the protection of the Party were youths who wished to avoid the draft. From their viewpoint, there was no legitimate reason to leave their families to enter military service when they perceived no threat to their families or their villages. The demand of a remote central government for military service in some distant part of the country was viewed in these circumstances as an illegitimate exaction, strengthening communist claims that the Diem regime was preparing for war against the North. By relying on the Party's network of agents and sympathizers to warn them of the approach of draft officials or soldiers, such individuals were actually able to remain at home most of the time despite their delinquent status. When the need arose to leave for a longer period, the Party would hide them in one of its camps in the Rung Sat or the Plain of Reeds, or with its organization just over the border in Cambodia. Ultimately, of course, these individuals were forced to take up arms as the pace of governmental military and police activity increased, but the transition was a gradual one and, from their viewpoint, forced by the government, not the Party. While no figures are available on the number of individuals evading the draft in Long An when it was begun in 1957, the number was running at the rate of several hundred a year by 1959. Such individuals formed the pool from which revolutionary military units were rapidly expanded in Long An starting at the end of 1959.

The Party's reaction to the agroville program in Long An is interesting, because the construction of the agroville straddled the Party's transition from nonviolent to violent action. When construction began in mid-1959, the Party reacted with an intensive propaganda campaign denouncing the agroville as a disguised military base. Party propaganda played heavily on the fact that a week's labor without pay was required from every male in the province, something which had aroused considerable opposition even among government supporters, as the quotations in Chapter Two have shown. On the other hand, after January 1960, police reports record frequent instances of small armed units intercepting groups of from fifty to one hundred people being escorted by the army to work as laborers at the agroville site. The people would be sent home, as would the escorting soldiers a short time later, after receiving a lecture on their evil deeds and being relieved of their weapons. The subsequent communist reaction to the strategic hamlet program, which had a far more damaging impact on popular livelihood than did the agroville, was not nearly so tender. Strategic hamlets in Long An, however, are remembered with such distaste that even many of the local government officials charged with their construction and defense viewed their collapse as a blessing in disguise.

A final note on the Party's policies of protection will serve to illustrate how little they were hobbled by any narrow doctrinaire outlook. One small but important source of recruits into the movement lay in individuals fleeing prosecution for ordinary criminal offenses such as murder, embezzlement, or rape. Several defectors interviewed mentioned that such individuals were regularly accepted and protected by the Party, whose principal concern was not with "ideological purity" in an abstract sense but rather with increasing its forces. The use to which such individuals were put was best expressed by An. "They were praised and treated as heroes," he noted, "and then given the most dangerous assignments."

Summary

The separation outlined above between strategic, organizational, and policy differences was a somewhat artificial distinction introduced to facilitate discussion. We may summarize these same phenomena from a different perspective that will illustrate their essential unity.

Party doctrine correctly identified the fact that the critical element in victory is a superiority of forces, that is, people willing to take risks to influence the actions of others. To create such forces implies rewarding certain kinds of behavior and penalizing others. To do this the Party developed the set of policies described above, the common characteristic of which is that they offered *contingent incentives*. A contingent incentive may be defined as an incentive which is contingent both on certain kinds of behavior by the target individual and on the continued existence of the sponsoring organization. In this way a link of interdependence is created between the two, which is as strong as the individual's desire for the reward offered, and as enduring as the contingency.

Examples of each of the three types of policies will demonstrate how they were structured to provide contingent incentives. The policies relating to economic redistribution offered an incentive which was contingent from the point of view of the individual's behavior in that each beneficiary of land redistribution retained his land only as long as he did not oppose the revolutionary movement, and indeed only as long as he assisted it in required ways. Should he serve as a government spy or fail to pay his taxes, or should his son desert from the movement's military forces, then his land would be forfeit. Moreover, the incentive was contingent from the standpoint of the sponsoring organization, the Party, because of government policy itself: new owners retained their land, and the benefits of a progressive tax system, only as long as the Party was not driven out of the area. Should the government return, so would the old landholding and tax systems. This is in fact exactly what happened in 1955, when the government enforced the signing of a rental contract on some 28,000 tenant farmers in Long An, thereby confirming the titles of the former landlords after the Vietminh redistribution.

A similar situation prevailed with respect to power and status. The power roles and status roles offered by the revolutionary movement were available only to the extent that the individuals behaved in conformity with the criteria established by Party policy—by leading struggle movements or military units against the government, by maintaining intimate relations with the population, etc. Moreover, they were also contingent from the viewpoint of the sponsoring organization because of government policy: were the government to return, the power and status roles would vanish or be filled by others. It is also important to note that at the village and hamlet level the contingent incentives available through the Party were much greater than those available through the government, because the Party maintained a continuous vertical career structure for both its political and its military organization. In contrast, government village and hamlet officials and members of the Dan Ve or Combat Youth were already at the "peak" of their career structure: there were no promotion incentives the government could hold out to an individual to induce him to take greater risks. This resulting weakness of the government's village organization represented an enormously important vulnerability which the Party effectively exploited.

The Party's policies of protection were likewise structured to provide contingent incentives. The Party would only shield those evading the national draft, or those fleeing the Cong An, as long as they in turn cooperated with the revolutionary movement. It would provide leadership and weapons to resist the strategic hamlet program only as long as individuals cooperated to build "combat villages."

What is crucial to observe about each of these policies is that, although the contingency aspect was manipulated by the Party to demand certain kinds of behavior, *the contingency itself was lent by the government*. As Chan commented: "But if the communists were to go and the government to come back, the peasants would return to their former status as slaves. Consequently they must fight, to preserve their interests and their lives, as well as their political power." The significance of this is that the government could have had a policy of preemption: it was within the power of the government to cut this link of contingency which shifted social groups against it and in favor of the Party.[18]

---

18. "Contingent incentives" as used here is a variation on the concept of "selective incentives" discussed by Mancur Olson in *The Logic of Collective Action* (Cambridge: Harvard University Press, 1965). The important structural identity of the two is the divisibility of the collective good according to the individual's contribution, which was integral to the design of the revolutionary movement's policies but not to those of the government. The

Here it is crucial to note why "development" was not a pre-emptive measure: it did not offer contingent incentives, and therefore it did not motivate forces. Economic development would go on regardless of who won, although it might be delayed while deciding who would win. Thus it was simply not an issue in the struggle. Moreover, such development programs as existed brought benefits to members of rural communities (or harm, as was often the case) regardless of their behavior. Government programs were focused largely on providing a general *increment* of wealth or income, whereas what attracted people to the revolutionary movement was that it represented a new society in which there would be an individual *redistribution* of values, including power and status as well as material possessions.

Several examples from Party propaganda will illustrate how this worked out in practice. What use, the Party cadres would ask, is the school that the government just built, when power in this society lies with holders of the *tu tai*, which no poor peasant can hope to achieve? What use is the road the government has just built, when permission to use it to travel to the next village depends on the goodwill of authorities appointed by Saigon? What use is the fertilizer you have just bought with the government loan, when the landlord takes half the crop and the district chief refuses to prosecute him? What use is the farmers' association when the poor always have been and always will be treated like trash?

If these criticisms were valid—and they come from people who became communists for just such reasons—then we can see why development programs failed to prevent the growth of the revolutionary movement in Long An: they were simply irrelevant to the reasons why people cooperated with the movement. Those unsympathetic to the government were glad to have dispensaries, roads, loans, and farmers' associations, but they went right ahead and cooperated with the revolutionary movement, for *the same groups were still going to be at the bottom no matter how much assistance the government provided.* This, of course, is just another aspect of the government's reinforcement strategy, which permitted "development" and "assistance" as long as these did not involve a shift in the distribution of values in the society. In concrete terms, the

---

point emphasized here in the use of the word "contingency" is that what Olson calls selective incentives were contingent upon the maintenance by the government of the existing distributive system and of its various policies of persecution.

making of an agricultural loan could have been truly meaningful only if the government village chief had also had the power and the inclination (as did his Party counterpart) to arrest and imprison an exploitative landlord. Yet it was just this and similar powers which the government declined to grant.

A second summary theme is that of *assimilation of forces*. Communist attention focused on rural Vietnam as the strategically decisive area. The Party leadership consequently structured its forces so that they were inextricably bound into the social fabric of rural communities by ties of family, friendship, and common interest.

Four criteria implicit in Party doctrine may be used to judge the degree to which forces are assimilated:
1. the forces are of local origin, and are representative of the local ethnic, religious, family, class, or productive groups;
2. the forces perform functions distinctly perceived as useful within the local community;
3. the incentives used to motivate the forces are regulated (to some degree) by the local community;
4. the forces are locally supplied in terms of pay, food, labor, intelligence, etc.

The logic of these criteria is dictated by the communist view that human action is determined by interest. To ensure that a sympathetic environment exists into which forces may be assimilated, it is essential that the forces be representative of the people composing the environment, and enforce a distribution of values acceptable to them. Moreover the best way to ensure that forces once recruited remain responsive to local interests is to structure their incentive, intelligence, and logistic systems around the local community, in such a way that responsiveness is a condition for survival: if the members of the forces are responsive to local interests, they survive and prosper; if they are not, they die.

Each of these four criteria was addressed by specific Party policies in Long An. For the first, for example, were the requirements as to local and class origin for upward movement in revolutionary organizations. For the second were the Party policies relating to land redistribution, progressive taxation, the decentralization of political power, and protection from governmental repressive measures. The third criterion was served by various Party working principles which placed a high value on relations with the population in determining upward movement; typical of these were such principles as criticism and self-criticism and "the higher-ups go down." The fourth criterion was addressed by the requirement that each community supply its own forces—a specific instance of the general communist doctrine that revolutionary movements must be self-sufficient.

On the other hand, by these criteria government forces were poorly assimilated. Those rating highest were village and hamlet officials, informers, Dan Ve, Combat Youth, etc., because these groups were all composed of local people. Yet, as noted in preceding chapters, all these forces were involved to a greater or lesser degree in opposing the redistributive measures advocated by the Party, or in forcing the execution of measures such as the strategic hamlet program in opposition to local interests. The central government's conventional military forces and its administration down to district level lacked even this feature of being local in origin, for this was excluded by specific government policies. Moreover, their incentive, intelligence, and logistic structures were centrally oriented rather than being decentralized and focused on rural communities. Thus, while the government often spoke of the importance of the rural areas, in fact its forces were led by urban people, were supplied from urban areas, and were serving urban interests.

Two interesting consequences derive from the differing requirements of the Party and the government on assimilation of forces. First, the Party's decentralized logistic and intelligence systems, based in each rural community, greatly reduced the need for security forces to defend lines of communication, depots, administrative centers, etc. On the other hand, the government's centralized logistic and intelligence systems, based on ministries in Saigon, demanded the use of heavy security forces, further aggravating its already heavy need for troops. Thus a series of doctrinal failures—centralized intelligence and logistic systems, "protecting the population," and an exclusively tactical conception of security—led to the erroneous view that a numerical superiority of troops (for example, the oft-quoted ratio of ten to one) was necessary to defeat the enemy. Yet, as the revolutionary movement demonstrated, victory was possible with a numerical inferiority.[19]

---

19. The alleged necessity of such a numerical superiority is argued, for example, in Seymour J. Deitchman, *Limited War and American Defense Policy* (Cambridge: MIT Press, 1964), chap. 18, and is simply assumed without argument in most of the "counterinsurgency cookbooks." Sir Robert Thompson does not make this mistake; instead he notes correctly, "The magic figure of ten to one, therefore, is not a prerequisite but an indicator," in *Defeating Communist Insurgency* (New York: Praeger, 1966), p. 49.

A second consequence of the Party's decentralized logistic and intelligence systems was that it permitted the Party to do away with outposts: its "outposts" were simply the homes of each of its sympathizers. This in turn was permitted by the Party's social policies, which ensured that a sufficient portion of the population would shelter and supply the Party's forces to maintain the requisite level of combat. Thus the Party's agents living among and responding to rural people were every bit as necessary as government officials living in outposts and responding to Saigon. In each case the forces clung to and nurtured their lifeline.

A third summary theme is that of *communalism*, which encompasses an extremely important difference in approach between the Party's and the government's efforts to gain the loyalty of the rural population. A central feature of the Party's effort was its focus on developing forces assimilated into rural communities. This effort was communal in the sense that it took place within the framework of the peasant's span of interests, largely limited to issues within his own community. It was revolutionary in the sense that it effected a redistribution among social groups within the rural communities. Thus the Party's approach was to develop bonds of loyalty between individuals and the local community leadership on the basis of the latter's ability to resolve concrete local issues of importance in the peasant's life: land, taxation, protection from impressment into the national army, or a personally satisfying role in the activities of the community. That such communities would then behave in conformity with the demands of the national communist leadership was assured by the previously secured loyalty of the community leadership itself to the revolutionary movement through the continuous vertical career structure from hamlet to Central Committee on which Party organization was founded.

Thus "nationalism," as commonly understood, was not a principal motive in the behavior of the rural population in ways demanded by the national communist leadership, although it was a constant legitimizing theme. Instead, local, or communal, issues were the motivating factors.[20] The genius of the Party lay in its

---

20. Communist cadres interviewed by the author emphasized that it was seldom sufficient in recruiting merely to mention the need to "liberate the country from the American imperialists." Such a statement would gain nods of approval, but action was conditional on explaining how the individual himself would be "liberated," e.g., by gaining land, by opportunities for education through the revolutionary movement, by gaining a position of power in the local community.

ability to harness these local interests of the rural population to its national revolutionary goals. It accomplished this by strengthening community leadership, whose prior loyalty to the revolutionary movement had been assured through the kinds of policies described above. Thus in fact most of the participants felt themselves fulfilling their own or their community's interests, not those of some remote communist leadership. This was particularly true after the formation of the National Liberation Front, when the role of the Party, which had previously been quite open, was muted considerably.

In contrast, the Saigon government's approach in its quest for "control" of the rural population may be summarized in the word "nationalism": the attempt to create direct bonds of loyalty between individuals and the central government. Contrary to the Party's policy of developing local leadership, the government suppressed local leadership and allowed it no authority. "Nationalism" and its corollary, a diffuse anticommunism, instead of being legitimizing themes, were the substance of the government's appeal, in the name of which rural people were expected to make sacrifices in their personal interests: controls on movement, free labor at the agroville site, abandonment of one's home and fields to move into the strategic hamlet or to establish the free strike zone. While such interventions by the central government were often described as "revolutionary" or "modernizing," in fact they were not revolutionary in the sense of effecting a redistribution of values among social groups, although they were disruptive. We have seen which approach proved viable in Long An.

We may summarize the argument thus far by noting three elements in the collapse of the government presence in Long An:
1. the existence of strongly felt distributive conflicts within Vietnamese society;
2. the weakly motivated and poorly assimilated nature of government forces; and
3. the failure of governmental leadership to understand the process taking place—indeed, its lack of even the means of conceptualizing the process.

The distributive conflicts in Vietnamese society allowed the Party to motivate a small core of supporters to such a point that they would risk death to intimidate and finally to destroy the government's weakly motivated local apparatus. The central government's inappropriate reactions to this threat, based on a failure of understanding, were a pivotal element in the Party's strategy of victory. Had government leaders understood that the conflict was not a military one to overthrow a particular government, but instead a social conflict to overthrow a particular social system, then they might have seen that the existing system was not defensible at any level of mobilization (that is, that the force equation was past the crossover point), because those called upon to defend the system had little incentive to do so. In fact, the leadership did not conceive of the problem in these terms, and so it fell into what we have called a reinforcement strategy, although government officials had no conceptual categories corresponding to reinforcement and preemptive strategies, and were thus unaware of the risks and costs of choosing the former over the latter.

In contrast, the Party's ability to develop a decisive superiority in the balance of forces within each rural community was founded on its superior conception of revolutionary war as a social process involving the motivation of forces through a series of policies offering contingent incentives. The Party opted for what we have called a strongly preemptive strategy, projecting a picture of a new society with a more equal distribution of values, which threatened an absolutely minimum number of people, and in which a significant number would experience a sharp upward movement: in ordinary language, a more just society. Once this had been done, the government's attempts at escalation rebounded against the government itself. How this worked out was well expressed by the hamlet chief from Thu Thua quoted in Chapter Three, in recounting the reasons for the collapse of his strategic hamlet:

You want to know how the communists got into our strategic hamlet? All of us in the Combat Youth were poor people. We asked ourselves, why should we be carrying rifles and risking our lives when Xoai's son doesn't have to? His family is rich and has used its power to get him out of it. When the communists come in, they never bother us—they go to the homes of those who got rich by taking from others. Are we so stupid as to protect them?

What was true of this hamlet was just as true of the social system as a whole.

A Brief Historical View

It is worth while to review the course of events in Long An from 1954 to 1965 to show how the kind of analysis just outlined is useful in understanding many of the changes that took place during those twelve years.

The period from mid-1954 to mid-1956 was a time of indecision for the Party, during which the shadow of the recent war obscured the course events would take in the future. By mid-1956, however, the Central Committee had reached several important conclusions, which were embodied in its long strategy document, "The Path of the Revolution in the South." The first of these was that, contrary to the Party's expectations, the Diem regime had successfully consolidated its position and would therefore have to be eliminated, although neither by invasion nor by diplomatic measures ("international solutions"). The second principal conclusion was that the existing balance of forces was not sufficiently favorable to the revolutionary movement to permit immediate armed action. This was owing partly to the regroupment of Vietminh military forces to the North and to the corresponding countermovement of "reactionary elements" to the South. Another extremely important factor in the unfavorable balance of forces was the "fake nationalism" of the Diem regime—its appearance of providing a true nationalist alternative to the Party.[21] The third principal conclusion was that, despite the apparent strength of the Diem government, there existed a number of fundamentally favorable factors, which, if properly exploited, would bring about a shift in the balance of forces. What this would then lead to was purposely left vague. We know from the testimony of defectors like An that at this time the Party leadership counted on seizing power through a coup but was prepared to fight a second war should the coup strategy prove unsuccessful. The latter point was not discussed below province level, however, to avoid "confusing" lower-level Party members. The policy actually passed on to the Party's district and village cadres in the South was one of peaceful political activity to aggravate the three general contradictions which the Party leadership felt would be decisive in altering the balance of forces: peace and reunification, freedom and democracy, and popular livelihood. The slogan adopted was that quoted at the end of Chapter One: "To lie patiently in ambush, gathering one's forces, waiting to strike at the right moment."[22]

---

21. Numerous individuals interviewed in Long An, even those cool to the Diem regime, gave Diem credit for his rapid removal of the French after the signing of the Geneva Accords.

22. Although this document fell into the hands of government intelligence agencies in March 1957, the government did not develop appropriate policies

What happened during the next three years shows that the errors of judgment were not all on the government side, for, under the new policy spelled out by the Central Committee, the Party organization in the South was almost wiped out. The critical element in the nearly total destruction of the Party was the reestablishment of the government's local apparatus in almost all rural areas. Although military operations by mobile army forces had some impact in disturbing the Party's previously impenetrable base areas, the government's most effective action in its destruction of the Party's apparatus among the population was the expansion of its own local apparatus, consisting of hamlet and village officials, police and their networks of informers, and paramilitary and political organizations such as the Rural Defense Youth and the National Revolutionary Movement, composed of local people, often former Vietminh, who were intimately acquainted with the local area and population (i.e., those government forces most closely meeting the criteria of assimilated forces outlined above).

Nevertheless it is significant that, despite the high losses of the revolutionary movement during this period, the Party was still able to motivate some people into accepting the risks of involvement. In general, despite the high losses, the period of peaceful political activity attained its objectives of demonstrating, as An said, "if not to a majority, then at least to a certain number" that participation in the revolutionary movement was the only means of defending their interests, and perhaps even their lives. The Party succeeded in this due to widespread dissatisfaction with the existing distribution of values and to the government's one-dimensional view of anticommunism as suppression—aggravated as necessary, of course, by the Party's policies of provoking the government into repressive and unpopular actions. The point which comes through clearly from discussions with Party members active during this period is their judgment that the Party could not subsequently have advanced to the stage of violence had the government not played its "assigned" role during the 1956–1959 period. In part, this government role was to enact measures that would be important sources of recruitment

---

to head off the exploitation of the issues enumerated in the document. Moreover, despite the availability of this document and other intelligence establishing the communist leadership's intention to overthrow the Diem regime by internal revolution and not external invasion, the government nevertheless tailored its military establishment to the threat of conventional invasion, though this course had been repeatedly excluded by the communist leadership.

into the movement—the draft, the persecution of former Vietminh, the agroville, restrictions on personal freedom, etc. Another essential aspect of the government's role was to demonstrate to the population something the revolutionary movement could not prove by itself: that there was no alternative to violence. By adopting an almost entirely defensive role during this period and by allowing the government to be the first to employ violence, the Party—at great cost—allowed the government to pursue the conflict in increasingly violent terms, through its relentless reprisal against any opposition, its use of torture, and, particularly after May 1959, through the psychological impact in the rural areas of the proclamation of Law 10/59.

We may conclude from the events of 1956–1959 that the Party's judgment on the existence of contradictions and the possibility of aggravating them was basically sound, although the Party grossly underestimated the costs of the policy it laid out—costs which would have been much higher had it not been for the "extermination of traitors" policy, the sole exception to its official policy of nonviolence. Yet by suffering these high and unanticipated costs, the Party created the conditions without which the advance to the stage of violence would have been impossible.

The rapid reversal of roles after the revolutionary movement passed into the violent phase in January 1960 demonstrates the correctness of the Party's judgment that the situation was basically favorable in the rural areas. What had previously permitted the government apparatus to survive and the Party apparatus to be ground down had been the asymmetry of risks imposed by the Central Committee's policy of nonviolence, and not any intrinsic superiority of the government apparatus. The fragility of the government apparatus was masked by the Party's decision not to employ violence except in limited circumstances. When the risk was equalized, the Party apparatus proved viable, and the government apparatus simply did not. Moreover, the high incentives by which the Party had been able to recruit even under conditions of heavy risk led to a large increase in the number of people entering the revolutionary movement under the new conditions.

Some Examples

It is worth while examining in detail exactly what happened in Long An in the critical months after January 1960, because of the profound implications these events have for an understanding of what might have helped or hindered the measures the Party employed. The hamlet of Ai Ngai in Phu Ngai Tri village will serve as an illustration of the process which sooner or later occurred throughout almost the entire province.[23] When the Party's hamlet and village organizers visited the hamlet chief of Ai Ngai to "warn him of his crimes," he had four choices: to quit his post, to cooperate with the revolutionary movement, to retain his post but leave the hamlet, or to stay and fight. This hamlet chief, like the overwhelming majority of his counterparts throughout Long An, did not select the fourth choice, the only one which might have stopped the advance of the revolutionary movement. Why not? We may answer this question by examining the array of incentives available to him, and the situation in which he found himself, and having done this we can see why he inevitably took the course that he did.

The decisive new element in the post-January situation was that the conflict had been presented in new terms to the government local apparatus: is cooperation with the government worth the risk of dying, if the probability of dying is very high? Previously, involvement with the government had not had a high cost attached, and many people elected, or accepted, involvement for unsubstantial reasons such as supplementing their income or "being a good citizen." Only now did the new terms of the conflict test the intensity of their commitment by attaching a high cost—the probability of death. We can easily reconstruct the calculations that these numerous local officials made. Those who were rich—the first "pure type" discussed earlier in this chapter—clearly had "everything to lose and nothing to gain" by continuing to cooperate with the government, particularly because they were offered the option (initially at least) of retaining part of their land at reduced income. Some among this group elected to remain but cease working for the government, although as time went on an increasing number chose to leave the revolutionary areas entirely, sometimes retaining their posts and sometimes not. The second group of less well-off "faithfuls," the "pure type" to which the Ai Ngai hamlet chief belonged, also clearly had no personal incentives worth the risk of death. For many the position had been an unwelcome burden in the first place, and the new threat proved a welcome opportunity to quit. Those who took the post merely for

---

23. The history of events in this hamlet, recounted by Nguyen van Cu, the hamlet's first activist and ultimately the village secretary until his defection, is included in the collection of interviews deposited with the Center for Research Libraries.

the salary were allowed the option of retaining the post but cooperating with the movement. This was possible, from their viewpoint, because the revolution did not represent a threat to their personal interests—their position in the new society, they believed, would be very much the same as in the old. Such a state of affairs had of course been consciously created by the Party's electing a strongly preemptive strategy, that is, one which threatened an absolutely minimum number of people. A major part of the movement's propaganda effort during the preceding three years had been in explaining its policy of clemency toward those officials and soldiers who elected cooperation with the revolutionary cause—what it called *chanh quyen van* and *binh van*. Now this effort began to pay off. For example, in Ai Ngai, the hamlet chief ultimately elected to return and cooperate with the revolutionary movement.

What about the fourth alternative: to stay and fight? This might have taken either of two forms, one of living in a heavily defended compound or bunker, and the other of taking up a mobile "underground" existence like the revolutionary apparatus. In fact, the first of these was adopted in a number of areas, but it did not prove viable over a long period because of the movement's increasing ability to mass superior forces against any static defensive system. Thus, gradually, the hamlet officials who adopted this approach were forced to move from their hamlet to the village compound, and as the village compounds were in time reduced in number, the inhabitants were forced to move to the district compounds. The second approach, that of living like a guerrilla, was never a viable alternative, for the required condition—a sympathetic environment—did not exist. The government's social policies and the unpopular measures that the local officials had been charged with enforcing had produced a hostile environment, of which the local officials themselves were well aware. It is for this reason that with only one important exception not a single official adopted this approach, as far as can be determined several years after the fact.

This important exception, which might be said to prove the rule, is the village of Luong Hoa, whose population, except for a half-dozen people, is entirely Catholic. Here the local officials opted partly for the defensive bunker approach (feasible because of their favored position in receiving weapons and defensive materials from the government), and partly for the "underground" approach, in which they simply slept in a different house each night. By 1965 Luong Hoa was miles from the nearest government outpost and approachable only by air, yet despite heavy pressure its local officials remained at their posts. For religious reasons the alternative of remaining in place and cooperating with the revolutionary movement was unacceptable, and at the same time these local officials could survive while remaining in place, because of the sympathetic environment provided by their fellow Catholics. It is significant that the village which best resisted revolutionary pressures in the whole province was the one which most closely resembled in form the approach which the Party itself had employed in developing its strength: Luong Hoa had strong community leadership, closely tied to the overwhelming majority of the local population by ties of critical interest, and there had been little interference in its affairs by the central government, because of its loyalty to the national cause. The distinctive difference between Luong Hoa and a communist village was that these conditions existed in Luong Hoa because of the perceived common interest of protecting the Catholic faith, while the Party employed social and economic policies to develop strong local leadership and ties of critical interest.

On the other hand, what had made the Party apparatus viable even under conditions of high risk? The answer lies in two complementary elements: the Party emphasized recruitment from the lowest and most marginal groups in the social and economic scale,[24] and it offered them high personal incentives. Aside from reducing the threat to their physical survival represented by the government, the revolutionary movement offered a redistribution of property for even its lowest-ranking members; similarly, it put considerable decision-making authority at very low levels. These were very high incentives in the view of the elements low in the social scale from among whom the movement recruited its leadership in the rural areas. In contrast, decision-making authority was placed at a much higher level in the centralized government structure, and recruitment came principally from elements much higher in the scale of social stratification. Motivation was thus correspondingly lower. The relatively higher incentives offered and relatively lower social standing of the recruited groups permitted the revolutionary movement to motivate much larger numbers of people than the government to take an active part in its organization, and to exact greater discipline, more expenditure of effort, and more risk-taking from them.

---

24. Although an important segment of Party leadership—in some areas a majority—was drawn from other social elements not in a hopeless position, as the document quoted in footnote 16 above illustrates.

Moreover, it is interesting to note the relatively small number of people required to eliminate the government presence. Here Ai Ngai is fairly typical: the movement there had only one activist, yet one proved adequate. The revolutionary movement, despite a relative inferiority of numbers, represented a greater force in the sense that we have used the term, because of a relative superiority of motivation: when it came to a face-down, the government apparatus (the hamlet chief and his half-dozen soldiers) elected to quit, leave, or cooperate, rather than risk death. Thus the common observation that the movement represented a small but determined minority is accurate—although the same could be said of the government. The critical factor deciding which small but determined minority could survive was which had a sympathetic environment. For the answer to that question, one need only look at the map of Long An as of 1965.

After losing its local apparatus, that is, assimilated forces, the government could no longer collect taxes or recruit troops; similarly it did not have sufficient intelligence on which to base military operations or to direct its police activities. Had the Party been unable to destroy the government's local apparatus, it could not have developed the human and material resources necessary for its subsequent advance to higher stages of military conflict. On the other hand, without its local apparatus, nothing the government subsequently attempted to do was effective, from military operations, which floundered for lack of intelligence, to the establishment of the strategic hamlets, which collapsed for lack of forces to defend them. The activities of the participants had been determined by the personal incentives available to them, and all the orders from Saigon to "stay and fight" could not change this.

Beyond this, what happened in Ai Ngai hamlet teaches us another important lesson: that there was an enormous difference between the Party's destroying the government's organization, and the building of its own. For the first, violence—sharply limited to object—was essential. For the second, only personal incentives could be employed, not "terror."[25] Indeed, the government's use of "terror"

---

25. Lest the emotional connotation of these words cloud our analytical ability, it should be noted that communist "terror" was viewed by the Party as punishment carried out according to established procedures against the "rebel authorities"—themselves the practitioners of indiscriminate terror. The logic of this view was understandable, and persuasive, to much of the rural population: communist executions—at least the official ones—actually were the consequence of extensive investigation and approval by higher authority

against the general population of Ai Ngai had been one of the key elements in destroying its position there. This belies the commonly heard argument that "the communists only have to destroy, while the government has to build." As Ai Ngai clearly shows, the very ability of the Party to destroy rested on its prior creation of a superior apparatus, and the government's attempts to "build" without first building a superior apparatus were irrelevant. What happened later only serves to confirm the truth of this point: it was not until more than two years afterward that the Party was able to establish a functioning front organization which had the capability of pushing the struggle into other areas—two years of continuous political activity to show how the movement's policies would be of personal benefit to the residents of Ai Ngai. Even then only some seventy people were motivated to take an active part, still a small minority of the village population—though this was far more than the government had ever motivated to take part in counterrevolutionary activities.

Another important aspect of the events of January 1960 deserves mention: the rapid weakening of the government position once the conflict was brought to the stage of generalized violence, because of a number of what may be called "downward spiral effects." These became operative only when widespread violence was employed by both sides. Thus violence accentuated the weakness of the government's already weak position.

The first of these downward spiral effects was a consequence of the changed situation of the local officials responsible for moving in rural areas: hamlet and village officials, police, and cadres of the central ministries based in the district seats. Earlier in this chapter we noted one useful distinction in the types of activities these officials carried out: some were conflict-aggravating, such as tax collection and the arrest of draft evaders. These were the minimum functions of the local apparatus which district officials insisted be carried out. On the other hand, there were some other functions which might be called conflict-minimizing, such as visiting the sick and traveling

---

(the province committee); the government clearly was one that had been imposed from outside the village and was not responsive to majority village interests, and the government clearly was responsible for terrorizing many people not involved with the Party.

According to the reports of defectors, the Party actually exercised much tighter control over the procedures for approving executions after 1954, because of the unfavorable consequences of the many careless executions that occurred during the Resistance, when the Party did not have the absolute command of the movement it gained after 1954.

around inquiring about grievances, which were more or less up to the goodwill of the official himself—they were not of an obvious and quantifiable nature like a decline in tax receipts or a failure to produce the required number of draftees for the national army. As security declined in the rural areas, local officials sharply minimized their own movement, but since the "conflict-aggravating" functions were the minimum standards of performance, these were the last to disappear. When questioned about their activities during this period, local officials note that they would never move around in insecure areas without a squad or more of troops, and then usually only to collect taxes or payments on communal lands, to enforce land-rent payments to private landlords, or to round up draft evaders. As a consequence, the government became identified even more firmly than before as a hostile outside force.

The increase in violence also brought about similar consequences through a second, somewhat different mechanism: the changed direction of policy adopted by decision makers in the new circumstances. The latter felt forced into ever more demanding "control" measures to reestablish "security," explicitly postponing attention to projects of reform or improvement in popular livelihood until after "security" had been restored. We saw the germ of this phenomenon in Duoc's comments that it would have been desirable to hold elections for village government in 1957, but that it was not possible at that time because of communist activity. As the physical threat increased in 1960, Duoc shifted his attention even more into security-related efforts, in accord with his Confucian theory of "peace and prosperity," in which "we must first of all provide peace, for without peace there can be no prosperity."

Yet this peace, or security, was security according to the definition the government had employed all along, based on a confusion between tactical and strategic conceptions of security and the inevitable paradox this confusion involves. Government programs which might be considered preemptive in nature, for example, the land-distribution program, simply ceased to function an attention was turned to implementing a series of reinforcement measures such as curfews, increased controls on movement, and forced mobilization into mass organizations. When by 1961 the government began to respond in a systematic fashion to the new communist policy, these reinforcement measures were combined into what represented the high point of the government's reinforcement strategy: the strategic hamlet program To judge the impact of this program on popular attitudes, we need only think back to the opposition created by the agroville, which was far less disruptive in its demands than the strategic hamlets that followed. The greatly increased demands of the reinforcement strategy fell on a rural population which for the most part had been preempted by the revolutionary movement. Thus government programs that might have alleviated the situation to some extent were cast aside in favor of programs that aggravated it and increased sympathy for the revolutionary movement. Moreover, the deaths which subsequently occurred through military engagements tended to lock participants into the movement even though their initial commitment may have been weak.

A third downward spiral effect was the consequence of the changed situation of the rural population. We have noted earlier that decisions to become involved with the revolutionary movement were made on the basis of sober calculations of probable benefits against probable risks. Prior to January 1960, a great many people were favorably inclined toward the movement, but elected not to cooperate overtly because of the risks entailed by the continued government presence and by the seeming impossibility of the movement's fulfilling its promises, such as land distribution and community government responsive to majority local interests. Yet, as the presence of the central government was eliminated, the probability of achieving what the movement promised greatly increased, at the same time as the risks of involvement greatly decreased. Consequently, a number of people now became active in the movement who had previously been receptive to the idea of joining but had calculated that it was not expedient to do so. Just as in 1955 and 1956 the government's apparent strength and survival capacity caused many to join it who would not otherwise have done so, so now the apparent defeat of the government caused a corresponding shift in the other direction. Thus the limited initial success of the movement in 1960 was the foundation for greater successes in the years to come.

Needless to say, these downward spiral effects had been anticipated by the Party leadership and were an important part of its strategy of victory. Government officials, however, did not appreciate the snowballing effect of the steps they took. Instead, they believed that these steps were right and natural—indeed, that there were no alternatives. Only a far deeper understanding of what was occurring would have directed them away from the trap they entered by their responses to the events of January 1960. Yet it is reasonable to assume that, had such an understanding existed, the situation would not have developed as unfavorably for the government as it had by that time.

The strategic hamlet episode just mentioned deserves analysis in more detail because it clearly demonstrates the hopelessness of the government position once its local apparatus was crippled—and the pointlessness of issuing orders, reorganizations, and physical defense plans from Saigon if sufficient incentives did not exist in the rural areas to carry them out. Today the comment is frequently heard that the strategic hamlets would have been a good thing if the program had been properly executed. For example, Thanh, province chief during the strategic hamlet period, considered that the two critical problems were the lack of cadres and the attempt to "move too fast." In fact, the conditions did not exist for the proper execution of the strategic hamlet program, and if they had, then there would have been no need for the program in the first place. In other words, the strategic hamlet program was simply not a relevant response.

The strategic hamlet concept exemplifies in clearest form the government's reinforcement strategy. It might be said that the program gathered into one effort all the government's strategic errors: the incentives for living in the strategic hamlets were not relevant to the reasons for assistance to the revolutionary movement (and in fact these incentives, irrelevant as they were, never materialized in any case); the program devoted its resources to a physical reinforcement of the existing social system and of those who held power under it; the form of physical reinforcement adopted was founded on an explicit conception of security as the physical prevention of movement; security was explicitly intended to apply to the population in general, although the population was not the object of attack; and the thinking which led to the adoption of the strategic hamlet program was based on a severe miscalculation of its conflict-aggravating consequences—a consistent characteristic of government efforts in the rural areas.

What was the logical chain of events that determined the collapse of the strategic hamlets in Long An? In the simplest terms, no physical obstacle to movement is worth anything if it is not defended. Yet, given the inadequacy of government military forces, this meant that the population itself had to be mobilized to defend the strategic hamlets. The strategic hamlets, however, represented no positive value to the majority of their inhabitants—on the contrary, as the testimony of even government officials showed, they were a terrific annoyance, through controls on movement which interfered with making a living, through demands for guard duty which interfered with sleep, through the destruction of homes and fields. The pointlessness of this annoyance was amplified by the fact that, for a majority of the population, the supposed enemy was not even perceived as a threat, and for a significant segment the "enemy" even offered substantial positive incentives. These problems were recognized to some extent by government officials, but they were intended to be overcome by organization which would "compel" each citizen to take part in the defense of the strategic hamlets, even if they could not persuade people of their value. Yet, as stated earlier, the very ability to coerce lies in a decisive superiority in the balance of forces, which is exactly what the government did not have, once its local apparatus was destroyed. Beyond this, there is reason to doubt that the government's local apparatus, even before it came under strong attack after January 1960, would ever have been adequate to enforce a program as ambitious as the strategic hamlet program against the combination of indifference and active hostility that existed among the population in Long An. Here again we see the significance of the Party's constant emphasis on the strengthening of the chi bo as a strategic task of first-rank importance. The construction of "combat villages" in revolutionary areas—far less ambitious or demanding than the strategic hamlets—depended on a level of motivation at the local level considerably greater than that achieved by the government.

A Retrospective View of Some Other Explanations

Each of the government officials interviewed in the course of the research had some favorite explanation or set of explanations to account for the collapse of the government position in Long An, many of which have been quoted in earlier chapters. It is instructive to review these explanations in the light of the analysis in the previous pages to discover on what points these explanations are valid. Some fit the evidence and are relatively significant; some fit the evidence but are relatively insignificant; and some are completely mistaken.

1. "Insufficient Security"

Insufficient security was the most common explanation offered by government officials. Nevertheless, this explanation is founded on a misleading interpretation of events. As the figures in Table 1 show, communist cadres were constantly moving in "insecure" areas, and suffering high losses in doing so. On the other hand, as the risk for the government of operating in the rural areas increased, its response was to withdraw, with the justification that "those areas are insecure." Yet this was not an absolute imperative—it was so only because the government lacked a highly motivated apparatus that would operate under conditions of high risk, like that of the revolutionary movement. The appropriate response by the government to maintain its position could have been only a twofold action, on the one hand to develop policies to create a highly motivated apparatus, and on the other hand to create security in the strategic sense by pre-empting additional segments of the rural population. Yet neither of these occurred: the incentives for and the social basis of recruitment into the local apparatus remained the same, as did the government's policies on the key issue of the distribution of values among the various classes of society.[26]

The reason always cited by government officials for the "lack of security," and hence the need for withdrawal from certain areas, was, "We haven't enough troops." Yet how did the revolutionary movement gain victory with so few troops? As we saw in the previous pages, it did so by using a different conception of security from that employed by the government; by distinguishing between the legal position of the people and the illegal position of its apparatus, and by protecting only the latter; and by motivating an apparatus to operate under a higher level of risk. The government's failure to employ a strategic conception of security, its insistence on "protecting the people" when the people were not the objects of attack, and the low level of risk which its apparatus demanded, created impossible demands for military forces, given the level of opposition which existed.[27]

---

26. One change worthy of mention is the adoption of a formal surrender program in 1963, known as Chieu Hoi. However, this program was not in any sense redistributive—it simply eased the return of those who elected to do so for other reasons. In fact, the number of those returning under the Chieu Hoi program in Long An, while increasing in absolute numbers in 1963, 1964, and 1965, was actually a constant to declining proportion of revolutionary forces each year.

27. The fact that there were "not enough troops" was the analogue in real terms of the theoretical conclusion that the force equation had passed the crossover point, i.e., that the existing social organization was unable to motivate sufficient forces to defend itself. Government officials in Long An, however, never drew this conclusion, for they did not understand that the number of troops and their level of motivation were a consequence of social

A more subtle argument frequently raised by government officials to account for the government's comparatively greater need
for troops asserted that "we must protect physical installations and
lines of communication." It is true that, on the basis of the military
strategy the government adopted, it had to defend physical installations and lines of communication. Yet this was not a winning
strategy. The revolutionary victory in Long An showed that roads,
buildings, seaports, and even cities were conveniences but were not
necessary to victory, if one's strategic horizon was broad enough.

Party strategists correctly identified the rural areas as strategically decisive,[28] and hence they developed policies that allowed the
movement's forces to live directly off the people, minimizing the
need for physical installations and lines of communication. By contrast, the government recognized that the rural population would
not supply its military forces, and so it elected a strategy of supply
through the cities and seaports, thus requiring the protection of extensive physical installations as well as lines of communication for
its forces to survive.[29]

---

organization. The only alternative they saw was to call on foreign assistance
to make up for the forces which could not be raised internally. The very
"need" for such foreign assistance in suppression should have been a warning
that there were severe underlying structural vulnerabilities in Vietnamese
society.

28. This was so as long as the strategy was a take-over by armed force. It
is true, however, that during a brief period the leadership expected that
victory would come about through political upheavals in Saigon, and thus it
directed its principal efforts into the populated areas. This period was the
approximately eighteen months following the signing of the Geneva Accords,
before the leadership realized that this strategy would not be successful. The
strategic decision to concentrate on the urban areas had manifested itself in
the movement of large numbers of political cadres from the rural areas into
the cities in 1954, as well as in the relocation of COSVN from Ca Mau to
Tay Ninh, just a few miles from Saigon.

29. It is not clear to what extent the choice of a conventional military
machine was the result of conscious deliberation or of unconscious acceptance
based on an ignorance of the alternatives. Nevertheless, there was an explicit
decision that the source of support of this military machine would be the
American and not the Vietnamese taxpayer, for the simple reason that the
Vietnamese taxpayer, as the government well knew, would not stand paying
for the kind of military forces which the government elected to build. This
conscious decision was reflected in the establishment of the Commercial Import Program, financed by the American treasury, which generated the Vietnamese piasters to pay for the defense budget. Thus the implements of war
literally came through the seaports and cities over the lines of communication
to the countryside, while the salaries of the military establishment also followed the same path but in a more roundabout fashion: they were paid out

On the other hand, had the government adopted a truly rural strategy, in the sense of assimilating its forces into rural communities as well as conducting operations in rural areas, then there would have been no need to devote such extensive troop levels to the protection of physical installations and lines of communication. Of course, such a rural strategy could not have been successful without the proper policies—indeed, we may view the strategic hamlet program as a semirural strategy which failed precisely because it lacked the proper supporting policies. Ironically, if the proper policies had existed, the revolutionary movement could never have come to represent the threat it did, since the "proper supporting policies" would have been just those policies which would have preempted the rural population for the government.

2. "Terrorism"

A second commonly cited reason for the declining position of the government was that the revolutionary movement was able to use "terror" to "force people to support it." One reason for the currency of this explanation is that it pointed (in the view of its proponents) to an asymmetry between the government's position and that of the revolutionary movement which justified the "we had no choice" attitude of government officials. This asymmetry, in their view, was that "the communists are inhumane and bound by no moral demands, hence they can terrorize at will; the government cannot terrorize for humane and legal reasons."

Yet the history of events in Long An clearly contradicts this interpretation. The lessons of Long An are that violence can destroy, but cannot build; violence may explain the cooperation of a few individuals, but it cannot explain the cooperation of a whole social class, for this would involve us in the contradiction of "Who is to coerce the coercers?" Such logic leads inevitably to the absurd picture of the revolutionary leader in his jungle base, "coercing" millions of terrorized individuals throughout the country. In fact, the asymmetry was not at all the moral one government officials had in mind, but rather the asymmetry of motivation between the operatives of the two sides and of the environment in which they circulated. Revolutionary violence crippled the government apparatus

---

of local funds generated by the American-financed import of consumer goods, brought into the country through the seaports and consumed principally in the cities.

because it was so exposed; but the government could not then create a viable "underground" apparatus like the Party's, because of the low level of motivation of the government's operatives and their lack of a sympathetic environment.

The history of events in Long An also indicates that violence will work against the user, unless he has already preempted a large part of the population and then limits his acts of violence to a sharply defined minority. In fact, this is exactly what happened in the case of the government: far from being bound by any commitments to legality or humane principles, the government terrorized far more than did the revolutionary movement—for example, by liquidations of former Vietminh, by artillery and ground attacks on "communist villages," and by roundups of "communist sympathizers." Yet it was just these tactics that led to the constantly increasing strength of the revolutionary movement in Long An from 1960 to 1965.

3. "Infiltration"

A third commonly cited explanation to account for the inability of the government to cope with revolutionary activity was infiltration from the North. This was one of the explanations prominent in Duoc's thinking: "Without the infiltration from the North, the Vietcong would be an empty name like the Pathet Lao." For several reasons Long An is useful in evaluating the role of infiltration and the accuracy of such judgments as Duoc's.

Two considerations outlined earlier in this chapter will assist in this evaluation. First, the revolutionary leadership—in this case the Party apparatus—performed, as did the government, an organizational function for certain constellations of forces motivated by the existing distribution of values. Thus neither the government nor the revolutionary leadership could have been any more effective than the forces available to them. The second consideration is a historical one: that the extent of infiltration into Long An was extremely low, gradually increasing (according to some defectors' reports) from about ten a year in 1960 to less than one hundred a year in 1965. These numbers are negligible compared with the size of the forces recruited within the province. (Nevertheless, the importance of the infiltrated personnel was out of proportion to their numbers, because their impact was not in adding their own persons to the balance of forces, but rather in the organizational and leadership skills that they brought to the entire movement in Long An.)

When we examine the possible courses the government could have taken, we can see, first, that efforts by the government to limit the infiltration of personnel during this period would have been un-rewarding, because of the difficulty of capturing small groups of infiltrators. This is particularly clear when the resources necessary for such a program are compared with the probable results of the same resources devoted to efforts aimed at the Party leadership al-ready in the province. Second, even if some foolproof system for closing the borders of Long An had been possible, it still would have been of dubious worth in the long run, because the leadership infiltrated could in time have been developed within the province, once it had completed its first and most important strategic task of destroying the government's local apparatus. As noted earlier, this task was well on its way to completion by the time the infiltration began. Thus the final conclusion is that, from the viewpoint of feasibility as well as long-range results, the best course for the gov-ernment would have been to develop programs to reduce the forces which the society had made available for organization by the revolu-tionary leadership.

One corollary to the infiltration theory which deserves mention at this point is that "the people just wanted to be left alone." Such a comment, frequently encountered in the course of interviewing gov-ernment officials, is characteristic of the unscientific, one-dimensional approach that led to the defeat of the government in Long An. Such a statement views "the people" as undifferentiated and thus fails to make the crucial distinctions between segments of the population which are essential to developing a winning social strategy. From the point of view of social analysis, "the people" do not exist as individuals, but instead as elements of status relations, power re-lations, and economic relations: in short, as members of society. While it is true that some people just wanted to be left alone, it is also true that they were not the ones causing difficulties for the government. Others obviously wanted to improve their life situation to the extent that they were willing to risk death to do it. Thus the statement that "the people just want to be left alone" is partly wrong, and to the extent that it is true, it is irrelevant. The critical and un-asked question from the viewpoint of the government was, "how to motivate people who only want to be left alone to behave in useful ways." It was exactly this question that had been addressed by the revolutionary leadership and had resulted in its winning social strategy.

4. *"Insufficient Propaganda"*

The most common response of government officials to account for the apparent ease with which the population was "deceived" was, "we did not propagandize sufficiently," or "the communists are more clever propagandists than we are." When pressed on the critical issue of why their opponents were better propagandists, government officials offered a variety of ideas. One prevalent idea was that government propaganda efforts were severely limited by the lack of mechanical aids such as vehicles, projectors, public address systems, and portable generators. The validity of this view can be judged from the fact that Party agents had none of these.

A second view frequently encountered in the course of the interviewing was that "the people hear only one voice, and thus they don't know the government's story." The first part of this statement is true to a large extent, but the reason was simply that the government had failed to motivate an apparatus to operate in areas of high risk, as the revolutionary movement had done. When this idea was put forth, government officials replied that it was not possible to operate in enemy areas, "because they control movement much more closely than we do—they do not hesitate to shoot someone they suspect, while we are bound by legal restrictions." Again this is a mistaken interpretation of events: the Party was able to control movement more closely because it had motivated many times more manpower at the local level than the government. Despite this, movement still would have been possible—many areas were held very weakly—but only at the risk of death, a risk which the government propaganda apparatus refused to undergo.[30] The second part of the former statement, "the people don't know the government's story," must be assigned to the conclusively wrong category. The population was quite aware of those government policies critical to their life situation: the policy of maintaining the existing landholding system; the policy of military service far from one's home; the policy of persecuting former Vietminh; the policy of denying local organs sufficient authority to punish offending soldiers and officials; the policy of building strategic hamlets; and the policy of maintaining a government recruitment pattern which

---

30. One of the striking conclusions from interviewing defectors is the total absence of government movement in revolutionary areas for years at a time, except on occasional large-scale sweep operations which had little impact on the Party's local apparatus.

denied advancement to those from majority elements of the rural population.

A third and more perceptive reason commonly offered for the Party's success in propaganda was, "communist cadres are close to the people, while ours are not." Yet here again government officials when pressed were at a loss to provide a reason consistent with the facts. Some were surprisingly frank and replied, as Ba did, "This is something I have never been able to figure out." Others, for example, Si, felt that the problem lay in the inadequate funding of propaganda programs which prevented the government from hiring "trained people." In fact, the reason why government cadres were not "close to the people" is easy to see in the light of events in Long An. In the first place, because of their low motivation, with few exceptions, they did not physically live with the people in "insecure areas," that is, the areas where they were needed most. Second, because of the educational requirements for recruitment into the appropriate civil-service grade,[31] government cadres were drawn from the social elements least able to deal empathetically with the rural population. Thus it was structurally impossible for government officials to be "close to the people," because of the nonassimilation of government forces. Ironically, the people best able to deal with the rural population cost no money at all, as the success of the revolutionary movement demonstrated. Moreover, the Party leadership did not leave to chance such an important matter as assimilation of forces: it was institutionalized through requirements of class and local origin for cadres, and such fundamental working principles as criticism and self-criticism, "from the masses, to the masses," and "the higher-ups go down." It is significant that none of these critical factors was mentioned by any of the government officials interviewed.

Finally, it should be noted that the most important factor in the success of the revolutionary movement's propaganda was never mentioned by government officials: that the movement offered concrete and practical solutions to the daily problems of substantial segments of the rural population, and that the government did not come forth with equal or superior solutions. It is true that there were numerous shortcomings of a technical nature in the government propaganda effort. How much of an improvement the resolution of these technical shortcomings might have produced is unknown, because

---

31. For most cadres the requirement was *trung hoc de nhat cap*, one grade below the *tu tai*.

the government devoted so little effort to propaganda. Nevertheless, it is clear that these technical deficiencies were insignificant compared to the fact that the government simply had very little to propagandize.

5. "Underdevelopment"

A basic fallacy underlay the government's development programs in Long An: that people "supported communism" because they were poor, and therefore that reducing their poverty would reduce the appeal of revolution. Thus this approach viewed the problem as incremental rather than distributive.

As noted above, what permitted the Party to motivate its forces was its policies offering contingent incentives. Contingent incentives in turn derived from the offer of redistribution of power, status, wealth, or income, or the offer to protect against some repressive action by the government. In each case the contingency was the consequence of government policy itself. Development, an incremental effort, simply was not relevant to ending the Party's ability to motivate forces, because it did not break this link of contingency.

Consequently, the hypothesis that the revolutionary movement succeeded because of underdevelopment or because of inadequate government programs of assistance must be viewed as disconfirmed, because governmental development efforts—and there were many— were not responsive to the distributive conflicts in Vietnamese society which permitted the revolutionary movement to motivate its forces.

6. "Corruption"

Corruption was another factor commonly cited by government officials to account for the rise of the revolutionary movement, particularly in two roles: first, in diverting material resources and thus sabotaging the effectiveness of government assistance programs; and second, in alienating specific individuals who then sought revenge through the movement. Two issues are important in discussing the significance of corruption: the actual role of corruption in leading to the collapse of the government's position in Long An, and the extent to which corruption was an independent factor which could have been altered apart from the social system itself.

What was the role of corruption? In earlier pages we noted the great difference in perception between government officials and members of the revolutionary movement as to the reasons for sympathy for and assistance to the movement. The former—most prominently Duoc—assigned to corrupt practices the principal role in the creation of this support and assistance. Yet in contrast, former members of the revolutionary movement allotted only some weight to the role of corruption, emphasizing far more the fundamental role of grievances against the social system itself, which would have existed regardless of the honesty or corruption of government officials. Moreover, despite all the talk of corruption in Long An by government officials, an objective appraisal must conclude that the majority of officials in Long An were honest, if not always hardworking, and the most commonly cited examples of corruption on closer investigation turned out to have been caused by lack of funding, poor planning, or administrative breakdowns. While this may not have been true in other provinces, the administration in Long An in retrospect looks very good when examined from the standpoint of corrupt practices. The prominent role which government officials assigned to corruption in defeating the government seems to have resulted from the need for a satisfying and acceptable excuse on which to blame the more fundamental but less clearly understood failures of the social system. Thus we may conclude that, while corruption played some role in affecting the rate at which the government collapsed, it was not decisive in determining that the government would collapse: that was determined by more basic aspects of the social order.

A second, equally important aspect of the issue of corruption is the extent to which corruption was an independent factor for which a few corrupt individuals were to blame, and the extent to which it was a product of the system itself. The view that it was an independent factor for which a few evil officials at the top were responsible was popular among former officials in Long An—they particularly liked to blame Diem's brother Nhu and his wife. In fact, this view is another manifestation of the unscientific analysis of government officials, which tended to view events or phenomena in isolation and thus, for example, failed to establish the relationship between corruption as a social phenomenon and the social order of which it was a part. Three aspects of this order were crucial in fostering corruption: the locus of authority, the social origins of the decision makers, and the "theory" on which they based their decisions.

The issue of the locus of authority has already been discussed to some extent. The point particularly relevant to this discussion is Duoc's own testimony that the retention of disciplinary authority at such a high level (even out of his hands for appointees of the central government) was instrumental in the retention of corrupt and abusive elements. Even had those with final disciplinary authority been men of the best will—as they were not always—nevertheless, their job would have been an impossible one: the disciplinary procedures were too cumbersome to respond adequately to petty but significant incidents in creating ill will for the government; and the required span of attention was simply too great for adequate coverage.[32] The issue of the social origin of decision makers has also been considered in earlier pages: that recruitment requirements ensured that they were drawn from the social elements least able to empathize with the rural population. Thus many appointees of the central government were simply unaware of existing abuses they might have learned of, had they been able to inspire sufficient confidence among the population they ruled.

The third issue of "theory" is more diffuse, for it was more diffuse in the minds of government officials themselves. Two examples, however, will show how commonly expressed views of government officials on the subject of corruption were devoid of a conception of revolution as a coherent social process. On the subject of troop discipline, many officials responded that "it is just not possible to know what every soldier is doing all the time," thus justifying in their minds the impossibility of achieving better discipline in the army. Yet this view overlooks the sharp difference in discipline between the government and the revolutionary military forces, a difference attributable to the voluntary and more highly motivated nature of the revolutionary forces, which permitted the imposition of tighter discipline. The possibility that the government army might have been a volunteer force had the proper incentives been employed was again a "blank area of consciousness" in the minds of government officials. Their explanation of tighter revolutionary discipline was that communists were "fanatics," "ideologues," or "machines." Likewise, Duoc's justification of the rigging of the 1959 elections in Long An—that it was necessary "to prevent communist or procommunist elements from entering the government"—was based on the confusion of tactical and strategic conceptions of security discussed earlier. A "reliable" National Assembly representative might ensure that the government would pass the necessary anti-

---

32. It is significant that the communist disciplinary system was organized differently, with judgment meted out to malefactors immediately by the echelon to which they were assigned, with review by the next higher echelon. Moreover, the incidence of malefaction was reduced within the revolutionary movement by such preventive measures as criticism and self-criticism, etc.

communist laws to ensure "security," but the vote-rigging required
to elect him also created the popular dissatisfaction which destroyed
that security in the strategic sense.

The same point applies to the view occasionally expressed by
military commanders in Long An, that it was necessary to use corrupt officers because they were "effective in killing communists."
Such a view is again founded on the failure to make the crucial
distinction between tactical and strategic conceptions of security.

Thus we may conclude that corruption was not an independent
factor which could have been altered at will, but integral to the
organization of the system itself and to the views of decision makers.
While there was some latitude for honest officials, the structure of
the system limited both their impact and the number who could exist
in the system at all. The corollary to the fact that the government's
collapse was not due to a few evil men is that honest men could not
have saved it. The talk of "better leadership" and "better military
operations" does not contradict this: the very conditions for better
leadership and better military operations would have been changes
in the social system. Even with a government of saints, the situation
in Long An would have moved in the same direction, although perhaps not as fast, and perhaps only to some kind of equilibrium of
forces short of the totally vanquished position that the government
occupied by 1965. In short, corruption, like underdevelopment, was
one of the leading false issues of the war in Long An. Had the system
of powerholding been structured differently, there would have been
little corruption. Thus the anxiety over whether there should have
been a "get tough" policy on corruption by the government's foreign
supporters was based on a failure to understand the phenomenon.

7. "No Ideology"

Another explanation frequently offered by government officials
in Long An for the government's lack of effectiveness was the lack
of a government "ideology." Such an explanation does not coincide
with the evidence in one sense, but it does in another.

This explanation is erroneous in the sense usually used by government officials, that an "ideology" is a magic intellectual formula
capable of blinding reason and turning individuals into fanatics.
Such a view springs from a spurious understanding of communist
ideology. All the former Party members interviewed were able to
give persuasive personal reasons for joining—reasons centered not
on "ideas" but on interests. It could be said they were "willing to

die for an ideology" only in the sense that the revolutionary ideology was a systematic expression of these interests.

This explanation is also erroneous in the sense occasionally used by government officials, that the revolutionary ideology was "doctrinaire" and "dogmatic." Communist efforts in Long An were marked by pragmatism and flexibility. This is demonstrated by one Party working principle that prescribes conducting limited tests of new policies in selected villages and then drawing conclusions. Similarly, the Party's land-reform policy to "outbourgeois the bourgeoisie" is an apt illustration of the Party's willingness to make expedient moves to win ultimate victory. Indeed, in this area the Party's pragmatism was in sharp contrast to the government's "doctrinaire," "ideological" insistence on the inviolability of private property.

As the previous chapters have shown, communist ideology was not a substitute for an appeal to practical interests but rather a systematic expression of them. Thus the government's lack of an ideology cannot justifiably be understood—as it was by government officials—as a lack of a "magic formula," but rather as a lack of concrete policies serving practical interests.

On the other hand, the view that "we had no ideology" is true and extremely significant, if this is understood to mean that the Party had an integrated conception of social change which proved an effective guide to action, while the government did not. As we saw earlier, one critical element in the collapse of the government in Long An was the failure by government officials to understand the process taking place: they lacked any explanation of the interrelation of different aspects of reality, Marxist or otherwise, which would have guided them to the proper responses.

8. *"Poor Administration"*

It was the judgment of several officials in Long An—for example, Doan and Duoc—that the low level of administrative competence was an important factor in affecting the position of the government. Yet in retrospect it can be seen that this account of events was not significant, and indeed in one sense it was dangerous. First, efficiency in carrying out administrative tasks was not relevant to the basic problem of the level of distributive conflict in Vietnamese society: what was significant was the content of that activity, not the efficiency with which it was carried out. The preoccupation with administrative efficiency thus diverted attention from the underlying issue of distributive conflict. Second, as noted earlier, many of the central government's activities in Long An were conflict-aggravating in nature; the more "efficient" these activities became, the more damaging they became.

9. "Lack of National Consciousness"

Many government officials in Long An believed that one factor aiding the Party was an alleged "lack of national consciousness." Consequently, they devoted considerable efforts to propaganda programs emphasizing national symbols such as the flag, photographs of national leaders, and the duty of "loyalty to the state." Their view was that an increase in "national consciousness" would lead to an increase in "support."

This misapprehension was permitted by the superficial understanding of the situation possessed by government officials. It was noted above that one component of the strength of the revolutionary movement was a combination of risk-taking, expenditure of effort, and coercive ability; these were a function of the high level of motivation of the movement's operatives, permitted by the movement's redistributive policies. A second component was identified as a "sympathetic environment," which permitted the movement's operatives to move undetected over wide geographical areas, while destroying the government's functional capabilities in these areas. However, since the second component required a minimal expenditure of effort on the part of the individuals involved, the rewards could be much lower; indeed, for many a mere congruence of values was sufficient.[33] "Nationalism"—if by this is meant a commitment to oppose foreign intervention—certainly played some role as a legitimizing theme in creating a sympathetic environment for the revolutionary movement. However, we can see that the important structural factor in generating the sympathetic environment was the strengthening of *communal* loyalties by the revolutionary movement, through the assimilated nature of its revolutionary organization. In neither event was it the loyalty of individuals to an abstract national community which produced the sympathetic environment. Nor was such a loyalty at issue for the motivation of the movement's operatives: here there was instead a ladderlike progression of loyalties from the individual to the community leadership,

33. "Values" in this context of course has a different meaning from its earlier use in the phrase, "distribution of values"; "preference orderings" would be a more accurate expression of this second meaning.

from the community leadership to the district leadership, and so on, because it was in just such a ladderlike system that the contingent incentives were manipulated.[34]

It is ironical that what might be called the too-advanced con-ceptualization of government officials stood in the way of their strengthening communal loyalties, because it was dissonant with the dogma of Western political thought that "nationalism" and "mod-ernization" mean "more inclusive loyalties." Following this dogma they felt it their duty instead to break down communal loyalties, thus unwittingly undermining their own position. The revolutionary movement handled the same problem by strengthening loyalties to communal leadership, and then binding the resulting great number of communities together with a national "skeleton" of a continuous vertical promotion system within the revolutionary organization.[35]

In summary, it is fair to say that none of the foregoing govern-ment explanations, alone or in combination, is sufficient to account for the collapse of the government in Long An, because none was founded on a systematic conceptualization of revolution as a social

---

34. Because what generally comes under the name of "support" in the literature of political science can be seen here to consist of two very different components, this analysis suggests that in the interests of clarity the word "support" might profitably be eliminated from discussions of revolutionary war. Similarly, scientists might fruitfully abandon use of the term "control," which, like coldness, is epiphenomenal in nature and unsuited to describing a structural model of the social process occurring in a revolutionary war.

This analysis also suggests a more general framework into which to fit the "behavior versus attitudes" debate among theorists of "counterinsurgency." An attitudinal change may be sufficient to bring about a sympathetic en-vironment, but not sufficient to bring about risk-taking behavior, for which contingent incentives are required. Both are necessary but distinct components of victory, a fact generally elided in the "behavior versus attitudes" debate. See for example Charles Wolf, Jr., *United States Policy and the Third World* (Boston: Little, Brown, 1967), chap. 3. It should be noted that Wolf's input-output model, like most of the writing on the subject, omits consideration of how the government under attack might motivate the forces required to carry out the measures he deems necessary.

35. This analysis has important implications for policy on ethnic minorities. The bias—often quite explicit—in the prevailing "nationalist" view is one of forced or not-so-forced assimilation of ethnic minorities into the predominant culture of the national entity, i.e., creating direct ties of loyalty from the individual to the state. The communist approach, based on a chain of loyal-ties, is in sharp contrast: loyalties of ethnic minorities are focused on the leadership of the minority, and the loyalty of this leadership to the Party is in turn ensured through a policy of co-optation and the selective elimination of noncooperators.

process, and thus none established the intellectual connection be-tween the particular factor it pointed to and the nature of the social system itself which the government maintained.

Conclusion

As noted earlier, three elements stand out in the collapse of the government in Long An: a level of distributive conflict which per-mitted the Party to motivate a core of forces to risk death;[36] a series of structural vulnerabilities in government organization, centering on nonassimilation of forces, which dictated that government forces would be poorly motivated, unresponsive, and ineffective in com-parison with revolutionary forces; and a failure of understanding on the part of the government leadership, which dictated a vicious circle of self-destructive responses. The lesson of Long An is that what was attacked was a particular form of social organization, and only consequentially the government itself. But because the government relied upon a certain constellation of social forces, it died when its host died. A viable defense, rather than defending "the government" in terms of physical manifestations of power, would have had to expand the social forces on which the government relied. Yet, just as in a conventional military conflict the defense of a piece of ground might demand some changes in it such as the construction of earth-works, so the strengthening of the social foundation of the gov-ernment would have required significant distributive changes in social organization, and hence in government structure itself, to be successful.

In retrospect we can see that the nine explanations offered by government officials to account for the government's collapse in Long An were ways to avoid recognizing the basic fact that the Party, because of the kind of society which it promised, was able to motivate greater forces than was the government, and because of its superior strategy, to employ them more effectively. The same

---

36. Every society has distributive inequalities; it is also a historical fact that societies with highly skewed distributions of values have sometimes been revolutionary and sometimes not. Thus there is clearly operative a mediating factor of subjective perception of a particular distribution of values as just or unjust. What circumstances correlate with this change of perception is an important subject for empirical research.

The model developed in the preceding pages accordingly describes the factors important to the differing performances of the two sides, *holding this element of perception constant*. In this writer's judgment the major change in popular perception occurred prior to 1954.

population groups were available to either side, and which side they elected to cooperate with was determined by which side developed superior policies.

In an intellectual sense the problems were far more complex than the simple issues of corruption, underdevelopment, or terror: they were a question of the form of social organization the government maintained. What happened did not have to happen, except as a consequence of a limited understanding by the principal government participants and their foreign advisors. In retrospect, perhaps the most significant aspect of talking to government officials was their belief that the steps they took were inexorably demanded by the situation itself, with no alternatives possible. In fact, there was a whole range of alternate strategies which were not apparent to them, because of their limited understanding of the processes taking place.

CHAPTER FIVE

Ignoring the Lessons: The American War in Long An

Actually the communists are not strong . . . the increase in their strength has come about because of the weapons and troops provided by the communist countries.

COLONEL NGUYEN VAN NGUU, Province Chief 1966–1969

In 1968 Long An represented in miniature the problems of the South as a whole. It was such an important area that both sides had the mission of holding it at all costs. Both sides escalated their commitment until all available local manpower was exhausted, and then both sides brought in external forces. Moreover, the situation in Long An represented well the unarticulated strategic dilemma faced everywhere by the Saigon government: its opponent was so strong that with the internal forces at the government's disposal the existing reinforcement strategy could not lead to victory in any sense, yet the changes necessary to move in the direction of a more preemptive strategy were largely unacceptable to the current government leadership. As a consequence, what might have been the cutting edge of a more preemptive strategy—the rural construction program[1]—remained form without substance. Finally, Long An was an interesting study not only of the reactions of the native leadership to a revolutionary social movement, examined in previous chapters, but also of the reactions of the American government, which was employing its latest doctrines in Long An for dealing with the problem of "insurgency."

On the other hand, Long An was different from most other provinces in two important ways. Because of its proximity to Saigon and the consequent steady stream of high-ranking visitors, Long An

---

1. Rural construction is the correct translation of *xay dung nong thon*, erroneously rendered in official publications as "revolutionary development."

was considered a "model province" and received special attention from the Vietnamese and American commands in the supervision of existing programs and the development and application of new ones. Likewise, because of its considerable strategic importance, most of Long An lay in the "national priority area" and thus received material resources on a scale unmatched in most other areas of the South.

Several important changes took place between 1965 and 1968 that had a significant impact on Long An. First and perhaps the most significant in the long run was the return of political stability to the Saigon government. The importance of this point can hardly be overstated, because, although this did not in itself lead to an improvement in the government's position in Long An, it was a necessary condition for that improvement to take place. The return of political stability did not expand the core of forces aligned with the government, but it did permit a consolidation of those forces which in 1965 were ineffective because of the collapse of central leadership —another interesting consequence of the government's policy of centralizing authority. This consolidation of the forces aligned with the status quo allowed the government to regain some ground which it would not have lost in 1963 and 1964 had the organs of the central government in Long An not been paralyzed by the political upheavals in Saigon. This consolidation of core forces in turn had a cumulative impact on expediency calculations and thus led to a further accretion of peripheral forces.

A second important change was the injection of sizable external combat forces into the province. The first of these was a battalion of the American 25th Infantry Division, which arrived in September 1966. Subsequently this battalion was replaced by a brigade of the Ninth Infantry Division. The second substantial increment of external combat forces occurred with the arrival between December 1967 and February 1968 of three PAVN main-force battalions, whose mission was to launch attacks on Saigon from bases in Long An. The arrival of these external forces had its own impact on the forces within Long An. In particular, the American forces, which occupied areas formerly held tenuously by the government, expanded the so-called "secure" areas and had a corresponding impact on expediency calculations. They likewise brought about a severe degradation in the effectiveness of revolutionary combat forces. At the same time, the tactics employed brought extensive physical destruction and loss of life to the province. All considered, the presence of external forces considerably clouded the relative underlying strength of both sides, which was quite clear in 1965.

A third change occurred in government strategy. Increased American involvement brought about somewhat greater intellectual and organizational rigor and a program which, on paper at least, was analogous to the communist social strategy. Nevertheless, the actual strategy employed in the field differed markedly from what had proved successful for the Party in Long An during the preceding decade and a half, and it represented no significant departure in concept from previous government efforts, although it did represent an enlargement of scale.

Yet despite the presence of large numbers of troops, despite the expenditure of resources on a scale matched in few other areas in Vietnam, and despite the favorable developments after 1965, the government position in Long An remained tenuous at best. As of 1968, only two of the forty-four provinces in the southern zone were considered by American officials to be less secure than Long An: An Xuyen and Chuong Thien at the very southern tip of Vietnam, both revolutionary strongholds for more than two decades.[2]

Some figures may prove helpful in grasping the situation in Long An.[3] In 1968 approximately 17,600 government and American

---

2. According to the Hamlet Evaluation System, discussed below.

3. The following is a list of revolutionary and counterrevolutionary military forces in Long An in late 1968:

Revolutionary forces:

Main- force units	506th Battalion	200	
	2nd Independent Battalion	250	
	265th Battalion (PAVN)	200	1,050
	K-3 Battalion (PAVN)	200	
	Phu Loi Battalion (PAVN)	200	
District companies			700
Combat support troops			500
Local guerrillas			1,450
			3,700

Counterrevolutionary forces:

2 ARVN regiments	5,500
28 Regional Force companies	4,600
71 Popular Force platoons	3,050
National Police	1,100
Provincial Reconnaissance Unit	300
	14,550
Third Brigade, Ninth Infantry Division (and supporting units)	3,000
Advisory Team 86	100
	3,100

troops were stationed in Long An, opposed by approximately 3,700 revolutionary troops. Of the government forces, Popular Force platoons (successors to the Dan Ve) were used principally in a defensive posture for village and hamlet security and to protect small isolated installations such as bridges and culverts. Regional Force companies (successors to the Bao An) were used to provide security for each of the district headquarters compounds and other major district installations, as well as in an offensive role as mobile forces under the control of the district chief. Two ARVN regiments were used as mobile offensive forces under the control of the ARVN 25th Division in Hau Nghia province. In addition to their mobile offensive role, the two ARVN regiments had certain static defensive roles, principally in providing security for the Tan An and Ben Luc bridges and Route 4. Of the 1,100 National Police in Long An province, substantial numbers were assigned to intelligence work and to a Police Field Force company, organized and equipped much like a Regional Force company and intended principally for use as an offensive force. The Provincial Reconnaissance Unit was a highly trained and mobile force intended for use against the communist apparatus on the basis of "hard" intelligence.

American military forces in Long An consisted of the Third Brigade of the Ninth Infantry Division, and Advisory Team 86. The Third Brigade had its headquarters in Tan An, the province capital, and was employed mainly as a mobile offensive force, primarily through the use of helicopter transportation. Advisory Team 86 consisted of about a hundred members of the military and an equal number of civilians, who provided professional advice to various members of the Vietnamese province staff and liaison with American supporting agencies, both military and civilian. Five-man teams in each district performed a similar function for the district chief and his staff.

Revolutionary main-force units indigenous to Long An province consisted of two battalions, the 506th and the 2nd Independent, whose mission was similar to that of the two government regiments, although with far less attention devoted to security of physical installations. The 506th is the same unit that appeared in 1959 in various antigovernment propaganda documents. By 1965 it had expanded to over 500 men and was unwieldy for its mission. Consequently, it was split into two units, resulting in the original 506th Battalion as well as the new 2nd Independent Battalion. Beyond these two locally recruited battalions, various PAVN units were also operating in Long An after the end of 1967. Their mission was to support the local revolutionary forces, under severe pressure from American and government offensive forces, as well as to attack Saigon in the anti-city phase of communist military strategy following Tet of 1968. District companies and local guerrillas performed missions analogous to the Regional Force and Popular Force units of the government. They were under the control of the district committee and the village committee respectively.

To gain an idea of the situation in Long An as seen through American eyes, we may refer to the results of the Hamlet Evaluation System, a computerized reporting system employed to judge progress in the rural construction program. The HES relied on data supplied by American district advisors each month on each hamlet in their district. It placed each hamlet on a six-level scale on the basis of its standing on nine "security-related factors," such as revolutionary military activity or government defense capabilities, and nine "development-related factors," such as the existence of a government census grievance program and education and welfare activities. It is important to note that the HES measured only government "inputs" to the pacification process and not, except inferentially, "outputs," i.e., changes in popular attitudes. The actual quantity it measured is best described as "the number of people living in areas of specified levels of government activity." Its usefulness is that it provides a fairly consistent indicator of certain changes in Long An after January 1967, when the Hamlet Evaluation System was instituted.

Table 3 indicates that from January 1967 through December 1968 a significant improvement came about in the quantity measured by the HES. If we assume, as did American officials, that a "C" hamlet was the minimum acceptable, then we see that population in satisfactory (i.e., A, B, and C) hamlets increased to 52 percent from 22.8 percent over the twenty-four month period. The large jump in the "C" category in the last six months of 1968 occurred because of the so-called "Accelerated Pacification Campaign," a concerted effort, related to the Paris negotiations, to gain at least a minimal government representation in as many hamlets as possible. Nevertheless, as subsequent pages will demonstrate, the Hamlet Evaluation System was a misleading indicator of "progress," and in fact revolutionary activity in many "C" category hamlets was more extensive than that of the government. Moreover, the HES format was misleading, because it created the impression that five of the six categories represented government "control," versus only one for the opposition, when in fact an "A" hamlet from the government viewpoint was equivalent to a "VC" hamlet from the revolutionary viewpoint. Thus when the scale is viewed symmetrically, it can be seen that most of the population still fell in the "VC" range of the scale. Consequently, the HES itself suggested that by the end of 1968 the government still occupied a decisively minority position in Long An.

Furthermore, it is noteworthy that even the improvement reflected by the HES was brought about principally by the arrival of a brigade of American troops in Long An. In one form this improvement occurred through the simple military occupation of areas formerly occupied by revolutionary forces, such as Long Huu Island at the southern end of Can Duoc district and parts of the newly established Rach Kien district north of Can Duoc. Another form that this improvement took was the movement of residents of revolutionary areas into government areas, because of the tremendous increase in the level of destruction accompanying the arrival of a

TABLE 3: POPULATION BY HAMLET CATEGORY ACCORDING TO THE HAMLET EVALUATION SYSTEM (IN PERCENT)

	January 67	July 67	January 68	July 68	December 68
A	0.0	0.0	0.0	0.0	0.0
B	10.5	11.8	12.8	18.9	20.3
C	12.3	18.6	19.4	19.2	31.7
D	17.4	17.2	18.2	15.8	11.2
E	12.9	8.2	8.5	7.8	7.4
VC	46.9	44.2	41.1	38.3	29.4

NOTE: Official category definitions are as follows:
  A: Adequate security forces, communist infrastructure eliminated, public projects under way, economic picture improving.
  B: Not immune to communist threat but security organized and partially effective, communist infrastructure partially neutralized, self-help programs under way, and economic programs started.
  C: Subject to infrequent communist harassment. Infrastructure identified. Some popular participation in self-help programs.
  D: Communist activities reduced but remain an internal threat. Some communist taxation and terrorism. Some local participation in hamlet government and economic programs.
  E: Communists effective although some government control evident. Communist infrastructure intact. Government programs nonexistent or just beginning.
  VC: Under communist control. No government or American advisor presence except on military operations. Populace willingly or unwillingly support communists.
SOURCE: MACV-CORDS.

brigade of American troops and a step-up in the level of offensive operations by the Saigon forces during 1968. Six specific hamlets, shown in Table 4, exemplify the population shifts that produced a consistent upward bias in the HES after January 1967. These six hamlets are all located in Can Giuoc district in eastern Long An, the scene of heavy destruction and loss of civilian life, owing both to a number of bitter clashes between American and PAVN forces and to the extensive use of harassing air attacks and artillery fire. Thus, while the HES may have reflected fairly accurately changes in "the number of people living in areas of specified levels of government activity," it was not an accurate index of the relative underlying strength of both sides based on the internal forces at their disposal.

We can gain a very different picture of the situation in the province by looking at several factors not included in the HES. Perhaps the most significant of these was the rate of surrenders to the government, because it aggregated on a province-wide basis the expectations of the participants themselves. Surrenders during 1966 totalled 580, or an average of 48 per month, a slight increase over 1965. A sharp rise from January to February 1967 (45 to 227 surrenders) coincided with the adoption of new tactics by the battalion of the American 25th Infantry Division operating in Long An at that time, and the continued abnormally high rate of surrenders for several months may be viewed as a process of shaking out the more weakly motivated members of the revolutionary movement.[4] It paral-

---

TABLE 4: TYPICAL POPULATION SHIFTS IN CAN GIUOC DISTRICT

Hamlet	Population September 1967	Population October 1968	HES Classification
Ap Cho	4,708	5,348	B
Hoa Thuan I	3,526	5,150	C+
Loc Tien I	1,133	1,536	D
Phuoc Ke	660	265	VC
Long Duc II	561	310	VC
Chanh Nhi	603	91	VC

SOURCE: MACV-CORDS.

---

4. Monthly figures are as follows:

Year	Jan	Feb	Mar	Apr	May	Jun	Jul	Aug	Sep	Oct	Nov	Dec	Total
1966	49	52	62	46	44	50	39	36	34	87	37	44	580
1967	45	227	362	175	177	114	152	100	46	56	39	32	1,525
1968	17	14	22	28	20	12	34	37	45	90	69	62	450

The arrival in Long An of a battalion of the 25th Infantry Division in

leled the sharp rise in surrenders that took place between 1961 and 1962 when the government began its concerted counterattack against the new phase of the movement with the strategic hamlet program. However, it is significant that by September 1967 the surrender rate had returned to its pre-February level, suggesting that the morale of the revolutionary forces had recovered from the initial severe impact of the American presence. A precipitous drop in the surrender rate beginning in January 1968 paralleled the similar fall-off that occurred beginning in Januray 1960. In its series of assassinations during Tet of that year the Party had launched the new violent phase of the revolution in the South, just as it launched a new phase at the end of January 1968 with its widespread attacks on urban areas. It is clear from the 1968 figures, as it was from the 1960 figures, that in each case the new phase had a strong salutary effect on morale within the movement. In 1968 this revealed itself in the fact that surrenders, despite a rise at the year's end, were at the lowest level since 1964.[5]

A second important indication of the strength of the movement lay in its rate of recruitment. Accurate overall recruitment figures were impossible to obtain, but thanks to extensive identity records maintained by the National Police, it is possible to present a comparison of what happened to three comparable age groups—those reaching seventeen years of age—in each of the years from 1965 through 1967.[6] Table 5 shows that the total accounted for in each year—those in government service or in school in a government area —was considerably less than half the age group. Government officials estimated that of the number registered but not accounted for, one-third had entered a branch of military service elsewhere in the country which had failed to notify province authorities of their induction, or else were (until 1968) in a draft-evading status in a

---

September 1966 marked the first deployment of an American combat unit into the Mekong Delta. Because of many questions surrounding the use of American combat units in an area where there had previously been a negligible American presence, initial operations were conducted with great circumspection. Results were judged to be poor in view of the effort expended, and in February 1967 more aggressive tactics were adopted. These figures illustrate the impact of the new tactics.

5. It is significant that the surrender rate in Long An was far lower in January 1968 than at any time since January 1965, thus anticipating by a month the wave of urban attacks which occurred during Tet. The significance of this fact escaped government officials, however.

6. Regrettably, records of this type were not maintained after 1967.

TABLE 5: STATUS OF MALE YOUTHS REACHING SEVENTEEN YEARS OF AGE FROM 1965 THROUGH 1967

	1965	1966	1967
Totals			
Total age group (est.)	3,300	3,300	3,300
Total registered	2,215	2,663	3,058
Status of Accounted			
Drafted into ARVN	198	226	258
Officer or in officer training	180	71	73
In RF-PF	267	513	524
In National Police	36	91	. . .
In rural construction program	105	96	85
Deferred	226	283	511
Total accounted	1,012	1,280	1,451
Unaccounted			
Since registration	1,203	1,383	1,607
Nonregistered[a]	1,085	637	242
Total unaccounted and nonregistered	2,288	2,020	1,849

NOTE: [a] Difference between total registered and estimated total age group.
SOURCE: National Police identity records.

government area. The other two-thirds, they estimated, had entered the revolutionary movement.

The estimated nonregistered, having no identity documents, must either have been in the revolutionary movement or living under its protection. Total unaccounted and nonregistered is perhaps the most interesting. By the end of 1968 the government's vigorous enforcement of the general mobilization law and the Party's policy of impressing into service all down to eighteen years of age virtually eliminated the "draft-evading" status. Thus, by comparing the total registered with the total unaccounted and nonregistered, it appears that although through 1967 the government was able to register more youths each year in Long An, this did not result in an increase in the number entering government forces: the total registered increased by 800 from 1965 to 1967, but the total unaccounted and nonregistered dropped by only 400, which in turn was certainly more than compensated by the virtual disappearance of the draft-evading category. Thus it seems likely that through 1968 the revolutionary movement consistently claimed some 1,500 youths a year in Long An, or almost half of each group. Moreover, because of the relative ease of crossing sides, it is probably fair to say that everyone who felt strongly about the matter was on the side he wished to be on. This seems to be confirmed by the high desertion rate of government military forces, reproduced below in Table 7.

A third significant indicator is the percentage of assessed land taxes collected. As noted in Chapter Three, this percentage gives some indication of the existence, as well as the vitality, of the government's local apparatus, because village authorities maintain the land-tax rolls and are expected to "remind" landowners to pay their taxes. After reaching an eight-year low of 20.9 percent in 1964, this indicator then fluctuated generally upward: 1965, 23.1 percent; 1966, 26.1 percent; 1967, 21.9 percent; and 1968, 33.5 percent. Nevertheless, from this viewpoint the government position in Long An in 1968 was still weaker than that existing in 1963. Consistently low land-tax collections, accompanied by a sharply "improving" HES index, record what was obvious on the ground: much of the "improvement" consisted of coerced population resettlement.

A fourth indicator, one which supports the belief that the revolutionary movement retained enormous strength in Long An, is the number of men under arms in revolutionary military units, shown for years 1966 through 1968 in Table 6. This table reveals that estimated revolutionary military forces continued their annual increase of earlier years through 1966, and then declined somewhat in 1967, probably under the initial impact of the arrival of American combat units in Long An. This decline correlates with the sharp temporary increase in the surrender rate which appeared from February through August of that year. Then in 1968 indigenous

TABLE 6: ESTIMATED REVOLUTIONARY MILITARY STRENGTH, 1966-1968 [a]

	1966	1967	1968
Village guerrillas	1,200	1,290	1,450[b]
District companies	550	370	700
Province battalions	650	520	450
Combat support	...[c]	...[c]	500
Total	2,400	2,180	3,100

NOTES: [a] Including PAVN troops assimilated into Long An units, estimated to be 20 percent of strength of both province battalions in late 1968; not including PAVN units.
[b] Confirmed figure; estimated 2,000.
[c] Category not employed in 1966 and 1967 formats.
SOURCE: Long An sector J-2 intelligence estimates.

revolutionary military forces rose sharply to their greatest strength thus far, even subtracting the contribution of PAVN replacements into local units, and not including an estimated 2,000 members of the Party and Front political apparatus at the village and hamlet level. This increase was doubly significant in view of the fact that it took place in spite of total revolutionary losses (including an undetermined number of PAVN troops) of at least 4,000 men in 1968. Moreover, despite the relatively weaker position of district and province units, village guerrilla forces continued their steady annual increase. Thus it seems fair to say that the government, having lost the guerrilla war before 1965, continued to lose it through 1968. Figures on the size of the political apparatus in previous years are not available, but it is reasonable to believe that it was proportional to the size of the local guerrilla forces which protected it. Because it was exactly this political apparatus, protected by the local guerrilla forces, that made possible the replenishment of losses in the district and province units, it also seems fair to say that by the end of 1968 the most basic organizational element of revolutionary strength had yet to be weakened.

A nonquantitative but clearer picture of the relative strengths of both sides in 1968 can perhaps be gained by examining the probable consequences of three hypothetical situations: "every tub on its own bottom," cease-fire, and neutralization. Under the first of these, we may imagine that both sides would have had available only the manpower recruited within the province. For the revolutionary side, this would have meant the elimination of the various PAVN units and replacements, but the retention of the two local main-force battalions at almost full strength, as well as the district companies and the local guerrillas, because the Party leadership followed the "local employment" policy. However, if applied to the government side, the "every tub on its own bottom" requirement would have eliminated the majority of its offensive forces in Long An. Regional and Popular Force units would have been retained, because they were recruited and employed locally, but the entire American military establishment would have been removed. Beyond this, some 3,600 of the 5,000 troops in the 46th and 50th Regiments would also have been eliminated, i.e., five of the eight maneuver battalions, because ARVN operated under the "employment anywhere" principle. Because of its critical importance, Long An was reinforced with main-force troops far beyond its estimated recruiting capacity.[7] Thus revolutionary forces would have returned to the 1966 level, while government forces would have dropped to the levels which had existed around 1961. It is likely that in this event, the situation would rapidly have returned to and soon surpassed that which existed during 1964 following the collapse of the Diem regime, when the government presence in Long An was effectively extinguished.

A second situation we may envisage would have been a cease-fire, which, if it had occurred, would probably have provided in some fashion for the maintenance of existing village and hamlet authorities, whether government-controlled or not. In this situation the "progress" shown by the HES would almost certainly have evaporated as people moved back to work fields then in revolutionary areas which they had abandoned because of the increased level of fighting in Long An after early 1967. Another 10,000 to 15,000 refugees would probably have moved back to the free strike zone declared in a large area of Thu Thua district in 1964. The result of a cease-fire, then, would have been to establish even more firmly the minority position of the government in terms of dominant influence over the population. The government would still have held the principal lines of communication and all the towns, but the revolutionary movement would have dominated the majority of the population and most of the productive areas.

A third hypothetical situation is neutralization, which might have taken a variety of forms. In one form it might have provided for the removal of external (PAVN and American) forces, the forbidding of the import of armaments, and the resolution of political organization through elections or some other means. Coming (as it almost certainly would have) on the heels of a cease-fire, neutralization would have left the government in the weak position just described in terms of physical domination of the population. Moreover, neutralization would have brought into play another extremely significant factor: the marked psychological dependence on foreign assistance displayed by government personnel at all levels in Long An, who felt (realistically in the case of Long An) that only American manpower and physical resources were keeping the revolutionary forces at bay. Had the psychological reinforcement of

---

7. This estimate is obtained by averaging the annual recruiting into the ARVN for years 1965 through 1967 (Table 5) and multiplying by four years, the period of service then required in the ARVN.

continued American support been removed by neutralization, it is doubtful whether government personnel would have continued to resist, even in a stage of political maneuvering. It is likely that considerable numbers at all levels would have sought individual accommodations with the Party, salvaging the best personal situation possible out of the anticipated government collapse. In this way such a collapse might well have become a self-fulfilling prophecy.

Another useful aspect of neutralization to consider is the consequence of a resumption of armed hostilities following neutralization, such as occurred in Laos. Indeed, it is difficult to conceive of a viable cease-fire in Long An in the context of 1968, regardless of national or international agreements, because there were so many areas of opposition over distinctly local issues between the two sides. A cease-fire agreement would probably not have concerned itself with a myriad of technical and administrative issues such as rent payments, back taxes, and land redistribution, because these were precisely the issues on which differences were the most bitter between opposing sides at the local level, and on which mutual agreement could not be found. Yet, were these issues to be left uncodified, then the only resolution at the local level would have been violence—in other words, a resumption of the conflict. On the other hand, hostilities might also have been resumed on a national basis through the decision of one side to liquidate the other by force, as occurred in the genesis of the current round of the conflict.

In either situation, neutralization would have had a much severer impact on the government's armed capabilities than on the Party's, because the government relied to a far greater extent than did the Party on external assistance. In communist revolutionary doctrine, self-sufficiency is the standard, whereas American "counterinsurgency doctrine," on which the thinking of the Saigon leadership was based, called as a matter of routine for the use of external support. Beyond the matter of manpower, there is the fact that the government's forces were modeled on American forces, and hence they relied for effective operation on a complex logistic system supplying high-technology material such as helicopters, communications equipment, and attack aircraft, all of which might have been denied or limited under neutralization. In contrast the revolutionary forces operated, partly by necessity and partly by choice, with much more primitive—though improving—material support, drawn largely from within the province and often from the government itself. Thus the revolutionary forces, having better adapted themselves to the existing circumstances, would have been able to function far more effectively than government forces in the new environment created by neutralization. This, of course, is not to mention the fact that under the conditions of neutralization, guerrilla activity would have been the likely form of conflict, a form in which the government forces simply ceded superiority to the Party without contest.

To the extent that Long An typified the situation elsewhere south of the 17th parallel, it is reasonable to believe that neither a cease-fire nor neutralization were acceptable to the Saigon government or to the United States in 1968, precisely because of these weaknesses. The foregoing also seems to suggest that the Hamlet Evaluation System, far from recording "progress in pacification," as was intended, instead reflected principally the consequences of the military occupation of Long An by government and American forces. The reason that the HES yielded such a misleading picture of events in Long An is that it focused on precisely those superficial factors which over the years consistently monopolized the attention of government observers.

The conceptual confusion on which government strategy was founded thus carried over to the measurement process as well, which tended in turn to support the existing strategy. The Hamlet Evaluation System had four specific weaknesses. First, the HES, in common with government strategy, was not founded on any explicit conceptualization of revolution as a coherent social process, which would focus attention in measurement on the specific factors to be evaluated, and in strategy on the specific processes to be manipulated. Second, the HES, again like government strategy, focused on "security" without making the crucial distinction between a tactical conception of security based on the suppression of opposition and a strategic conception based on the absence of opposition. Third, the HES failed to distinguish among the relative impacts of forces internal to the province, domestic forces external to the province, and foreign forces. Fourth, the HES combined two incommensurable quantities: as noted earlier, it was based on nine "development-related factors" and nine "security-related factors." Development, as measured against an ideal "developed hamlet," might justifiably be measured as an absolute value. "Security," on the other hand, may be viewed as a circuitous way of describing the balance of forces, which can only be quantified as a proportion, and not as an absolute value. From these four conceptual weaknesses of the HES derived the misleading results demonstrated by the case of Long An.

The Government Strategy

In 1968 the government strategy aimed at destroying the revolutionary position just described was a two-fold effort, referred to in Party documents as a "two-pincers strategy," consisting of what will here be called the violence program[8] and the rural construction program. Within and between these two programs there existed numerous contradictions, out of which no sense can be made without understanding the strategic dilemma into which the Saigon government and its allies had maneuvered themselves: the currently employed reinforcement strategy could not bring victory, yet the force reallocations and redeployments and the policy changes necessary to move in the direction of a more preemptive strategy were largely unacceptable to the current leadership, because such changes would have had an adverse impact on those social elements which composed the current leadership, as well as on the logistic system demanded by the then current structure of government military forces. Frequent reference will be made to this strategic dilemma in the following pages, as examples occur which illustrate how certain changes whose importance was widely recognized could not be implemented because of the effect they would have had either on the current leadership, its constituents, or its military forces.

The shape of the overall strategy employed in Long An can be understood from the following excerpt from the testimony before the Senate Appropriations Committee in early 1968 of General Harold K. Johnson, then Army Chief of Staff. Although the principal issue at the time was to refute proponents of the so-called "enclave strategy," in this testimony General Johnson persuasively argued both the shape and the merits of the current strategy:

In order to appreciate the consequences of these proposals [for an "enclave" strategy], it is first necessary to have an understanding of the organization of the enemy effort and of the interdependence of the various levels of his forces. These forces consist of:

Regular North Vietnamese Army (NVA) units. These range up through divisions in organization and strength.

Main force Viet Cong (VC) units. These also include divisional organizations and have a high percentage of NVA personnel.

---

8. Violence program is a useful term borrowed from Douglas Pike's *Viet Cong*; it here refers to all government-sponsored violence: military, paramilitary, and police.

Local force VC units of up to and including battalion size.

Local guerrillas.

The less effective VC Self Defense Force ranging from the individual part-time guerrilla to small teams in the hamlets and villages.

In addition, there is the political apparatus or "infrastructure."

The viability of the enemy's posture—and hence the efficacy of his strategy—is dependent upon the establishment of secure prestocked bases in areas assessed by him as relatively inaccessible to Free World Forces. He depends in large measure upon the support—voluntary or enforced —of the local population for maintenance and replenishment of the material and human resources of these bases.

His strategic concept is this:

Regular NVA and main force VC units operate from secure bases as mobile forces, capable of rapidly reinforcing the regional and local force units or of launching attacks against targets judged to be of high value to us and of a propaganda value for them.

Regional and local force units, in turn, form the screen behind which a campaign of terror, assassination, intimidation, sabotage, and hit-and-run warfare can be carried on to achieve the goal of domination of South Vietnam through a process of destroying confidence in the Saigon government, or, alternatively, of holding selected areas by force and terror.

It is thus clear that without the reinforcement capability and the direction provided by each higher echelon in turn, the lower echelons would become ineffective. Conversely, the higher echelons are dependent upon lower echelons for replacements, laborers, and guides for larger force movements.

The strategy which has been pursued by General Westmoreland is designed to disrupt this mutual support and break up the chain of command by divorcing each successive echelon from its next higher echelon, so that the total effort is fragmented and can be defeated in detail.

The first undertaking is to separate the enemy regional and local forces, local guerrillas, and the political apparatus from NVA and VC main force elements. To accomplish this, operations are conducted to push NVA and main force VC units back to the unpopulated border areas and a few remote mountain and jungle areas, inflict casualties, and destroy the prestocked bases in South Vietnam which support these units.

A second element of this strategy is the wearing down and elimination of enemy regional and local forces by conducting small-scale operations designed to kill, capture, or induce defections. These smaller-scale operations are carried out systematically by U.S., Free World, and South Vietnamese forces. The preponderance of them are conducted by the South Vietnamese who are better able to distinguish friend from foe.

The final element of the strategy seeks the elimination of the political apparatus. This is primarily a function of the national and local police and other civil or paramilitary governmental agencies. However, this very important activity can be carried out only with the protection of friendly military forces.[9]

This testimony by General Johnson is well argued from the conventional military standpoint, following as it does the traditional doctrine of dividing enemy forces and defeating them in detail. Given a different social context with a different balance of social forces, such a strategy, though inefficient, might have been successful.

The reason why it was not successful in Long An can be seen by noting that this strategy is exactly the reverse of the strategy successfully employed by the Party, despite the fact that by 1965 the government in Long An was in a position roughly comparable to that occupied by the Party in 1959. Thus the strategy outlined by General Johnson called first for the destruction or expulsion of the enemy's conventional forces of divisional or regimental size, then the elimination of company and battalion size local units, and finally the mopping up of guerrillas and the political apparatus. While this strategy acknowledged an interrelationship between these various force echelons, it made a decisive error in fixing the direction—up or down—of the critical tie of dependence. Thus it is no accident that General Johnson devoted considerable space to describing main-force units and their importance, while mentioning last and in only one sentence the revolutionary political apparatus.

Moreover, General Johnson's testimony typified the American military approach: nowhere did it include one word about the conditions in Vietnamese society that permitted the relatively unhindered mobility of the revolutionary forces and that permitted the in-place political apparatus to do its work, or even to exist. This strategy was based on what might be called an "umbrella theory," which points to the allegedly decisive role of the enemy's conventional military forces and of his "secure, prestocked bases" in protecting his movement, and hence to the need first to destroy these conventional forces and supporting bases with similar but superior conventional forces. Such an "umbrella theory" might be contrasted to the Maoist "ocean-fish" theory, according to which proper social conditions are decisive

---

9. Senate Hearings Before the Committee on Appropriations, Department of Defense Appropriation, 90th Congress, 2d Session, FY 1969 (Department of the Army), pp. 592–594.

and, once these are achieved, make the enemy's conventional military forces largely irrelevant.

As can be seen from this analysis of the strategy outlined by General Johnson, the violence program was the core of the current strategy, and in fact it received the overwhelming share of men, money, and attention in Long An. For this reason, "political, economic and social development" received only a passing reference in General Johnson's testimony. It is thus appropriate to discuss first the violence program.

The Violence Program

A theoretical basis for the violence program, consistent both internally and with objective conditions, was never articulated, despite the number of lives it consumed daily. The basis for using violence was a residue of military doctrines developed to deal with friendly military units operating on hostile foreign territory, or on friendly territory against a foreign military force, and typified by the foregoing testimony of General Johnson. When asked to explain the purpose of military operations in Long An, for example, both Vietnamese and American officers gave the textbook answer, "to close with and destroy the enemy," and considered that sufficient. It may be useful to analyze the differing goals, assumptions, and means of conventional and revolutionary war in order to discern the implications when doctrines valid for the former, such as the answer just given, are applied to the latter.

The goal of warfare is a decisive shift in the power relationship between two forces. In terms of this definition, what has come to be known as conventional warfare must be viewed as only one way of organizing and confronting the resources represented by two societies, nations, tribes, and so on, in order to resolve a conflict. The distinguishing feature of conventional warfare is that it is a means to bring about a decisive shift in the power relationship between two forces *drawing on territorially distinct bases of manpower and supplies*. Its principal underlying assumption is that each side possesses such a territorial base, in which popular allegiance is substantially unchallenged. Because the actual confrontations must logically take place in an area different from the territorial base of at least one of the parties, and possibly both, conventional war organizations are designed to operate, to the required extent, *independently of their immediate environment*.

This logical consequence of conventional warfare has thus required that conventional combat organizations, as well as the logistic
systems which connect them with their territorial bases of supply,
be differentiated and physically separable from the social organizations occupying their territorial bases of supply. Accordingly, the
objectives in conventional war are the physical destruction, first, of
the enemy's combat forces, second, of his logistic system, and third,
of the productive system, or by extension the very society which
supplies his combat organization. Obviously, the latter is strategically the most decisive, but, as applied to the nation-state, it became
feasible only with the advent of the airplane.

On the other hand, revolutionary war, as an alternate form
of organized social confrontation, differs from conventional war in
several respects, all derived from two fundamental differences: revolutionary war is a means of bringing about a decisive shift in the
power relationship between two forces, *differentiated by social class,
and drawing upon the same territorial base of supply, with the physical confrontations occurring within the territorial base from which
both parties draw their personnel and their logistic support.* These
two pivotal differences—the one social, the other physical—lead to
a significant difference in the relative feasibility of attacking the
three targets described in the preceding paragraph, as well as in the
means of attacking these targets. As noted above, the underlying
assumption of conventional war is that the popular allegiance to
each side within its territorial base, and thus the motivation of its
operatives, is substantially unchallenged and unchallengeable except
through physical destruction, which thus becomes the principal
means of attack. In contrast, the underlying assumption of revolutionary war—we might call it the first principle—is that popular
allegiance is precisely what is at issue.

Thus the physical proximity of opposing sides in a revolutionary
war leads to the feasibility of attacking the third and strategically
the most decisive target: the social organization of the enemy. At
the same time, the social differentiation of the opposing sides permits
an alternative to the means employed in conventional war. Rather
than physical destruction, the principal emphasis of revolutionary
war is on the *preemption of existing social functions or of desired
but unfulfilled functions.* Violence itself is secondary and is employed only to eliminate the residue of forces left after the selected
degree of preemption has been achieved. A further important characteristic of revolutionary war, as it has evolved out of the social

and productive patterns of the areas where it has occurred, is its extremely decentralized and dispersed nature: combat organizations, and the logistic systems supporting them, are little differentiated from the basic form of social organization itself (e.g., "combat villages" in the case of Vietnam).

The consequences of the application of conventional war combat organization to a revolutionary war context may now be analyzed. Such an application is possible, but, owing to the inherent nature of conventional war combat organization, it is inefficient and, given the proper conditions, possibly self-defeating. First, because conventional war combat organizations are designed to operate independently of their environment, they require a differentiated logistic system to connect them with their supply base, and thus require extensive rear security forces which play little or no role in engaging the enemy. Second, because the principal means employed by conventional war combat organization is physical destruction rather than preemption of social function, and because of the actual assimilation of revolutionary war combat organization into its supporting social structure, the application of conventional war combat organization to a revolutionary war context necessarily implies the physical destruction of some greater or lesser portion of the society itself. Third, the application of conventional war combat organization to a revolutionary war situation will bring about greater or lesser counterproductive effects, owing to the second factor just mentioned and also to the relative imprecision of the instruments of destruction of conventional war combat organization (characterized by concentrated forces operating at some physical distance from the enemy) when applied against revolutionary war combat organization (characterized by dispersed forces and proximity to the enemy). If social conditions are such that the force equation is past the crossover point described in Chapter Four, then these counterproductive effects will be such as to make the application of conventional war combat organization literally self-defeating.

The evolution of the situation in Long An through 1968 illustrates well the limited relevance of conventional war doctrines of organization and tactical deployment to a revolutionary war context. First, of course, is the fact that the counterrevolutionary establishment in Long An, despite the employment of a staggering level of firepower, failed to destroy an opponent one-fifth its own size. Second, the employment of conventional war organization and tactics in Long An, as suggested by the above analysis, led to extensive disruption of the society itself. Because doctrine did not call for, and organization did not permit, developing a superiority of forces assimilated into rural communities, the only alternative was to eliminate those communities, either through destruction (bombing) or dissolution (forced resettlement). While such intentional destruction and dissolution of Vietnamese society could not lead to victory in any recognizable sense, it was the inescapable consequence of current doctrine and organization. Nevertheless, the actual combat commanders were generally convinced that this was the proper mode of attack, because the means employed conformed to the conventional prescription which they were taught at the Infantry School: "to close with and destroy the enemy."

The third and most significant conclusion is also illustrated well by events in Long An: that the application of conventional war combat organization (inherently a reinforcement measure) without accompanying preemptive measures to move the force relationship to the correct side of the crossover point, will lead to open-ended escalation. While a successful strategy—that is, the appropriate mix of preemptive and reinforcement measures—would logically have led to a decline in revolutionary force levels, exactly the opposite occurred in Long An. As shown in Table 6, locally recruited revolutionary forces (except for one year) continuously increased in number in Long An, reaching in 1968 their highest level theretofore. Moreover, this table clearly demonstrates the basic weakness of conventional war combat organization in Long An: although the revolutionary concentrated forces, represented by district and province units, suffered heavy losses and an actual numerical decline, the village guerrilla forces experienced an uninterrupted increase in strength.

The demonstrated ineffectiveness of existing combat organization did not go entirely unnoticed within the American establishment in Long An. A prominent example is the judgment of Colonel James A. Herbert, the senior American advisor in Long An from mid-1967 until early 1969. Colonel Herbert's own perceptiveness and his five years of experience in Vietnam had led him into fairly fundamental disagreement with many of his fellow officers, particularly, of course, those with the authority to make the necessary changes. Contrary to the view widely expressed in Long An that what was needed for victory was more troops, Colonel Herbert was convinced that adequate forces existed but that the principal obstacle to the destruction of revolutionary forces in Long An lay in the deployment and tactics of friendly forces. For example, he replied as follows to a question as to whether existing forces were sufficient if employed differently:

I will give you a short answer on that: yes. In general there is enough strength to handle the defense of the establishment as well as to do the necessary fighting in the countryside. The problem is that of all the strength that is left over for doing the fighting, a large percentage of it is not properly employed. In general the employment of forces over here—ARVN, RF, PF, and US—has been to put them in such places as to provide the forces some protection, but not to provide protection to the people in the hamlets.

An evaluation of the accomplishments in 1968 of four of Saigon's military and paramilitary components—ARVN, RF, PF, and PRU—similarly suggests that force allocations among the various components and favored deployments and tactics were seriously mistaken. Tables 7 and 8 suggest that in all respects but one, the ARVN was the worst performing force in Long An, while the PRU, operating principally in small units, in revolutionary areas, and at night, was by far the most effective and suffered the lowest casualties. Moreover, the type of target attacked by the PRU was strategically the most significant. The desertion figures also reveal one of the important costs of the ARVN policy of nonlocal military service. The ARVN soldier was better paid, better armed, had better living conditions for himself and his family, and saw less of the war

TABLE 7: SUMMARY OF ARVN, RF, PF, AND PRU ACTIVITY IN 1968

	Strength[a]	Desertion Rate[b] (percent)	Friendly KIA[c]	Enemy KIA	Enemy Captured	Enemy KIA Friendly KIA (ratios)	Enemy KIA and Captured Friendly Strength (ratios)
ARVN	5,500	66[d]	488	1,213	231	2.5	.26
RF	4,000	29	200	637	168	3.2	.20
PF	2,700	18	85	260	105	3.1	.14
PRU	300	0.0	19	125	39	6.6	.55

NOTES: [a] Figures given are approximate weighted averages for the entire year. Since unit strength changed continuously, these figures do not all agree with those shown in note 3.
[b] Annual percentage of strength.
[c] Killed in action.
[d] 46th Regiment only.
SOURCE: Long An sector J-3.

TABLE 8: RELATIVE RANKING OF ARVN, RF, PF, AND PRU BY FOUR CRITERIA

Enemy KIA	Enemy KIA and Captured	Desertion	Support
Friendly KIA	Friendly Strength	Rate	Cost
PRU	PRU	PRU	PRU
RF	ARVN	PF	PF
PF	RF	RF	RF
ARVN	PF	ARVN	ARVN

than either the RF or PF soldier; thus the enormously high desertion rate experienced by the ARVN in Long An could only be attributed to this policy of nonlocal service. This policy clearly had an impact on other aspects of ARVN performance as well. Thus these figures demonstrate quantitatively the cost of supporting in Long An a conventionally organized miliary force, recruited from other parts of the country, and engaging almost without exception in large-scale daytime operations from bases in urban or semi-urban areas.

Another point of some bitterness to Colonel Herbert and to other officers who shared his views was that convincing their Vietnamese counterparts to alter their inappropriate deployments and tactics had now been made virtually impossible by the presence of an American conventional military establishment in Long An which exhibited identical failures to adapt its organization and tactics to the type of war being fought there. This is well illustrated by Colonel Herbert's comments on his vain attempts to dissuade his counterparts from such an extensive reliance on outposts:

> I must say it beats me [why they are deployed that way], because I can only talk about the fight of advisors against the outpost approach to military deployment over a period of years. Our hand was not strong enough—we just didn't have enough leverage—to come right out and demand that the ARVN commanders deploy their forces so as to protect people and not just to be in big mud forts to protect themselves. We have plainly failed as advisors in getting the Vietnamese ground forces deployed where they should be. Now it turns out that in general when American forces come over here they go into bigger outposts and bigger bases, and do not deploy their forces so as to provide security for the people in the hamlets. So you can see the position of the advisor here: it is very difficult to get the Vietnamese to do what the U.S. doesn't do.

The internal inconsistencies of the violence program in Long An were exemplified by the knotty issue of civilian casualties inflicted by conventional operations in populated areas. The strategy of violence described by General Johnson (the attrition of main-force units through the use of large-scale operations and massive firepower) was based on the assumption of conventional warfare concerning geographically distinct bases of supply, according to which civilian casualties are of negligible operational significance. Noncombatant casualties inflicted in friendly areas by friendly forces are regrettable but will be borne by the population as the price of removing the enemy, while noncombatant casualties inflicted in enemy areas, owing to the predetermined hostility of the enemy population, are of no importance and may actually be desirable as a means of bringing pressure to bear on the enemy leadership.

Long An, however, fell into neither of these conventional war categories. It could not be considered by the Saigon government as friendly territory whose population would tolerate sacrifices as the cost of removing the "invader," for the "invader" was a part of the society itself. It was just this erroneous assumption that led to the disaster of the strategic hamlet program in Long An. Yet neither could Long An be viewed as enemy territory whose entire population held an unshakable hostility to the Saigon government. Instead, Long An occupied a third position, different from either of the two categories of conventional war. Rather than being "enemy territory" or "friendly territory," it formed the recruiting pool for both sides, that is, *both sides had to develop their forces from the very population among whom the actual combat engagements were conducted.*

In an attempt to work its way out of this problem, the American command developed a set of "rules of engagement" designed to inflict a "minimum" of civilian casualties. In essence, the rules of engagement provided that American forces might not bring a populated area under fire unless the failure to do so would endanger either the mission of the tactical unit involved or the unit itself. Despite these rules, however, heavy civilian casualties still occurred. One example out of many is an incident in 1967 near My Le village in Rach Kien district. An American unit moving along Route 18 near My Le received small-arms fire from the village, and in reply the tactical commander called for artillery and air strikes on the village itself, resulting in heavy civilian casualties and extensive physical destruction. Such a reaction was permitted by the rules, and indeed, in Colonel Herbert's judgment, the tactical commander would have been relieved had he failed to respond as he did.

The following exchange regarding this incident well illustrates Colonel Herbert's inability—or anyone else's—to formulate a consistent intellectual justification for this kind of action.

Q. What do you believe is gained by attacking the Vietcong in populated areas when you know this is going to imply civilian casualties?

A. This is a very elusive judgment but it has to be the judgment of the commander on the spot. You can take a long-term view of it and say we shouldn't shoot at Vietcong in hamlets, but that is where they all will be if that is your rule. And in fact the majority of them that we encounter take refuge in old houses or in populated areas. Now if we are to grant them that refuge then we will never be able to get them. . . . We will have to go in and get them with Bowie knives perhaps. . . .

Q. Can you think of any feasible alternative tactics?

A. What's done is done. I think there were some big mistakes made, partly because of a lack of understanding of the possibilities, and partly of course because of the VC counter-tactic of hugging the population and daring the U.S. to go after them. Of course the U.S. did, and so that meant there were a lot of innocents wrapped up in the fight.

Q. But what do you believe is accomplished by killing Vietcong if you have to take a lot of civilians with them?

A. Very little. But what could be done is simply by effective surrounding of the area for a long period of time you could in fact get the Vietcong to come out.

Q. Why wasn't that tactic adopted?

A. I cannot say. I wasn't in Long An at the time that the tremendous destruction took place in the early months of 1967.

Q. Have you made the suggestion since then?

A. I have on numerous occasions suggested that a bit more discretion be used. I think it is now being used. We worked out rules of engagement for U.S. and Vietnamese forces that I think were about as appropriate as could be, and I find in general that they have been improved upon and adopted countrywide.

Q. Except that under the rules of engagement that you have described, if an allied force comes under fire from a populated area it is authorized to bring firepower to bear on that populated area. That is going to result in civilian casualties, purposely intentioned that way by the Vietcong. How do you think the present rules of engagement prevent this kind of provocation by the Vietcong from bringing ill consequences to the government?

A. You know as well as I do that these rules do not prevent a firefight in a hamlet. However, you will find that the rules are so written that it takes a decision by a fairly high commander before one can even fire small arms into a hamlet. I think this is appropriate although it does keep brigade and division commanders up pretty late.

Q. If you say that you don't think it is worthwhile to kill Vietcong if you have to take an equal number of civilians with them, and yet that happens under the present rules of engagement, then how are they justified?

A. This is a case where you want to know how the doctor can pronounce the operation a success if the patient dies. I don't know any military commander who takes any joy in causing civilian casualties, but their mission is to knock out VC and NVA units, and they try to be as discriminating as they can. They balance out the cost in American lives versus the cost in Vietnamese lives and the amount of destruction that may be caused, and they listen to the voice of their own conscience. The result of all this is a set of rules which is being followed to the best of my knowledge, but is not satisfactory to anybody. The rules are a little too tough on the civilians according to those who have worked close to the effort for a long time, and they are a little too tender according to the romping, stomping tactical commander. But overall they seem to be about the most acceptable set of rules that can be developed.

Q. You still have not answered the specific question I asked which is: how are they justified *intellectually*?

A. I think they are justified because they are about the most satisfactory set of rules that has been developed and is acceptable to just about everyone . . . except to the people on the ground.

What may be concluded from Colonel Herbert's defense of the rules relating to civilian casualties—and he has made about the best defense possible—is that they were arrived at by a compromise among competing interests within the American military establishment, rather than being the logical consequence of a comprehensive theory of the role of violence in the way, for example, that the Party's use of violence was derived from its comprehensive view of revolution as a stage-by-stage social process.[10] Colonel Herbert's view that when

---

10. The differing policies on violence of the Party and the American military command neatly illustrate the differing results obtained by the "rational comprehensive" versus the "successive limited comparisons" methods of decision making discussed by Charles Lindblom in his article "The Science of Muddling Through," *Public Administration Review* (Spring 1959), 19,

all was said there was no alternative to casualties—"that is where they all will be if that is your rule"—fairly represented the consensus among American officers. In fact, however, this bitter dilemma was forced on the American command only because of its failure to adapt its strategy, organization, and policies to the nature of the conflict. There was indeed an alternative, one demonstrated by the process by which the Party gained the initial victory in Long An.

A second important aspect of the government's violence program was the heavy use of "harassment and interdiction" fires, consisting of air raids and artillery, against suspected enemy concentrations or lines of communication. As did offensive operations, the harassment and interdiction program operated under a set of rules designed to limit civilian casualties, of which the most important rule was that fires would not ordinarily be placed within 1,000 meters of a populated area. American and Vietnamese officers considered harassing fires to be an appropriate use of the technological advantages they enjoyed, analogous to the heavy use of firepower in offensive operations. They justified this program by citing the serious impact it had on enemy morale. Defectors almost universally confirmed this government claim, but they went on to report what government officials did not: that the use of air and artillery attacks had a far more devastating impact on noncombatants than on combatants. When questioned about this, officials responded with the same half-challenging, half-plaintive, "What else can we do?" that characterized official attitudes toward casualties inflicted by offensive operations in populated areas.[11]

74–88. Under the "rational comprehensive" method, decisions are made so as to maximize values specified by the decision maker, while under the "successive limited comparisons" method, "the test is agreement [of opposing organizations or factions within an organization] on policy itself, which remains possible even when agreement on values is not. . . . In an important sense, it is not irrational for an administrator to defend a policy as good without being able to specify exactly what it is good for." While Lindblom's purpose was to argue the virtues of the "successive limited comparisons" method under certain conditions, in Long An this method led not to the "best" policy but instead to a disastrous suboptimization.

11. Government officials were guilty of a severe inconsistency on this issue, for they quickly pointed to the alleged damage done to the revolutionary cause by rocket and artillery attacks against populated areas, while neglecting to mention the impact of their own attacks. The province chief, for example, emphasized this point about the dozen mortar rounds fired into the province capital of Tan An during the Tet attacks of February 1968. Yet such attacks were only a drop in the bucket compared with what the government had been doing for years in Long An: during 1968 the average use of 105 mm and

A third aspect of the use of violence by the government was the so-called Phoenix program, a coordinated intelligence collection and reaction plan focusing principally on the Party's political apparatus. The Phoenix program, not begun in Long An until mid-1968, was the only serious recognition within the government violence program that the conflict in Vietnam differed radically from the kind of war to which existing doctrine and organization were adapted. Nevertheless, while the issue was confronted intellectually, it was not confronted from the point of view of providing adequate manpower or policy support to make the Phoenix program function properly.

The theoretical underpinning of the Phoenix program was the recognition of the crucial role of each side's local apparatus. Its goal was to wipe out the Party's local organization, just as the Party had crippled the government's local apparatus eight years before. If successful, the Phoenix program would thus have made it possible to break the endless cycle by which revolutionary main-force units were ground down time after time only to be rebuilt through the efforts of the Party apparatus working among the population. It will be recalled that it was the destruction of the government's local apparatus by the Party that permitted the latter to avoid a direct confrontation with government military units. Rather than destroying them in combat, the Party destroyed their machinery for resupplying materiel and manpower and obtaining intelligence. Thus, although government companies and battalions still existed and conducted perfunctory maneuvers in 1965, they were operationally ineffective and possessed such low morale as to represent a negligible threat to the final wave of attacks by which the Party leadership planned to seize the province. But it will also be recalled that underlying this military strategy was an organization which assimilated the majority of its manpower into village and hamlet society, and a social strategy consisting of preemptive policies aimed at creating a sympathetic environment in which one's own local apparatus could survive while the enemy's could not.

Evaluated by these two criteria, the Phoenix program as of 1968 did not stand up well. Strictly by the criterion of manpower,

---

175 mm artillery for harassing fires was approximately 150 rounds per night (at an average cost of $35 per round). Moreover this represented only a fraction of the total use of artillery in Long An, which was running at a rate of between 1,500 and 2,000 rounds each twenty-four hours. As a result, large areas of the province looked (in words of one official) "like the face of the moon."

the reaction capability of the Phoenix program, once good intelligence was obtained, was still weak. Its basic reaction forces were the Provincial Reconnaissance Unit (300 men), the Special Branch of the National Police (250 men),[12] and the intelligence squads assigned to each district (70 men).[13] Thus the specialized reaction forces available to the Phoenix program amounted to less than 5 percent of the armed strength existing within the province in 1968. The disproportion between the alleged critical importance of the program and the manpower assigned to it had not escaped Colonel Herbert, as shown by this exchange:

In my estimation the fight against the communist apparatus is as important as or even more important than going after armed Vietcong units or village guerrillas. We ought to put more effort into it than we are doing. . . .

Q. Why don't you put more effort into it?

A. Partly because it takes a specialized type of unit. You really have to use the surgeon's scalpel, and you can't get too many people in the operating room.

Q. Why don't you have more of these units?

A. Why I can't cause the formation of more of them is a very complex question. I can only say that I have been unable to cause the formation of as many of them as I would like . . . probably because I have just been unable to inspire people to believe as I do.

Colonel Herbert's confessed inability to develop more units capable of attacking the Party apparatus was simply another aspect of the strategic dilemma in which the government found itself: any increment in the Phoenix effort would have had to be at the expense of some other use of military manpower. Forces which might have been devoted to the Phoenix program were tied up in providing

---

12. Successor to the Cong An.

13. Ad hoc raid units also existed in both the ARVN regiments and the American brigade, but their existence would have to be considered as offset by the misuse of the existing specialized units. The most effective unit in Long An's history was the short-lived Combined Reconnaissance and Intelligence Platoon (CRIP), a thirty-man unit composed half of Vietnamese and half of American members. Far more effective than even the PRU in eliminating members of the Party apparatus, the CRIP effort nevertheless had to be abandoned after several months, owing to a lack of enthusiasm by the commander of the Third Brigade, from which the American forces were drawn. His coolness was reportedly influenced by the fact that the CRIP "body-count" did not accrue to the Third Brigade.

"security" for towns and lines of communication, in turn necessitated by the concentration in the cities of those who sided with the government, and by the importance of cities and lines of communication to the particular kind of army the government had developed. Thus the preoccupation with providing security tactically, the object of conventional military doctrine, stood in the way of measures which would have helped to bring about security in a strategic sense.

Two observations must also be made about the organization of the Phoenix program. First, the program was plagued by the same kind of overcentralization that perpetually hindered government efforts in Long An. Intelligence was collected from a variety of disparate sources, and then organized, collated, evaluated, and acted upon at district level, or possibly even at province level. Thus, as usual in government practice, the district was the lowest operational level, one having no significance in terms of social or living patterns, and staffed by outsiders whose interests bore no necessary connection to the district. By contrast, the revolutionary organization was the essence of simplicity. Each echelon was responsible for keeping its corresponding government echelon under surveillance and taking action as necessary, for which in each village there was a local apparatus trained in guerrilla and assassination techniques, and intimately familiar with the local population and terrain. The response of government officials when this was pointed out—"Our village people aren't competent to handle these matters"—is just another aspect of the government's continued failure to develop a highly motivated and trained local apparatus.

The second observation concerns the operating methods employed by the reaction forces under the Phoenix program. None of these forces met the four criteria for assimilated forces outlined in the preceding chapter. Instead, these forces, recruited from all areas within the district or province, were retained at district or province level and sent on missions—as indicated by the collection effort—one day to one village and the next day to another. Thus these forces operated in the manner characteristic of conventional war combat organization—independently of their environment—and so did not have the enormous advantage enjoyed by the Party apparatus of operating continuously in their home area through a personally responsive network of friends and relatives. This in turn severely handicapped their ability to locate intended targets and to recognize fortuitous ones. The program was also handicapped in developing a sympathetic environment by the use by the Saigon authorities of foreign troops and by the program's intended purpose of maintaining a distributive system perceived as unfavorable to their interests by much of the rural population.

Nevertheless, from the viewpoint of many officials in Long An, the principal failure of the Phoenix program was its unsatisfactory level of intelligence collection, rather than its reaction capability. In an effort to overcome this intelligence gap, attention was turned to the use of such new devices as starlightscopes, ground surveillance radar, and remote listening devices, as well as the previously employed infrared and radio transmission detection systems. An objective appraisal would have to conclude, however, that this shortcoming in intelligence collection was just another consequence of the government's failure to create a sympathetic environment by preemptive social policies.

It is also worthwhile to quote the reaction of two individuals to the suggestion that the government establish a guerrilla apparatus similar to the one instrumental in the earlier revolutionary victory in Long An, in order to show again the extent to which doctrines developed for conventional war hindered the development of responses appropriate to the situation in Long An. The first individual was an intelligent and perceptive American major who was serving as an advisor in Can Duoc district when interviewed. Prior to his assignment to Vietnam, he had attended the MATA course, a special training program for advisors given at the Army Special Warfare School. After a lengthy discussion of the idea of establishing a permanent government guerrilla apparatus operating in insecure areas, he concluded:

This plan might possibly work. To the best of my knowledge it has never been tried, and I'm all for trying anything that hasn't been tried before on the chance that it might work.

Q. Was the idea discussed at all in the MATA course?

A. No.

Q. Have you *ever* heard the idea discussed?

A. No.

The views of Colonel Nguyen van Nguu, province chief from July 1966 until early 1969, are also worth quoting on this subject. Nguu was the son of a minor civil servant in Go Cong province just south of Long An, and he attended the Vietnamese Military Cadet School in Vung Tau, graduating with the rank of lieutenant in 1952.

Prior to coming to Long An, he had held a variety of military and administrative posts.

> Q. Why doesn't the government establish guerrilla forces like the Vietcong?
>
> A. The reason that the Vietcong use guerrillas is because they are weak and do not have enough strength to attack us directly. Thus they must use guerrillas to wear us down. We could also do as the Vietcong do. However, the use of guerrillas is a long-range proposition, but our own men often will not undergo the difficulties [of a guerrilla existence]. We could send our men into communist areas, but there is a problem: if our soldiers wear uniforms, then the Vietcong will know who we are immediately and will attack us, but if we wear civilian clothes, we will not be able to distinguish our men from the enemy and thus might mistakenly shoot each other. Moreover, the Vietcong know everybody in the areas they control. If we enter even with civilian clothes, they will know and attack us.
>
> Q. If they attack with inferior forces, then you fight; if with superior forces, you withdraw.
>
> A. I agree that we can withdraw if we know they have superior forces. But consider this situation: they know we are in a hamlet and so they plan carefully and surround us. There are also some psychological problems as well. For example, the Vietcong come in with superior force and our men withdraw, and then the Vietcong seize their families and kill them. Since the Vietcong are guerrillas, we have no idea where their families are, and thus they have that advantage, too.

Nguu's comments are interesting because they show how he had learned too well the doctrines of conventional warfare. Thus he revealed a total lack of awareness of the *strategic* role in revolutionary warfare of the guerrilla and the local apparatus which he protects as the foundation of the effectiveness and the economy of force of concentrated units. This is exemplified in his initial comment that the Party used guerrillas "because they are weak and do not have enough strength to attack us directly." This view, that guerrilla techniques are "the weapon of the weak," and thus presumably are inappropriate once one is "strong," is fundamental in current American military doctrine. Nguu's comments also acknowledged two important continuing weaknesses in the government position. First was the low motivation of its soldiers, which would have stood in the way of their "undergoing the hardships" of a guerrilla existence.

Second was the absence of the kind of sympathetic environment which permitted the revolutionary forces to overcome the obstacles which Nguu foresaw to a true guerrilla mode of operation for government forces. Taken in total, Nguu's comments reveal how alien to his thinking was even the idea of military forces "like fish in water," integrated with and supplied directly by the local community.

A definitive evaluation of the Phoenix program would have to be based ultimately on the degree to which it proceeded in step with a program to put something in the holes it created, and, indeed, whether it was part of a viable grand strategy correctly weighted between preemptive and reinforcement measures. Both these issues are considered in the following section.

The Rural Construction Program

Because the classic victory by destruction of the enemy's forces was beyond reach in Long An, the only alternate path to victory—in the sense of achieving a decisive superiority in the balance of forces—lay in the satisfaction of the grievances which had led so many to take up arms against the status quo. The rural construction program represented the response of the Saigon leadership to the realization, at an intellectual level, that there could be no "military solution" to the conflict. It was thus analogous to the Party's social strategy. In the Party's effort, however, the social strategy was of paramount significance, with the military strategy (i.e., the violence program) derived from and always supporting the social strategy. In contrast, the government rural construction program represented an insignificant level of effort compared with the violence program. Almost an afterthought of the government leadership, it was the first to be sacrificed when "demanded by operational requirements." Like the Phoenix program, the rural construction program represented a significant intellectual recognition, but one not made good in practice owing to the lack of proper manpower and policy support, in turn a consequence of the strategic dilemma into which the government had maneuvered itself.

In its intellectual conception the rural construction program was considerably more sophisticated than the welfare program which it finally became. This may best be illustrated by distinguishing the proposed rural construction program from the one actually adopted by the Saigon government. The proposed program is perhaps most clearly represented by the writings of Colonel Nguyen Be, one of its intellectual fathers and in 1968 the commandant of the National

Training Center at Vung Tau. Be was born in the central Vietnamese province of Thua Thien in 1929. A former Vietminh battalion commander as well as poet and philosopher, Be somehow
survived the weeding-out process which generally tends to eliminate
genuine humane intellectuals from military organizations.

Be's approach to the situation was so different from that current
in the southern government that it is difficult to describe his strategy
in terms meaningful to those trained in conventional war skills. Be's
standpoint may perhaps be described in simplest form by saying that
the war in his terms ought to be reduced not to "How do we get the
people on our side?" but rather to "How do we get on the people's
side?" Thus his basic premise was that the central government should
be restructured around local interests, with the starting point in the
rural village, i.e., the "communal" approach, in contrast to the prevailing view that rural attitudes and organizations should somehow
be adapted to support the central government, i.e., the "nationalist"
approach. The consequence of this fundamentally different starting
point was a set·of prescriptions for social policies, political organization, and military organization and deployment radically at vari-
ance with contemporary practices in all these areas. This was both
Be's success and his failure: his success was in arriving at a logical
and well thought-out alternative to the unsuccessful efforts then
being employed in Vietnam; his failure was his inability, and that of
his backers within the Saigon and the American governments, to
persuade those in power to act.

In Be's view the reason for the mistaken response of the current
military leaders was that they developed their competence in a different kind of warfare and thus found it impossible to adapt to the
new kind of warfare confronting them:

Naturally in the development of military doctrine we must wait
several generations for change. The reason for this is that the military
experts—the generals and the entire officer corps—have studied and developed their understanding according to preestablished doctrines which
have brought them honors and pride. How can they abandon a system of
thought which they have believed and do now believe is right and effective,
in order to adopt a new system of thought? Moreover, each succeeding
generation gropes in the path of the experience of history, studies according to the experience of its predecessors, and is bound within the thought
of those who previously gained victories and accomplishments. How,
therefore, can they visualize the strange horizons of new systems of military thought . . . ?

When a military expert looks at a limited war, he is usually scornful of the rudimentary weapons and military tactics of the enemy, and thinks instead of such practical considerations as troop training, employment of modern weapons, and numerical superiority to defeat the enemy and to crush the limited war immediately.

But such military experts are wrong. They are wrong first because they do not understand the essential nature of these limited wars. More than anything else such limited wars bear the distinguishing features of struggle rather than war. Thus, the more the people are oppressed, the more it feeds the flame of the struggle spirit, and the flame rises ever higher until the combination of improved techniques, more weapons, and the fires of the struggle spirit itself enable the people to mount a general counteroffensive. Only then is the cycle broken.

The second error of the military experts is that they never seek to assimilate the army into the people, or in other words, the military experts have employed techniques and leadership activities attainable only by the army, and thus have separated the army from the people.

The question is, how to gain victory in such a limited war?[14]

Be's answer to this question was to seek a reintegration of combat organization with the basic social and productive units, an integration which Be correctly recognized had been lost through the misapplication of doctrines of conventional warfare to the context of Vietnam. This basic social and productive unit is the village, and the fundamental form of combat organization which Be envisaged was the "People's Self-Defense Force." The purpose of this force was not to enter into combat with the enemy main-force units, but only to make it impossible for them to move secretly, to draw sustenance from the local communities, and to maintain their political apparatus in them. Once the enemy was isolated from the people in this way, he could be destroyed by a relatively small number of friendly conventional forces held in reserve.

The People's Self-Defense Force is a broad organization that unites all people to fight for their own immediate and legitimate interests. . . . Once each person sees that it is his own duty and responsibility, then the enemy within will be assimilated or isolated immediately. The important

---

14. This quotation and those that follow are taken from two multilithed works: *Ban Tham Luan Ve Con Duong Tranh Dau Cua Dan Toc Viet Nam Hay Van De Giai Quyet Chien Tranh Viet Nam*, an exposition of the idea of the rural construction program, written in 1967; and *Nhung Y Tuong Tren Duong Xay Dung Que Huong*, a collection of essays written in 1967 and 1968.

thing is not to make the people feel that they are fighting for "the nation" or "the central government," but rather that they are fighting for things of immediate and practical significance for themselves. . . . Only when we have such an active organization can we separate the enemy from the people and defeat him. Once the enemy forces are separated from the popular "sea" by the People's Self-Defense Forces in the hamlets and villages, then at exactly that moment the enemy will destroy himself or become the prey of our regular military forces.

Be emphasized that the purpose of the proposed People's Self-Defense Force was not to "defend" villages in the conventional sense, but rather "to resist the enemy when he is few, to undermine his morale when he is many, and most of all constantly to show the enemy that the people are bitterly opposed to him." To illustrate how different the People's Self-Defense Force would be from existing military organization, Be pointed to the local forces as then established:

We have always felt that to provide security we must train ten, twenty, or thirty youths for each hamlet, for example the Combat Youth, supply them with weapons, give them a miserable pittance, and call that the force protecting the hamlet. *With that belief we ourselves have killed so many youths and destroyed so many hamlets.* Once we train Combat Youth in each hamlet and give them weapons, then we are furnishing conventional combat techniques to them. That very idea makes the platoon think in terms of defending itself, and thus digging trenches, building outposts, and putting up barbed wire. Moreover, such a platoon can no longer be mobile, but is fixed within the hamlet and must think of fortifications, barriers and fences, creating countless unhappy situations in the countryside. After all, fencing in a hamlet of two or three square kilometers demands more covering firepower than the platoon has. Thus such fortifications and barriers are absolutely worthless for preventing the entry of enemy forces.

Thus Be's conclusion:

At the same time as the communists attack the government and the allied forces with both conventional forces and people's guerrilla forces, we only fight back with a single hand: the army. Although the government and allied forces are powerful and well supplied with tanks, ships, jet planes, etc., they will never defeat the communists, because it is not possible to use a great quantity of napalm, fragmentation bombs, machine guns, mortars, and heavy artillery against a guerrilla ambush. It is not possible to use conventional warfare against a popular guerrilla war. Using bombs and modern weapons in a political conflict simply leads to failure. The more we use bombing on a battlefield where the principal force is the guerrilla, the more we are condemned as inhumane. . . . Not only are we condemned as inhumane, but we also unwittingly prolong the war, and our future becomes the darker. This is so because the larger government and allied forces become, the larger the communist forces become; the more bombs we use, the more people die. . . . The situation of Vietnam in the last few years is the troubled one of a backward country, in a crisis of spirit, following the wrong political line and the wrong military strategy.

It was a mark of Be's realism, however, that he stated clearly that the alternate strategy he outlined could not be carried out, because given the existing structure of Vietnamese society, the rural communities *could not* fight for their "immediate and legitimate interests." The precondition was, simply, a government-sponsored social revolution which would "unite the population and isolate the communists."

To unite the people in one bloc, the most important thing is to eliminate the contradictions within society, to reduce the extreme differences among people in their daily life. There is no way to bring together someone extremely wealthy with someone extremely poor and deprived; or someone with extensive influence and someone weak and alone "who calls out but no one hears."

If we want to bring about true unity in order to rebuild our country through common determination and united effort, then we must bring about social justice, something the communists always talk of but can never do. But we can surely do it, because we have both sufficient means and a sincere intent.

The situation of a backward country like Vietnam, heavily affected by long periods of feudalist and colonialist rule, and by the communists during a short period, which has nevertheless produced many upheavals, demands an all-round revolution. We cannot create anything in the present political and social void.

To overcome this void Be proposed a comprehensive and detailed set of reforms in the areas of political organization, landholding, education, and military service. These proposed reforms cannot really be viewed independently of one another, for they were all parts of his proposed general reorientation of priorities away from the cities and toward the countryside, away from centralization and toward decentralization, away from the middle and upper classes and toward the peasantry, and away from reliance on foreign assistance and toward national self-sufficiency. All these reforms added up to what Be called the "village of responsibility"— an independent, cooperative social unit responsible for its own fate, without outside interference. In time this "village of responsibility" would grow into a "village of prosperity" through the adoption of modern agricultural and industrial techniques.

The central reform in Be's scheme was the return to the village of its traditional right of self-rule, although not, as in traditional Vietnamese society, into the hands of a minority social class monopolizing the positions of power. Without this reform—without overcoming the errand-boy status of village and hamlet authorities— there was no way, in Be's view, that the rural population could feel it was actually fighting for its own "immediate and legitimate interests" rather than the interests of some remote ruling authority.

The kind of power that the self-ruling village would have is illustrated by Be's proposals for the reform of landholding. In Be's view, "We must reorganize and rebuild the countryside by eliminating all the injustices and contradictions in the rural areas, among which injustices and contradictions the problem of land is the most serious of all." According to Be, land had to be "redistributed fairly, rationally, and in such a way as to avoid the exploitation of the tenant by the landlords," and "only to those people present in the village or hamlet, who would themselves have to farm the land." The land issue would thus be taken out of the hands of the central government, to be handled at the village level according to the needs of each area. Ultimately, according to Be's program, each village would become a mechanized cooperative, handling the buying of materials and the selling of rice on a collective basis, thus eliminating the existing heavy burden of the moneylender, the rice miller, and the seasonal speculator.

Similarly, Be's detailed program for educational reform called for a shift in attention from the urban to the rural areas, a decentralization of authority over educational policy, and a redirection of effort into practical rather than literary education. Its goal was to do away with the current "basically colonialist system designed to produce a small educated elite." Military organization would also be reformed, although in this area Be was considerably less detailed than elsewhere—probably mindful that his most powerful enemies were located within the Saigon military establishment. Although he nowhere said so directly, the unavoidable implication of his prescriptions in other areas was the establishment of a system of local military service, with the great bulk of the youth retained directly among the population in the rural areas, rather than in regular army outposts protecting principally themselves. Be recognized the need for a limited number of conventional units to destroy enemy forces after they had been frozen out of the villages by the People's Self-Defense Force, but he emphasized that these would be composed only of people sufficiently "enlightened" to volunteer to leave their home village. In any case, this would clearly have meant the end of the ARVN as it existed and its replacement by a locally recruited force operating around its home area. The closest Be came to saying this, however, was in one passage in which he stated "We must cast aside every prejudice about army organization or combat organization which we have learned from foreigners, and come forth with a military system [appropriate] to our own country."

How can we evaluate Be's proposed rural construction program? Be's debt to his Vietminh experience should be apparent, as, for example, in his frequent use of Maoist metaphors, like that of viewing the army as a fish in water. Moreover, Be's final evolution of the responsible and prosperous village was in several senses basically communism without class warfare. First, in the economic sense, the responsible village ultimately would become a wholly cooperative effort. Second, in the philosophic sense, the prosperous village might be likened to the communist utopia in that it is not an immediate prospect but rather the result of a gradual evolution. Likewise, the "end of hate" to which Be frequently referred in his writings may be viewed as his own expression of the future classless society. Nevertheless, Be's departure from the Maoist tradition of class struggle, for love and cooperation, was an imperative arising from his own profoundly humanist philosophy.

An objective analysis of Be's program must note, however, that in many respects Be's proposed reforms did not go as far as the measures which the Party had already carried out. Moreover, his program had certain important organizational weaknesses, perhaps the most significant of which was the absence of a well-defined system of upward mobility such as strengthened the motivation of Party cadres. In addition, from a sociological viewpoint, Be's analysis was not nearly as rigorous as the Party's.

Nevertheless, Be's proposals recognized and appropriated the critical strengths of the communist strategy, which were explored in

Chapter Four. First, Be recognized the overwhelming strategic significance of the guerrilla conflict and the basic need to destroy the enemy's political apparatus by means of assimilated forces having no static security mission. To do this one must have one's own strong, highly motivated local apparatus, which Be proposed to develop through the return to the village of its right of self-rule. One must also have a sympathetic environment, produced by appropriate policies, which Be suggested in the form of a number of specific reforms. These three essential points were summed up in Be's projected self-governing "village of responsibility," in which he merely put into coherent form the pyschological reality which the Party has so effectively exploited: that Vietnam is not one nation (although it is one culture) but rather thousands of insular local communities. Thus Be's proposed program represented an enormous strategic and conceptual advance over the current government approach, although in practice the implementing social policies might have proved inadequate.

This program, however, was not the highly publicized rural construction effort carried out in Long An in 1968. Whereas the proposed program correctly recognized the need for redistributive measures, the program actually adopted by the Saigon and the American governments ignored the redistributive issues and concentrated instead on "development" and on certain suppressive and intelligence functions. But since "underdevelopment" was not the foundation of the strength of the revolutionary movement, "development" was not a relevant response to the problem the government faced in Long An. Moreover, this crippling lack of redistributive policies was compounded by serious interorganizational rivalries within the Saigon government, as well as by a generally poor understanding of the program on the part of the officials in the regular military and administrative system assigned to support it. Thus, for example, not one official interviewed in Long An—Vietnamese or American—recognized that the rural construction program in theory represented a strategic approach to the war that was fundamentally different from and fundamentally in conflict with the existing strategy. Instead, the program was comprehended simply as a highly organized public-welfare or public-works effort.

It is worth while to examine area by area this failure to adopt reforms to implement the rural construction program. The core reform—the one that would have given meaning to all the others—

would have been the shift of authority back to the local community. This was impossible, however, because Ordinance 57a of October 24, 1956, was still in effect. It will be recalled from Chapter One that this document set out in the form of a unitary state the basic allocations of authority among the central government, the province and district officials, and the local communities. It thus created a political structure fundamentally in conflict with the social and cultural reality of Vietnam. It is significant that Circular 001–a/ PTT/VP, dated March 1, 1968, was issued to reemphasize that Ordinance 57a and the accompanying Circular 115–a/PTT/VP were still "the basic texts regulating the responsibilities and competencies of local administrative authorities. . . ." and that "the *principal* principles in the texts should be strictly applied."

Similarly there was no significant change in the personal incentives to seek local office, in the social bases of recruitment, in the career potential of local service, or even in the continued refusal of the central government to issue personal weapons to local officials. The strengthening of local organs could have been considered significant only had it taken such forms as the selection of district and province officials from among village and hamlet officials; the authority of village government to arrest, try, and imprison corrupt or abusive military personnel or central government officials (for example, a member of the National Police, or even the district chief) who entered the village; the authority to retain youths locally for military service rather than having them inducted into the ARVN to protect central government officials in some other province; the authority to resolve land redistribution and tax structure locally, without reference to higher authorities; or the authority of the villages to remove district and province officials. The most critical power of all, of course, is who has the power to remove whom.[15]

Most central government officials, however, could not conceive of such reforms—they were simply a blank area of consciousness. The proof of this is that not one encountered in Long An was even

---

15. In particular it was virtually impossible for the government's local apparatus to be as highly motivated as that of the Party without establishing a vertical career system by drawing district and province officials from among hamlet and village officials. Government local military forces (the RF and PF) suffered from the identical problem: they could not be as highly motivated as their revolutionary counterparts unless the system were structured so that the officer corps in each area was selected from the most qualified soldiers in its respective area, and not from urban-raised and urban-educated holders of the *tu tai*.

aware of the greatly decentralized structure of decision making practiced by the Party. When pressed on this point, officials typically responded that if such reforms were adopted—that if local communities were given autonomy—then they would "go communist." This was probably true, but it was just another consequence of the fact that the social structure maintained by the government was bitterly opposed by a significant segment of the rural population. Clearly, the only solution for the government would have been a decentralization of authority in step with the adoption of preemptive social policies, i.e., reforms in the areas of landholding, military service, education, the social composition of government organs at all levels, and so forth.

Similarly, reforms in land tenure such as Be proposed were not enacted. Despite the evidence of twenty years in Vietnam, there were still strong objections from within both the Saigon and the American governments, on the ground that land reform was either unnecessary, desirable but "destabilizing," or urgent but impossible to carry out.

In the area of the social bases of recruitment into the military and administrative hierarchies, government policies likewise underwent no significant change. There was some marginal broadening in the opportunities for officer rank, brought about through the insistence of MACV on such programs as field commissions and an OCS system for training officers from enlisted personnel. Nevertheless, the basic requirement for officer status was still the *tu tai*, and as indicated by Table 5, less than 200 people a year attained the *tu tai* in Long An, out of a population of 350,000. There was still no preferential policy, such as that adopted by the Party, by which a poor farmer's or fisherman's son could attain officer rank while serving in his own community. Similarly, the civil service remained effectively closed to the rural peasantry. The regulations establishing the educational and hence the social qualifications for civil-service status had not changed since they were adopted almost two decades before. Decree 103–CV, for example, established in 1950 the requirement of the *tu tai* for the civil-service grade of *doc su* from which district chiefs would be selected if the position were held by civilians.[16] The far-reaching changes in the educational system pro-

---

16. The take-over of many civil-service positions by the military apparently served to some extent to replace a rural elite by an urban elite in the positions of power. An example of this would be Colonel Nguu, compared with Ho van Si, province chief from 1953 to 1955. This shift, however, would have

posed by Be, which might serve to weaken this link between social class and educational opportunity, remained only proposals.

A special comment is in order on the composition of local government bodies. It was noted earlier that one important means by which the Party developed a close relationship between its local organs and the rural population was a system of requirements concerning class origin. These requirements were intended to ensure that the class composition of local organs resembled the class—and even the religious—composition of the population itself. In government practice there was no similar provision to guarantee that the chief of a village composed overwhelmingly of poor farmers should not be a landlord or a merchant. Instead, the choice was left to "free elections,"[17] but, owing to the lack of incentives to seek local office, the elections were often meaningless. As a consequence, despite the political convulsions in Saigon since 1963, in many areas of Long An the same individuals had held office for a decade or more, whether appointed or elected.

In the sphere of military service there was one important change, namely, the option of service in the Regional Forces or Popular Forces in preference to service in the ARVN. However, because of ceilings on Regional Force and Popular Force recruiting, large numbers of youths were faced with the choice of entering the ARVN or joining the revolutionary military forces. As can be seen from Table 5, each year some 1,500 youths apparently chose the latter, in contrast to 400 for the former, and of these 400 who chose the ARVN one-third to one-half were officers. Within the ARVN the policy of nonlocal service remained in effect, resulting in the generally poor effectiveness and staggeringly high desertion rate shown by ARVN forces in Long An. Perhaps a more significant conclusion from extensive discussions with Saigon and American officials is that not one (except for the now retired district chief noted in Chapter Four) recognized this as one of the most important factors crippling the effectiveness of the ARVN. Instead, the most commonly noted were the lack of modern weapons, low pay, poor housing, lack of combat support services, and poor leadership. A

---

to be evaluated as a sidewise motion, not as progress toward the goal of bringing the social makeup of the rulers closer to that of the ruled.

17. "Free" was sharply qualified by the statutory exclusion from candidacy of those who offered a real choice to the electorate of alternative distributive arrangements, namely, those individuals associated with the revolutionary movement.

comparison of government and revolutionary forces in all these areas, however, would reveal that only the last cited factor was close to the mark. Yet poor military leadership was precisely the consequence of a whole complex of social factors such as those just discussed.

Finally, an objective assessment would have to conclude that in 1968 it was almost absurd to discuss the rural construction program at all, because it represented such an insignificant level of effort compared with the violence program. In terms of manpower alone, by the end of 1968 cadre strength was only one-fourteenth of the strength of conventional military forces in Long An. When questioned on this point, province officials typically responded that "we cannot use more cadres, because there are not enough security forces," revealing again a failure to understand what it was that would produce security.

Colonel Herbert's comments also revealed his dissatisfaction with this gross disproportion between the violence program and the rural construction program.

As an infantryman I would notice that it is very easy to get artillery support, air strikes, and the like. A phone call or a radio call will get you all you need, and I must say the U. S. support of Vietnamese forces in trouble has been outstanding. At the same time, if we're asking for engineer support of our ARVN, if we're asking for administrative support, or financial support, it takes an inordinate amount of effort to get it. . . . It's almost as if I called for fire support and was told "You've got to come up and help load the howitzers."
Q. How does this have an impact on your programs?
A. It just means that if we want to boost a program that's going to require money, contracts, delivery of material, that sort of thing —as an example a road construction program—it just takes one hell of a lot of effort to get the thing in motion. . . . I would like to be able to put in a call for money, and although I can get thousands of dollars shot out of tubes [by picking up a phone] it's very difficult—I mean it just takes time and effort—to get thousands of piasters shot out of the bank. . . . It just seems to me it takes one hell of a lot of work to cause effort to be invested here, and it's primarily because Long An was selected for a pilot pacification program that we are able to get even these benefits.

Some realism may be added to these comments by noting that the entire rural construction budget for Long An amounted in 1968 to approximately one million dollars, or just half of the amount expended on harassing artillery fire. Harassing artillery fire in turn accounted for only 10 percent of all artillery rounds used, which in turn represented only a small fraction of the expense of the total conventional military effort in Long An. Operations of the Third Brigade alone, for example, were estimated to cost ten million dollars a month, while if the entire American budget for Vietnam were prorated on the basis of population, Long An's share was approximately 600 million dollars a year.

We may conclude from this discussion of the theory of the rural construction program that the efforts carried out in Long An in 1968 represented no major change from those of previous years. Instead, government efforts were largely an expansion of the scale of earlier programs, often humanitarian, but irrelevant to the roots of the conflict—programs like the civic action program, the agroville, and the strategic hamlets, which had for good reason failed repeatedly in Long An over the preceding fifteen years. While there was much discussion of the generally disappointing achievements of the rural construction program, few pointed to the crucial fact that it simply could not effect the redistributive changes that needed to be made. As we shall see, the cadres frequently had good insights, and the desire to effect changes, but they were prevented from doing so by government policy itself.

To show how these theoretical conclusions about the rural construction program worked out in practice, it may be useful to trace the experience of one hamlet over a year's time, during and after the visit of a rural construction cadre team. The experience of this hamlet, Hoa Thuan II, located in Truong Binh village of Can Giuoc district, was representative of both the strengths and weaknesses of the current program. To the extent that the program's success in Long An was limited, it was for the reasons demonstrated by the case of Hoa Thuan II.

Prior to arriving in Hoa Thuan II in February 1968, the assigned cadre team had worked for four months in the nearby hamlet of Tan Thanh A. The team was somewhat demoralized by its experience there, and it may be worth while to recount the reasons for this to provide a perspective on the problems the team was to encounter in Hoa Thuan II. The first demoralizing event had been the encounter at Tan Thanh A with a member of the National Police whom we may call Chi. Because of the serious security situation, Chi had been detailed some years before to operate in this hamlet.

His financial requirements had consistently exceeded his salary, however, and he had resolved the problem by altering, for a fee, the identity papers of hamlet youths wishing to evade the draft. Another maneuver occasionally employed by Chi to supplement his salary was the extortion of funds under the threat of arrest for activities "threatening the national security."

Just prior to the arrival of the cadre team in September 1967, one hamlet resident had failed to meet Chi's financial demands and had subsequently been arrested and jailed in Tan An after Chi had "discovered" a grenade in the man's house. On his arrival, as the team leader later recounted in an interview, he found that Chi's depredations were widely known in the hamlet, but no one, including the village chief, dared to denounce him for fear of retribution. After a period of activity in the hamlet, the team succeeded in building some confidence among the inhabitants, and two months after the jailing incident the brother of the victim agreed to make a complaint against Chi. Shortly thereafter the brother himself was arrested and jailed after the "discovery" by Chi of additional incriminating materials in his house. The team leader reported the incident in writing to the Can Giuoc district chief, but receiving no reply then sent a message directly through cadre channels to Saigon. Two months after the second arrest both brothers were released, and at the same time Chi was transferred to the neighboring district of Rach Kien. The team leader concluded, "Chi should have been taken out and shot in the center of the hamlet, and even then the people would not have been satisfied. But instead he was just transferred to Rach Kien, where it is even easier to extort money."[18]

When subsequently questioned about this incident, Colonel Nguu, the province chief, commented that he had "heard something about a dishonest policeman, but the individual had already been punished." After being told of the cadre team's suspicion that Chi had only been transferred, Nguu immediately summoned the head of the National Police to his office and directed him to bring Chi's file. A few minutes later the head of the province office of the National Police arrived and revealed that Chi had indeed been transferred six months before. He had not been punished, however, since that

---

18. Rach Kien was a newly created district formerly totally dominated by revolutionary forces. With the arrival of the Third Brigade, a large American force was sent to seize and occupy the area. Chi's opportunities for extortion were thus greater because of the large number of people in Rach Kien who may have been involved in revolutionary activities, even if involuntarily.

exceeded province authority. Nevertheless, a report of Chi's activities had been sent to Saigon, but as yet—six months later—no instructions had been received.

A second demoralizing incident, capping a series of disasters similar to the one just recounted, concerned the People's Self-Defense Force. As noted earlier, the People's Self-Defense Force was the operational lynchpin in the rural construction program's strategy to isolate communist cadres from the population. During its four months in Tan Thanh A, the team had succeeded in recruiting and training eighteen young volunteers for the People's Self-Defense Force. When at the end of December the team departed along with its two companies of security forces, the eighteen now exposed youths fled the hamlet, because province authorities declined to distribute weapons to them. When questioned on this point in May 1968, Colonel Nguu replied that he had not authorized the release of the weapons because the People's Self-Defense Force "are not really soldiers and can't be trusted very much."

With this record of support by the Saigon government, the cadre team arrived in Hoa Thuan II. The populated area of Hoa Thuan II is a cluster of a few hundred houses, located just over a half-mile from the edge of the district town, and stretching for several hundred yards on both sides of Route 5. Within the area of the houses there are a number of trees and shrubs, but beyond the cluster of houses flat ricefields stretch in all directions. The physical area of Hoa Thuan II is roughly a third of a square mile, although most of the population of 2,500 is concentrated in the cluster of houses just described. When the team arrived, Hoa Thuan II was listed in the "E" category by the Hamlet Evaluation System. Except for a Popular Force outpost right on Route 5, there had been no government representation in the hamlet—despite its proximity to the district town—since the last hamlet chief had been assassinated in 1964.

A series of talks with several leaders of the team in May 1968 indicated that the team members had accurately recognized a number of outstanding grievances within the hamlet. Their greatest initial handicap, team members revealed, was the need to overcome the fear of hamlet residents that the team had come to force them to build a new strategic hamlet. After about a month, however, a feeling of confidence in the team began to build, and its members began to get information. One complaint had to do with occasional excessive fees charged hamlet residents seeking paperwork from the village council, and the need to sit outside the council office for hours while the paperwork was being done. Another concerned forced labor in clearing fields of fire or building obstacles demanded by a Regional Force outpost some distance away. "In form the people are invited to work," commented one cadre, "but in fact they are forced. The soldiers feel they are fighting all the time, so at least the people can help with the labor. It's stopped while we're here, but who will prevent it when we go?"

One of the farmers interviewed in the course of the visit complained bitterly about the now abandoned bidding system on communal lands. The well-to-do frequently won, he said, and if a poor person won and then failed to pay, he went to jail.[19] He expressed the belief that the bidding system had been used "because it meant more profit for the government, which doesn't care about the people." Although the bidding system was no longer used, the farmer was still disgruntled, for, he claimed, having no land of his own, he could not borrow money from the government and thus had to resort to moneylenders.

The cadres also had more general thoughts about the malaise of southern society. One team member, for instance, made this comment:

We are often very angry about our society, especially the mandarinism. Every time we have a visitor—even a captain—we must organize a big reception. If a general were to come, he'd have to have a platoon honor guard, and all the villagers and officials would have to come out and waste hours waiting for him. Of course it's very seldom a general would come here—the district headquarters is as close as they come. Yet we have seen how different it is in your own army—once we saw an American general just drop out of the sky unannounced in his helicopter. We are very angry about all these injustices, but what can we do?

The team leader indicated that this same separation between ruler and ruled had stood in the way of the team's success. When the team arrived in Hoa Thuan II, for example, the village council was so out of touch with the situation there that it had no idea who even lived in the hamlet. Thus one of the team's first projects was a complete census, but no village official would agree to come along with the team and walk around among the houses in the hamlet. The

---

19. The village chief later indicated that poor people had "seldom" been jailed for failure to pay.

team leader reported this problem to the district chief, who ordered the village council to provide a man to assist in the census project. This individual, one of the lower-ranking members of the council, refused to go any further than the highway, despite the fact that the cadre team had been walking around the hamlet for about a month. He repeatedly said, "I can't go out there [off the highway] because I'm not sure of the situation." This in turn was reported to the district chief with no results. In the words of the team leader: "We just got no answer. After all, no matter how you look at it, the village council is on the inside with the district, while we are just outsiders. . . . If I had my way, I'd eliminate these people first, because as long as they exist there will be Vietcong."

Unfortunately, some time after the May visit, this team was replaced by another, because of an incident in which one team member became involved in a firefight with members of a visiting culture-drama group. The new team's leadership was generally less perceptive than that of the first, but it provided nevertheless an interesting example of the variation in the caliber of personnel within the program. Like his predecessor, the leader of the second team was quite upset over the apathy of village officials toward the hamlet. Moreover, one of the requirements to complete the team's work was the election of a hamlet chief, but that could not be done, because only Saigon had the authority to approve a hamlet election, and approval had not yet been given. In the interim, the village council had appointed an individual from outside the hamlet, who, according to the team leader, "has never stayed here once for a whole day —he just comes for a few minutes in the morning and then goes back to the village office [located in the district town]."

On the reasons for opposition to the government, the second team leader was far less perceptive than the first. He indicated that there were "three identified procommunist families" in the hamlet, and that "we have them under observation, but we have not been able to arrest them yet." As to why they were "procommunist," he indicated that he had no idea. Another member of the team was able to account for the background of each case. In the first family the son had served elsewhere in the ARVN, then deserted to return home. While home, he had requested to serve in the local Popular Force outpost, but had not been permitted. Subsequently he had gone over to the other side. The husband in the second family had been killed by fire from a government airplane. The third family was a poor one which "had probably been promised land"—the team member indicated that each poor family had been farming about a half-hectare under Party grant prior to the arrival of the cadre team. When questioned about the enormous difference between government and Party land policies, the team leader replied the problem was that "the people are very shortsighted. We have come to explain to them that the Vietcong land program is a trick."[20] Likewise he explained that the people were "shortsighted" on the issue of "forced labor" which the first team had pointed out. "It is not really forced labor, but their contribution to the fight against the communists."

The accomplishments of the rural construction program in Hoa Thuan II were mixed. Among the easiest and first completed were those relating to the program's suppressive functions: making a detailed map of the hamlet, carrying out an up-to-date census, and establishing a list of "communist sympathizers" and youths who had left the hamlet to take up revolutionary activity. Between them the two successive teams also completed or took part in the completion of a number of physical construction tasks: a school building, four sets of permanent steps to ponds within the hamlet, twelve culverts, six hundred meters of newly surfaced hamlet roads, and a bulletin board. The program also furnished three water pumps and five sprayers for use in the hamlet. In addition considerable effort was put into the construction of a barbed-wire fence which stretched along one-fourth of the perimeter of the populated area parallel to the highway.

Lasting accomplishments in the area of popular attitudes were more difficult to find. Prior to its departure the team had organized the entire population into the groups—youth, old-age, etc.—called for by the program's format, but these admittedly existed in form only. Perhaps what is more telling is the fact that not one family elected to move into the hamlet from more distant areas of greater revolutionary activity, nor did a single guerrilla from the hamlet elect to come over to the government side. During the eight months of team activity, however, six guerrillas were shot while operating

---

20. Village tax records revealed that Hoa Thuan II contained twenty-three hectares of communal lands, as well as nine individuals owning less than one hectare, thirty-four owning between one and three hectares, eighteen owning between three and ten hectares, and two owning more than ten hectares. Most of the people owning more than three hectares lived either in the district town or in Saigon. The records were not a reliable guide to total holdings by these individuals, however, because the same people may have owned land elsewhere. Several tenants in the hamlet indicated that their landlords had extensive holdings elsewhere in the district.

within the hamlet, thus indicating that they still felt it worth while to risk their lives against the government despite the team's activity.

Yet it is not hard to understand why more favorable attitudes toward the government did not come about. The task of "eliminating oppressive individuals" called for in the program's plan could not be carried out because, in the words of the team leader "this is the most difficult task of all. They are all tied in with one another from the generals right down to the hamlet. We report them, but nothing happens." Moreover, there was no shift in power that would have put decisions about the hamlet's fate back in the hands of hamlet residents; the perfect example of how even minute details of hamlet life were regulated from afar was the need to wait for a signature from Saigon to hold the election for hamlet chief. Similarly, the cadre team was unable to effect any change in the landholding or land-rent pattern. Moreover, in the absence of government efforts to redress landholding inequalities, the "return of security" had meant also the return of the landlords.[21] The appointed hamlet chief still did not travel off the highway, and the village chief had yet to travel about within the hamlet a single time during his term of office. Party agents still moved frequently through the hamlet area, being careful only to stay a few meters off the road. The monthly HES report to Saigon, prepared by the American advisory team, nevertheless upgraded the status of Hoa Thuan II to the "C" category because of the "progress" it had shown.

Perhaps the final indicator of the central government's concern and support for Hoa Thuan II is the history of the People's Self-Defense Force there. As with the earlier experience of Tan Thanh A, the team recruited and trained twenty-one members of the People's Self-Defense Force, but when the team's time of departure arrived, no weapons could be obtained. Subsequent investigation revealed that in the intervening months since the Tan Thanh A experience, the province chief had been under considerable pressure from Saigon and had consequently issued weapons to the district. As of September 1968, however, the district chief himself refused to issue the weapons. The cadre team leader reported that when he asked the district chief why, the latter said "All twenty-one are within draft age, so let's wait until they go into the army." The real

---

21. The village chief approved of this state of affairs. He indicated in an interview that the previous situation had been very hard on the landlords, because they could go into the hamlet to collect rents only on military operations.

reason, according to a Vietnamese-speaking American civilian who worked closely with the district chief, was that the latter "opposes passing out weapons to the peasants."[22]

A reasonable conclusion from this experience is that the actual program carried out in Long An bore few resemblances to the program proposed by Be, except in its suppressive functions. As Hoa Thuan II demonstrated, the cadres were able to accomplish certain suppressive tasks and to construct certain artifacts, but they were unable to resolve the distributive conflicts over power relationships and social organization which lay at the root of the violence in Long An. The continued strangle hold of the central bureaucracy over even minor details of rural life was symbolized by the inability of the Tan Thanh A village chief to remove a corrupt policeman from the village.

Similarly, even the greatly weakened version of the rural construction program adopted by the Saigon government was stymied in execution by the bureaucracy in the field. This was exemplified by the experience of the People's Self-Defense Force in both Tan Thanh A and Hoa Thuan II. Even though weapons were finally supplied to the People's Self-Defense Force in those two hamlets, a basic problem still existed: insufficient manpower remained in the rural communities to carry out the goals of the rural construction program. This was a consequence of the government's continued strategy of supporting a large nonassimilated military establishment, a strategy fundamentally in conflict with the strategy on which the rural construction program was based. The impact of the government's strategy was to bleed the countryside of manpower in order to protect the urban areas, and its practical effect was simply to withdraw from the war a significant portion of the manpower of the country.

The experience of the rural construction program in Hoa Thuan II also highlights the misleading nature of the Hamlet Evaluation System. As noted earlier, the HES rating of Hoa Thuan II was upgraded from the "E" category prior to the arrival of the cadre team

---

22. During February 1969 the village chief reported with some pride that the People's Self-Defense Force was 100 percent complete, and that twenty-one weapons had been issued in Hoa Thuan II hamlet. A five-minute ride down the road to Hoa Thuan II revealed, however, that all twenty-one weapons were sitting in the Popular Force outpost on Route 5, and had been for two months. The outpost commander reported that "we'll give them out as soon as the district chief gives the order."

to a "C" after its departure. Yet despite the team's activities, no change took place in the only significant index of progress: the balance of forces. No member of the revolutionary apparatus in Hoa Thuan II returned to the government side, not one member of the hamlet was sufficiently motivated to accept the position of hamlet chief, no government-sponsored guerrilla organization was established within the hamlet, and no progress was made toward resolving the social problems underlying the conflict within the hamlet. Nevertheless, through its focus on a series of superficial indicators, the official index of progress recorded a sharp improvement in the status of Hoa Thuan II.

Yet another conclusion suggested by the experience of rural construction in Long An is that government officials continued to be seriously out of touch with the situation in the province, both factually and in what they considered important or just. Both Colonel Nguu and the village chief of Truong Binh, a Northerner, were examples of officials who were conscientious but whose background or training interfered with an effective response to the problems of Long An. Colonel Nguu, city-bred and well-trained in conventional military methods, denied that the communist land program had an impact in the countryside. Moreover, only under considerable encouragement from Saigon could he be induced to support the arming of the population, while his general disdain for guerrilla methods was illustrated by his words quoted in the discussion of the violence program. Similarly, the chief of Truong Binh village was an alert and intelligent individual. Indeed, he was the only official encountered in Long An who expressed an awareness of the Party's progressive tax system—yet, ironically, he disapproved of it. Likewise, his somewhat authoritarian personal manner and slightly contemptuous attitude toward Southerners stood in the way of good relations between him and his constituents.

These problems, however—particularly the lack of preemptive social policies—were not generally identified by Saigon or American officials as being responsible for the limited success of the rural construction program. One example of this may be seen in the following excerpt from a memorandum entitled "Thoughts on Pacification," written early in 1968 by a high-ranking American civilian official. This quotation may be considered representative of an important body of official thought because the writer played such a significant role in the workings of the rural construction effort.

Over the last six years there have been a number of pacification programs, none of which have really succeeded. Actually, we never found out whether or not these pacification programs would work because the first basic requirement, security, has never been achieved. You cannot expose the population to the inroads of the enemy each night and reasonably expect them to willingly cooperate with the government or to overtly reject the Vietcong. They know far better than most of the senior officials of the Vietnamese government or of our government that the type of commitment we are asking them to make would probably result in their getting their throats cut by the Vietcong. This does not mean that the job of pacification is hopeless. It merely means we have to recognize the overriding requirement for security. Whether security is 10 percent of the total problem to be resolved or 90 percent, it is, inescapably, the *first* 10 percent or the *first* 90 percent.

While subsequent parts of the memorandum contained many perceptive observations, this quotation reveals how the official was the victim of the same conceptual contradiction that had continually hampered counterrevolutionary programs in Vietnam: an obsession with a tactical conception of security, when this was meaningless in the context of Vietnam. By postulating security as an initial condition, he simply demanded at the start what could only be the result of the process. As we saw in Chapter Four, the Party's "pacification program" did not require large troop units providing territorial security to be successful.

Similarly, an earlier memorandum by the same official, devoted specifically to Long An province, identified one of the important shortcomings as the lack of material support.

We still have not committed, in my opinion, resources to the pacification of a province on a MASSIVE scale. Pacification programs must be more broad-based, consequently the Revolutionary Development budget and program must be amplified. Public-works programs must be accelerated on such an enlarged basis that it has a visible psychological impact on the minds of the people. Psychological operations in support of pacification must be increased and enlarged on a greatly magnified basis. An accelerated public-works program will create a favorable image of the government in the minds of the people and add to the credibility of psychological operations. At the same time we must intensify our attack on the VC infrastructure in the province as the plan envisages if our overall efforts are to be successful.

The concluding emphasis on the importance of the communist apparatus was well placed and paralleled Colonel Herbert's dissatisfaction with the scale of activity in this area. Likewise the observation that constructive programs received a disproportionately small share of the total effort mirrored Herbert's own feelings, and reemphasized the built-in bias of the current effort toward methods of violence and suppression. Nevertheless, the assumption that the absence of "resources . . . on a MASSIVE scale" was responsible for the rural construction program's lack of success was decisively wrong. Similarly, the emphasis on the need for an accelerated public-works program was the result of the unexamined projection of American middle-class needs onto the rural Vietnamese scene, remote from the factors which underlay the conflict in Long An.

As these quotations demonstrate, despite the extensiveness of military-sponsored research programs in Vietnam, official doctrine was still oblivious to the simple truth, so clearly proven by the case of Long An, that neither "massive resources" nor a numerical troop superiority over the enemy was necessary for victory. The preemptive policies required to establish a more just society in Long An, policies consisting of redistributive rather than incremental measures, would have required no money and few troops to carry out. The current program, however, called for the "development" of a number of superficial factors, while ignoring the critical distributive issues.

Conclusion

Any evaluation of the situation in Long An in 1968 must begin with the victorious position of the revolutionary movement by 1965 —that it had all but extinguished the government presence in the province, and that it had the ability, based on internal forces, to smash the remaining government units at will. Thus perhaps the most accurate description of the situation in 1968 would be to say that because of certain clear superiorities in strategy, organization, and policy, the revolutionary movement had won in Long An by 1965, but since that time the Saigon government, recovered from its earlier paralysis, had mustered certain additional Vietnamese and foreign forces to occupy the province.

Nevertheless, the factors responsible for the initial victory and continued strength of the revolutionary movement in Long An, and its rapid turnabout ability in 1960, had not been challenged, although a certain war weariness had clearly developed, just as it had by 1954. The complex of measures employed by the Saigon government and its allies represented the same reinforcement strategy which had failed repeatedly in the past, and the relatively minor efforts devoted to constructive measures, such as medical care, wells, roads, or electrification, were humanitarian, but, as before, irrelevant to the fundamental issues involved. Moreover, the basic conceptual failure that led to the initial collapse of the government in Long An had in no way been overcome, but was duplicated in the American establishment as well. By their actions as well as their words, it was clear that American decision makers were no more aware of the strategic alternatives in 1968 than they were in 1965. This was exemplified by the inability of officials to explain the earlier victory of the revolutionary movement without the use of massive resources or numerical troop superiority, except on the basis of a "terror" theory which is discredited by the historical experience of Long An.

Similarly, even alternative strategies of the use of violence were excluded by current official thinking. The strategy of violence outlined by General Johnson was probably the most expensive and inefficient approach possible in the context of Vietnam—in a situation in which expense must be calculated principally in human lives rather than in money. The statement of the American advisor in Can Duoc that, even in his specialized advisor training, he had never heard discussed the idea of an extensive use of locally-based guerrilla forces, is eloquent testimony on this point.

It is also reasonable to believe that these inappropriate measures came into use through the thinking of a conventional military establishment—Vietnamese and American—whose doctrine, training, and organization were unsuited to cope with the kind of conflict occurring in Vietnam. Thus many programs came about out of preexisting doctrines and organizations for which no clear intellectual justification could be provided, except in terms of a strategy inappropriate to the context of Vietnam. Typical examples were the use of artillery, air strikes, and large-scale sweep operations in populated areas. Although most existing forms of combat organization were unsuitable to carry out declared goals in Vietnam, the general response was to alter the nature of the conflict rather than to alter the organizations involved.[23]

In summary, then, the need to maintain more than 17,000 men

---

23. It is interesting to note that the three programs best adapted, in concept, to government goals in Long An—the Phoenix/PRU program, the rural construction program, and the Accelerated Pacification Campaign—all shared a common organizational parentage in the Central Intelligence Agency.

under arms in Long An in 1968 was simply the cost of maintaining the existing distributive system, and the strength of the revolutionary movement continued because the distributive issues continued. Moreover, one of the principal factors driving people into the arms of the Party in Long An was the continued inappropriate responses of the government, starting with its failure to adopt preemptive policies, and ending with the employment of highly counterproductive forms of violence. Consequently, the fairest conclusion to be drawn from the history of Long An is that through 1968 the principal benefactors of the revolutionary movement were precisely those who devised, supported, and executed the measures employed against it.

CHAPTER SIX

From War to What?

Victory will come to us, not suddenly, but in a complicated and tortuous way.

From a communist strategy document captured in mid-1969[1]

This policy [of Vietnamization] fulfills our objective of reducing American involvement. It cannot, except over a long period, end the war altogether.

PRESIDENT RICHARD M. NIXON[2]

For Long An, 1970 was a year of transition between a situation in which the internal balance of forces was swamped by external forces and one in which strictly internal factors would play a greater role in the relative strengths of the competing forms of social organization. The last American combat troops departed in October, but the "Vietnamization" program they left behind was supposed to produce a permanent advantage to the social forces favored by the American government, in a variety of ways: through a more favorable power ratio—by means of a differential distribution of weaponry, communications, and training between the opposing forces and certain changes in military doctrine—and through a more favorable force ratio, by means of certain social policies.

The nature of the counterrevolutionary effort in Long An was examined in detail in Chapter Five. This brief chapter will examine what changes had taken place in the areas found to be important earlier in this study. The reader may assume the persistence of 1968 forms in areas not discussed in the following pages.

Military Strategy

During 1969 higher-level American strategists began to realize that the strategy of violence described by General Johnson in the last chapter was not well adapted to the goals of American policy in Vietnam. A lengthy rethinking of the problem led to what was

---

1. *Viet-Nam Documents and Research Notes*, No. 64.
2. "United States Foreign Policy for the 1970's: Building for Peace," the President's report to the Congress on foreign policy, February 25, 1971.

called the "area security system," which established a system of geographically defined security zones. Certain kinds of security forces, ranging from conventional American combat units to indigenous police, would be the principal security elements in each zone in accord with the degree of security required in the zone. This area security system did not involve concepts analogous to those of the legal position of the population, a strategic conception of security, or assimilation of forces. Thus its practical consequence was not a restructuring of Saigon forces or a change in field tactics, but rather a reallocation of manpower among various types of government forces.[3]

The impact in the field of this doctrinal shift from the earlier strategy can be seen in the proportions of troops in the various Saigon forces in Long An. Under the new doctrine ARVN forces in Long An remained constant, but 54 RF companies were authorized, totaling 8,250 men, and 213 PF platoons, totaling 7,805 men. Another 27,000 individuals were formally enrolled as combat troops in the People's Self-Defense Force (armed with 9,000 weapons). None of these forces was well assimilated into village communities, but the biggest increases came in those least poorly assimilated. Thus the new doctrine increased, in a very roundabout way, the relative degree of assimilation of government forces. In a similar roundabout way it increased the proportion of manpower devoted to tactics better adapted to the nature of the conflict.

These forces still operated with a centralized logistic system and with varying degrees of accountability (ranging to zero for ARVN) to the village community. Consequently abuses of the civil population by Saigon military forces continued to be institutionalized in varying degrees.[4] Similarly, there was no change in the recruitment system for the officer corps that would have permitted the degree of upward mobility permitted under revolutionary military organization. Table 9 in fact shows a modest decrease in the percentage of those moving from noncommissioned to commissioned officer status through 1969. It may be inferred that motivation was still limited as well.

Correlating with the adoption of this modified strategy and the

---

3. Details of the area security system regrettably remain classified.
4. For the ARVN, no formal relationship of accountability existed; for the RF, there was some informal accountability because of the relative closeness of the home village of the troops. PF and PSDF were formally under the authority of the village chief.

TABLE 9: SOURCE OF OFFICER COMMISSION, 1966-1969

	1966		1967		1968		1969	
	number	percent	number	percent	number	percent	number	percent
Regular commission								
(*tu tai* II—Dalat)	233	3.4	173	4.7	...	0.0	92	0.7
Reserve commission								
(*tu tai* I—Thu Duc)	4,894	71.6	3,515	95.3	11,876	90.9	11,288	90.8
Special commission								
(OCS-Nha Trang)	1,716	25.0	...	0.0	1,195	9.1	1,063	8.5
Total	6,843	100.0	3,688	100.0	13,071	100.0	12,443	100.0

NOTE: The tripling in the number of those receiving reserve commissions resulted from the enforcement of the general mobilization law in 1968 on college graduates, eligible for this commission by virtue of their education but formerly exempt from war service. The rapid expansion in the size of the officer corps thus did not provide increased opportunities for promotion from groups of peasant origin.

SOURCE: General Political Warfare Department, Ministry of Defense.

relative shift in organization and tactics which it implied was a decline in the size of revolutionary forces in Long An province. In late 1970 intelligence figures showed that there remained only 182 village guerrillas, 12 members of the sole surviving district company, and 233 members of the province battalions. Surrenders to the government rose sharply during March and April of 1969, and maintained a high level through early 1970. The ultimate decline in the rate of surrender in late 1970 may have been due, as in 1959, to a decline in the number of surviving revolutionary activists.[5]

One possible inference from these data is that the former strategy of suppression finally began to show results in Long An, with the new strategy merely coming along at an opportune moment. In an interview in June 1970, Nguyen van Thanh offered some testimony to evaluate this inference. Thanh was born into a landless peasant family on the outskirts of Saigon in 1924. He became a Party mem-

5. Monthly surrenders were as follows:

Year	Jan	Feb	Mar	Apr	May	Jun	Jul	Aug	Sep	Oct	Nov	Dec	Total
1969	62	79	184	273	263	165	311	243	201	220	263	189	2,453
1970	131	155	119	84	128	83	67	66	41	39	17	22	952

HES statistics for 1969 and 1970 are not shown for several reasons. Chapter Five concluded that these statistics were of dubious significance for the type of analysis conducted here. In any case a new format was adopted during 1969 such that subsequent HES statistics are not comparable to those generated earlier. As an example, under the former system Long An ranked 42 (i.e., "42nd worst") among the 44 rated provinces. Under the new statistics its rank jumped to 17.

ber in 1947 and commanded various military units until his regroupment to the North in 1954. There he attended the infantry
school and later commanded the regiment protecting Hanoi. From
1961 to 1964 he taught at a school for company commanders located
near Svay Rieng, Cambodia, finally returning to Vietnam only in
1964. From the end of 1967 until his defection in May 1970 he was
deputy Subregion II commander.[6]

Thanh pointed out that there had been some decline in Subregion II forces as a consequence of an improvement in ARVN
operations. Losses had also continued at a high level because of
American operations in Long An. He also emphasized the enormous,
and unanticipated, losses in the Tet attacks of 1968.[7] Nevertheless,
the Tet attacks had not been uniformly unsuccessful. Manpower
losses had been extremely heavy, and popular confidence in the Party
leadership had been severely damaged, but after the Tet attacks the
United States had temporarily ceased bombing north of the 17th
parallel and had entered into negotiations in Paris.

Thus, revolutionary losses in Long An had been high for years
—ever since the start of serious American combat operations in early
1967. The decisive new element had been, Thanh felt, a number of
changes in the government approach which had begun to make themselves felt around May of 1969. One of these changes had been a
partial reconstitution of the government's village apparatus. A second had been the psychological impact of the government's land-
reform proposals, widely propagandized at the time. A third important change had been the considerable expansion of the Popular
Force and People's Self-Defense Force organizations.

The combined effect of these changes was to make it much more
difficult for revolutionary operatives to penetrate populated areas to
gather food, intelligence, and recruits. Many who might formerly
have joined the revolutionary forces now simply stayed home while
serving in the government village organizations. Around May 1969,
Thanh stated, Party chi bo began reporting a serious impact on the

---

6. Subregion II is one of several military command areas surrounding
Saigon established by the Party in late 1967. It includes several districts in
an arc from western Long An to Tay Ninh. See *Viet-Nam Documents and
Research Notes*, Nos. 23 and 93.

7. Because of excessively optimistic reporting from the village level, higher
echelons in the Party had erroneously believed that a general uprising could
be successful.

village organizations. This in turn made it increasingly difficult to replace the continuing high losses suffered by the concentrated forces which were engaging in company and battalion size operations. The effect became a cumulative one, such as we have seen before in Long An: an initial weakening of revolutionary organs increased the risk in cooperating with the movement; this led to a further weakening of the movement's ability to defend itself, and so forth. Finally it became impossible for concentrated forces to conduct military operations or even to move in groups larger than half a dozen individuals. It was in groups of such size that the battalions and companies mentioned above existed in late 1970. The impact on the village-level apparatus is also reflected in the sharp decline in the size of the guerrilla forces.

Thanh's views on the order of events by which revolutionary forces were weakened in Long An by late 1970 are consistent with the inferences from evidence recounted in previous chapters that the government's earlier collapse in Long An was due partly to inappropriate organization (affecting the power ratio), and partly to distributive conflicts (affecting the force ratio). That is, the weakness enforced on government forces by distributive conflicts alone had been compounded by errors of organization and military strategy as well.

Thanh based such optimism as he had for the future of the revolution on the failure of the Saigon leadership to overcome remaining errors in military organization and strategy, and in what we have called social strategy as well.

Social Strategy

This section will address those policies of the Saigon government which were part of its implicit social strategy, that is, those policies intended to affect the force ratio through their impact on the distribution of values. In some of these social policies there were major changes after 1968, in others only minor changes, and in others no change at all.

The greatest changes occurred in the area of landholding inequalities. The first significant action was the signing in February 1969 of Circular 033-TT/Th.T/PC.2, which froze rents and cultivation rights for one year in areas officially declared "Vietcong controlled," thus in theory eliminating the adverse consequences of the simultaneous arrival of both the landlords and the Saigon military

forces to reoccupy a formerly contested area. Circular 069-TT/
Th.T/PC.2, dated April 25, 1969, extended this freeze to all other
areas not falling under the provisions of Circular 033.[8]

The land program of the Saigon government was consummated
with the passage and signing in March 1970 of Law 003/70. The
law provided for immediate cessation of rent payments simply by
application of the tenant operator to his village council; free grant of
land to the tenant, with payment to the owner of record to be ab-
sorbed by the Saigon government; and no retention of land not
cultivated by the owner or his family, except for limited amounts
devoted to ancestor worship.[9]

A much debated but decisive feature of Law 003/70 was the
first priority it gave to the present tiller of the land. Opponents had
urged first priority for those who had cast their lot with the Saigon
government. On the other hand the drafters of the law, strongly supported by President Nguyen van Thieu, urged first priority to the
present tiller, even though installed by the Party, thus cutting the
link of contingency which had bound him to the revolutionary movement. To the extent that the law was executed in the proposed form
it thus ended the vested interest that many had in the victory of the
revolutionary movement, at least in regard to the one issue of landholding inequalities.[10]

Two points should be emphasized about Law 003/70. It will
be recalled that the Party's land redistribution had been explicitly
provisional: grantees retained their land only as long as they cooperated in required ways, such as by paying taxes, providing intelligence, or sending their sons to serve in the revolutionary military
forces. The conditional nature of the grant served as an important
control by the Party over the actions of individual grantees and their
families. This conditional aspect also made the grant, in the eyes of
the Saigon leadership, a fraudulent one. In contrast, Law 003/70
provided for a definitive distribution, which in the view of Saigon

---

8. It is apparently to the psychological impact of these two circulars that
Thanh referred.

9. An English translation of the text of Law 003/70 may be found in
Asian Survey, X (August 1970), 734–737.

10. It is another of the ironies of history that this program, which was
initiated by the Saigon government, was supported only slowly and reluctantly
by the United States. See Elizabeth Pond, "Viet Land Reform Gathers Speed,"
Christian Science Monitor, June 16, 1969; Jeffrey Race, "Land Without
Hope," *Far Eastern Economic Review*, LX (May 16, 1968), 349–352; and
Jeffrey Race, "The Battle over Land," *Far Eastern Economic Review*, LXIV
(August 20, 1970), 19–22.

officials was a just and desirable feature. Yet for this same reason the Saigon government could not reap the benefits from its program that the Party had gained from its own earlier redistribution.

A second possibility is that Law 003/70, while not motivating individuals through contingent incentives as had the Party program, might still create a favorable image for the Saigon government (thus expanding the sympathetic environment). It is probable that the law had a limited impact in this respect as well. The program was widely propagandized as a "revolutionary" step, and had it been carried out in 1945, it certainly would have been. In the context of 1970, however, it was hardly revolutionary and in fact little more than the Saigon government's stamp of approval on a land redistribution already carried out by the Party—in many cases a quarter of a century before. Communist defectors interviewed made the striking analogy that one is, after all, hardly grateful to a thief who is compelled by force of circumstance to return stolen property. These comments do not deny the importance of the program in reducing distributive conflicts in Long An; rather they point out some of the limitations built into the program.

In the area of village government, changes by 1970 were probably of less significance than those relating to land ownership. The improvements in village government cited in official claims of a strengthening of local government consisted of an expansion of the size of village and hamlet governing bodies, addition of technical cadre appointed by the central government, authority for the village council to decide on expenditures of up to 100,000 piasters without the need for approval by higher authority, and the granting to the village chief of operational control over rural construction cadre, National Police, and Popular Force troops operating within his village. These measures were intended to reduce the "errand-boy" image of village leadership roles and thus to enhance their attractiveness.[11]

Nevertheless, it must be emphasized that operational control, that is, authority over day-to-day activity, is not the same as authority over career incentives. This was, as in the past, still jealously maintained at much higher levels within the central bureaucracy. Despite considerable "command emphasis" from Saigon that district and province officials "pay attention to the wishes" of their village

---

11. The relevant legal documents are Decree O45–SL/NV, dated April 1, 1969, and Circular 093–TT/NV, dated June 2, 1969. These amended the earlier legal basis of local organs, Decree 198–SL/DUHC, dated December 24, 1966.

chiefs, the haughty and sometimes contemptuous attitudes of earlier days persisted in Long An in 1970. Complained one village chief in Can Giuoc district in the summer of 1970: "If I suggest [to the district chief] a punishment for a cadre in my village, nothing happens; if I suggest a promotion or a commendation for a particularly hard worker, it is ignored just the same." Similarly, though village officials had plenary authority to conduct military operations, "We have to notify the district in advance of an operation; the district chief immediately radios back that we can go on the operation if we want, but if we get into trouble, don't expect reinforcements, artillery, or medical help for the wounded." Thus since control over career incentives and over military resources still rested with district and higher level officials, the paper grants of authority to village officials were in practice hamstrung.[12]

Strengthening of Saigon's village organs was necessarily limited to cosmetic measures because of the continuance in force of Ordinance 57a, which a decade and a half before had tilted the scales against the village as an organ of significant political authority.[13] Most importantly, there was still no system of upward mobility for village officials to parallel that of the revolutionary movement by rewarding outstanding performance with promotion to district and higher levels, to integrate the village into the national political structure, and to preclude the dominance at the higher levels of urban-elite social groups. This third function of the upward mobility within the revolutionary movement of course was dependent on ascriptive criteria for promotion from the lowest ranks, and such ascriptive criteria similarly had no counterpart in government policy. When questioned on this government officials were generally horrified at the idea of applying "discriminatory" standards based on class origin. In reality, of course, government practice discriminated as well, but against those at the lower end of the scale of social stratification rather than those at the upper, and under the guise of "educational standards" rather than by explicit rules as in Party doctrine.

Evidence on village elections from Long An is consistent with the hypothesis that these measures did little to improve the attrac-

---

12. Thus Circular 093 stated, for example: "The village and hamlet chiefs have the right to *recommend* rewards for good work by Popular Forces and may also *recommend* punishment in case of fault. The district chief/subsector commander must respect the recommendations of the village and hamlet chiefs" (italics supplied).

13. Only reconfirming, of course, a political structure the French had created during their occupation of Vietnam.

tiveness of village government. In the April 1967 elections there were 220 village council seats, contested by 297 candidates, for a ratio of 1.3 to 1. For the May elections for hamlet chief and deputy hamlet chief, the ratio was 2.0 to 1. For the elections to the corresponding positions in 1970, the ratios were 1.4 to 1 and 2.2 to 1. A reasonable inference from these data is that the positions had been little enhanced by the reforms of 1969 and 1970.

A further word is in order on the subject of elections, since these played such a role in official claims of the strengthening of government at various levels or of its enhanced responsiveness. One conclusion from the history of Long An was that the distribution of values in the society was a key operative factor in motivating risk-taking for one side or the other. In official pronouncements, however, "participation," that is, casting a ballot or expressing an opinion in a public meeting, was viewed as sufficient to produce "loyalty" or "identification," even if it issued in no change in the distribution of values. Thus the official and sanguine view of the importance of forms or processes, irrespective of their results, is not supported by the history of events in Long An. A further illustration that there is no necessary connection between "voting" and a redistribution of values is provided by the Party's revolutionary redistribution of values in Long An without conducting any referenda on the issue.

We might also note two reasons why the Saigon-sponsored political system produced no revolutionary redistribution of power and status values. First, those most strongly advocating such a redistribution, Party members and those cooperating with them, were specifically excluded by statute from candidacy. Second, even opposition figures within the Saigon political system tended to come from the same kind of elites as the military who held the central executive positions in 1970. These individuals understandably had little reason to promote a reshaping of status and power relationships. Thus we may conclude that the survival of the Saigon-sponsored political system itself did not turn on its having electoral processes, as many Saigon officials erroneously believed.

In the sphere of economic doctrine, government thinking continued its earlier preoccupation with incrementalism, viewing the motive to revolution as absolute poverty rather than the relative ranking of various social groups. Both rhetoric and programs thus continued their focus on physical artifacts leading to a "better life," without dealing with the crucial distributive issues. As with elections, there was a direct equation of "participation" with "loyalty" or "identification," i.e., the view that if villagers participated in a self-help project paid for by Saigon, this would produce "loyalty" to Saigon.

Speaking only of Long An, the revolutionary movement in late 1970 was in a difficult position. The strategy elected by the communist leadership had not yet brought victory, but it had, as Vo van An had feared a decade before, provoked a lengthy and powerful foreign intervention and seemingly interminable bloodshed. Yet the revolutionary movement had been in difficult straits before, as in 1959, and was able to stage remarkable returns to life because it continued to satisfy needs that the authorities in Saigon did not.

Nevertheless, as communist documents from the time of Lenin and before have emphasized, the internal balance of forces is just one factor, albeit an important one, in determining the success of a revolution; at any moment international factors impinge as well in determining victory for the revolution, victory for the counterrevolution, or an endless cycle of civil strife.

Long An is not a poor province; the soil could provide a bounteous life for all. But man is moved by the need for spiritual values as well: a sense of power over his own destiny, a sense of respect from his fellow man. A humane society provides wide satisfaction for these spiritual needs, reaping domestic peace as its reward. Yet while material plenty comes from nature, societies are made by men. And so Long An might, as the very meaning of its name implies, have been a land of peaceful and prosperous cooperation between all its people. A decade and a half of killing and destruction in Long An provides evidence of the superhuman sacrifices which some men, deprived of these values, will endure to redress their deprivation; yet it also provides a melancholy example of the lengths other men will go, already abundantly enjoying these values, to perpetuate their privilege.

Appendix I

A Graphic Presentation of Concepts

The purpose of this appendix is to give a graphic illustration of several terms employed in the text, such as crossover point, preemption, and reinforcement, and particularly to point out the defectiveness of the conventional concept of security when employed in the context of revolutionary war such as occurred in Long An province. The following is intended only as a heuristic model, and not as a means of actually calculating the variables involved. For the purpose of this discussion the variables cited are assumed to have unique values, although as a practical matter the quantities they represent shade into one another. Moreover, linkages exist between variables which are not considered here, because they would complicate the discussion without contributing to its purpose.

There are many ways to model the various aspects of the process which occurs in a social revolution. This model will concern itself with the aspect of security as related to various aspects of social environment.

What is security? The effort to develop means to create it has suffered substantially from the lack of a commonly accepted definition. This in turn has been caused by the tactical-strategic confusion described in the text: it is pointed out by some that there is no such thing as "absolute security," because an enemy presumably may always mass superior forces against any defensive system. This problem of definition can be resolved only by adopting a probabilistic definition of security applicable to a whole national unit or theater of operations. The use of probabilistic quantities in warfare is accepted practice, for example, in weapon damage assessment, and it presents no difficulty from the point of view of current practice. Thus a general definition of security is: *the probability that a certain event or class of events will not occur within a defined area within a defined period of time*, for example, "the probability that the hamlet chief will not be assassinated within the boundaries of his hamlet during his term of office," or "the probability that there will be no movement of external hostile individuals within the hamlet area between the hours of 1800 and 0600."

In this model the population will be divided into five groups: enemy population over the threshold (where they are willing to assume high risks), enemy population under the threshold, friendly population over the threshold,[1] friendly population under the threshold, and neutral population. These variables as fractions of the total population group will be denoted by the symbols EP_{ot}, EP_{ut}, FP_{ot}, FP_{ut}, and P_n. For the sake of simplicity these symbols rather than the words they stand for will be used in the following discussion.

EP_{ot}, EP_{ut}, FP_{ot}, and FP_{ut} represent the *forces* involved in the conflict. EP_{ut}, FP_{ut} and P_n represent the *environment* in which these forces operate. EP_{ut} and FP_{ut} would correspond to each side's sympathizers among the population who continued their daily living as ordinary citizens but also served as "eyes and ears" and sources of material support for their respective sides. On the other hand, EP_{ot} and FP_{ot} would correspond to members of military units, police, government officials, in other words, those opting for roles involving great risk if captured (or discovered, as in the case of a penetration agent). For the purposes of the following model, let us simply note that force, represented by f, is some function g of these fractions of the population:

$$f_t = g(FP_{ot}, FP_{ut})$$
$$f_e = g(EP_{ot}, EP_{ut}).$$

A concept we will denote as the *force ratio* is simply the ratio of these functions:

$$f = \frac{f_t}{f_e} = \frac{g(FP_{ot}, FP_{ut})}{g(EP_{ot}, EP_{ut})}.$$

To maintain any given level of security (with a constant level of threat), a variety of combinations of FP_{ut} and FP_{ot} are possible. An intuitive sense of the relationship between these two quantities may be gained from the following simplified model. Imagine an area consisting of one hundred units, ten units on a side. A "security force" whose visibility is limited to a block the size of one unit square has the mission of interdicting an enemy force of equivalent

---

1. A practical complication arises concerning the two groups over the threshold: formal enrollment in a military organization is not sufficient to assign an individual to this category; risk-taking is the criterion. Unmotivated individuals coerced into military service would, in this model, belong to the neutral category. The history of Long An provides numerous examples of this situation.

size from moving into this one hundred square area. By stationing itself in any square on the perimeter, it can provide a maximum security of less than 3 percent, because it can occupy only one of the thirty-six perimeter squares. However, by placing a "sensor" in additional perimeter squares, security can be increased. If communications and mobility are assumed to be perfect, each additional sensor increases security by exactly the same amount as adding one more security force. In a situation of "village security," the sensors would be the sympathetic environment. The real situation would be more complex in that there might be multiple intrusion and security forces, less than perfect communications and mobility, and so on, but the same principle applies: each additional sympathizer is the equivalent of some multiple (unity or less) of the entire security force in existence at that time.

The multiplicative nature of this relationship means in real terms that, as the number of one's sympathizers among the population vanishes, one's suppressive forces must become very large. Yet this is empirically unreasonable. In fact, just the opposite happened for the government in Long An, for reasons obvious from the text: as the number of government sympathizers decreased, so did the number of those willing to take risks for the government. Thus the condition for maintaining security specified by this relationship could not be satisfied, and the intervention of external forces was required.

The most important consequence of the multiplicative nature of the relationship between FP_{ut} and FP_{ot} is that, over a considerable range, removing one member of FP_{ut} diminishes security more than removing one member of FP_{ot}.[2] Communist doctrine takes account of the multiplicative nature of this relationship, as exemplified by the fact that in the 1956–1959 period in Vietnam communist strategy aimed at eliminating the FP_{ut} element of government forces, and not the FP_{ot} element, that is, communist strategy aimed at eliminating the government's sympathetic environment rather than at attacking military forces. This proved decisive because, as noted above, when FP_{ut} approached zero, FP_{ot} declined as well, rather than increasing as would have been necessary to maintain security. It was this virtual disappearance of FP_{ut} in Long An by 1959 which

---

2. Within the limits: (1) that FP_{ut} is not so large that the marginal impact of FP_{ut} is less than the marginal impact of FP_{ot}; and (2) that FP_{ot} is not so small relative to EP_{ot} as to be inadequate for defense even when intelligence is obtained.

created impossible demands for FP_{ot} when the violent stage began in 1960. Moreover, it was the central government's continued demands on the population to satisfy the requirements for FP_{ot} (troops) which pushed additional elements of P_n into the EP_{ut} and EP_{ot} groups. The inverse of the situation just described is that adding one member to FP_{ut} increases security more than adding one member to FP_{ot}: increasing the sympathetic population by one person adds more to security than recruiting, training, and supporting one more soldier or policeman.

The degree of security may also be enhanced by exploiting a number of power-augmenting factors, such as improved weaponry or communications, better training, superior tactical deployment, etc.; in general:

$$p = h(a, b, c \ldots)$$

where p represents power and a, b, c. . . represent these power-augmenting factors. All these factors operate only as multipliers on the force level, however, and thus if one's forces are near zero, manipulating the power-augmenting factors will be of negligible benefit.

By dividing the power function for one side in the conflict by the identical function for the other side, we produce a concept which will be called the *power ratio*:

$$p = \frac{p_f}{p_e} = \frac{h(a_f, b_f, c_f \ldots)}{h(a_e, b_e, c_e \ldots)},$$

where p_f represents friendly power and p_e represents enemy power. This may be understood as the ratio of effectiveness of opposing forces according to some abstract scale, taking into account all the factors bearing on effectiveness such as weaponry, training, and communications; or, for the purpose of this discussion, it may be understood as the probability of one side interdicting the movement of the other, given forces of defined sizes.

In Figure 1 the force ratio is represented by the vertical axis, while the horizontal axis represents the power ratio. The multiple of the first variable, the force ratio, by the second variable, the power ratio, represents a quantity determining one's ability to enforce one's will on the enemy. Thus **fp** is the mathematical expression of the term "balance of forces" employed in the text. The balance of forces in turn is a general concept depicting the relative capabilities of the two sides, that is, the levels of security or disruption they will be able to enforce.

In terms of the vocabulary employed in the text, reinforcement

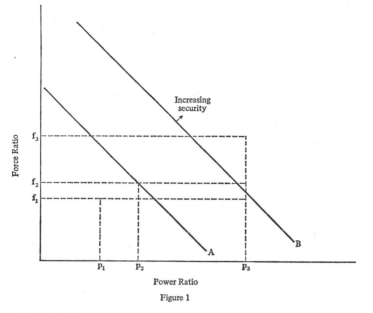

Figure 1

consists of shifting the power ratio out along the horizontal axis to progressively more favorable ratios. Preemption consists of moving up on the vertical axis by reducing the fraction of the population which wants to reduce security in proportion to the fraction of the population which wants to increase it.

A number of conclusions may be drawn from this graph:

1. Investigation of the history of Long An revealed that without a local apparatus, forces not assimilated into communities proved useless, i.e., once one's local apparatus is destroyed, one is strategically defeated, although one may still be able to fight some battles. Investigation also revealed that the local apparatus is more vulnerable than concentrated forces, because its members live among the population. The consequence for prediction is that the critical issue is to know whether one's local apparatus can survive and function; the fate of one's concentrated forces is a secondary consideration.[3]

In the accompanying graph points p_1, p_2, and p_3 represent three power ratios, each progressively more favorable to the government. For example, p_1 might represent government forces operating principally in company size or in larger formations, with poor weaponry,

3. This argument applies to each side; for ease of discussion the following is phrased in terms of the government.

and minimum police and small-unit operations; p_2 might represent an identical manpower allocation and deployment, but now with improved weapons; p_3 might represent improved weaponry and training combined with superior manpower allocation and deployment (e.g., emphasis on police activity, small-unit operations, night ambushes, etc.). If the central government's local apparatus (in any one community, or in the aggregate over the entire nation) requires a degree of security corresponding to line B, if the force ratio is represented by point f_1, and if the power ratio is represented by point p_1, then the government will have been defeated in that area, because its local apparatus will be unable to survive. The graph also reveals that, even if the power ratio is shifted to p_3, the government is still defeated. If p_3 in this particular situation represents the maximum advantage obtainable over the enemy through the manipulation of power-augmenting factors, then this situation would correspond to the one described in the text as beyond the crossover point. The crossover point is thus a shorthand expression for the point at which the force ratio is so unfavorable that even the maximum practicable augmentation of the power ratio will not permit one's local apparatus to survive. The concept of security employed in government military doctrine in Long An corresponded only to reinforcement (i.e., the manipulation of power-augmenting factors) or to the concentration of existing forces in a limited number of locations ("physical security"), rather than to preemption. B, f_1, and p_3 thus define a situation in which the forces available and the level of security required are such that this conventional definition of security is irrelevant: survival can come about only by shifting from f_1 to some value higher on the vertical axis.

2. If the government's apparatus requires a degree of security represented by A, and the maximum practicable power ratio is represented by p_2, then the government would have the choice between f_3 and f_2, i.e., more preemption and less violence, or less preemption and more violence. Thus in those societies in which social conditions are such that they do not lead to the collapse of the government's local apparatus, the impact of a reinforcement strategy is such that it leads to a higher level of violence than would be the case if a preemptive strategy were adopted.[4]

3. As a practical matter in Long An, reinforcement measures

---

4. On the assumption that the opposition organization chooses to actualize the capability for violence that it possesses. As we saw in Long An, the Party elected to limit violent activities during the 1954–1959 period.

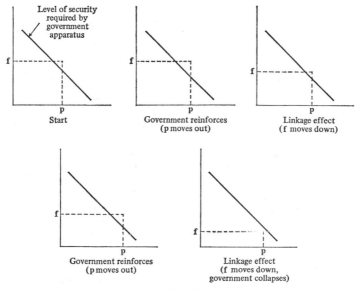

Figure 2

were such as to shift the force ratio against the government, e.g., population controls, martial law, harassing artillery fire and air attacks on populated areas, conscription. The diagrams in Figure 2 illustrate how this linkage leads to the escalatory spiral described in the text. In the case of Long An, the linkage was such as to lead to an open-ended escalation culminating in the defeat of the government. Under different social conditions the spiral might have reached an equilibrium at some point of less than total defeat for the government. The escalatory spiral and the higher level of violence it implies are integral to a reinforcement strategy, however.

Appendix II

The figures in the following pages are collations of the data presented year by year in the text.

PERCENTAGE OF ASSESSED LAND TAXES COLLECTED

Year	Percentage	Year	Percentage
1955	5.8[a]	1962	47.0
1956	16.2[a]	1963	40.3
1957	59.2	1964	20.9
1958	68.9	1965	23.1
1959	81.6	1966	26.1
1960	74.4	1967	21.9
1961	50.6	1968	33.5[b]

NOTES: [a] For the former province of Tan An.
    [b] After 1968 this information was no longer reported from village to province level.
SOURCE: Directorate General of the Treasury (1955–1956).
    Long An province Treasury Office (1957–1968).

MONTHLY TOTAL OF SURRENDERS

Month	1	2	3	4	5	6	7	8	9	10	11	12	Total
1958	...[a]	...[a]	...[a]	...[a]	...[a]	2	0	9	31	13	17	9	81[b]
1959	7	3	13	8	1	11	8	10	5	3	2	8	79
1960	6	3	0	0	0	2	4	0	0	1	2	1	19
1961	0	0	0	0	1	0	5	2	0	1	1	4	14
1962	4	1	5	4	3	6	14	5	14	7	19	27	109
1963	23	12	10	25	48	6	13	46	40	22	48	39	332
1964	58	41	47	54	13	31	38	10	13	8	6	19	338
1965	21	49	61	41	22	41	31	67	36	44	42	44	499
1966	49	52	62	46	44	50	39	36	34	87	37	44	580
1967	45	227	362	175	177	114	152	100	46	56	39	32	1,525
1968	17	14	22	28	20	12	34	37	45	90	69	62	450
1969	62	79	184	273	263	165	311	243	201	220	263	189	2,453
1970	131	155	119	84	128	83	67	66	41	39	17	22	952

NOTES: [a] Unavailable.
    [b] Seven months.
SOURCE: Long An province Cong An Office (1958–1962).
    Long An province Chieu Hoi Office (1963–1970).

ESTIMATED REVOLUTIONARY MILITARY STRENGTH

Year	Village guerrillas	District companies	Province battalions	Other	Total
1962[a]	800	...	...	...	...
1963	950	400	200	...	1,550
1964	1,100	480	500	...	2,080
1965	1,150	600	450	...	2,200
1966	1,200	550	650	...	2,400
1967	1,290	370	520	...	2,180
1968	1,450[b]	700	450[c]	500[d]	3,100
1969	...	...	...	...	...
1970	182	12	233[e]	...	427

NOTES: [a] For comparison purposes figures contained in *Ban Tran Liet Viet Cong* indicate that total revolutionary military strength in Long An in the last six months of 1959 was approximately 400.
[b] Confirmed figure; estimated 2000.
[c] Including estimated 90 PAVN replacements assimilated into local battalions.
[d] Category not employed in earlier formats.
[e] Including an undetermined number of PAVN replacements.
SOURCE: Long An sector J-2 intelligence estimates.

Glossary

The reader should consult the index for the sections of the text that describe these terms in greater detail.

agroville	A security-oriented resettlement program established in 1959
ap	A village neighborhood, translated as hamlet in the text
apparatus	A general term for the communist political organization
ARVN	Acronym for Army of the Republic of Vietnam
ban hoi te	Name of the village council until 1953
ban nong	In communist usage, one without sufficient land to support his family
Bao An	Civil Guard; a district-level military force during the Diem period.
battalion	A military unit composed of two or more companies
binh van	Propaganda activities directed toward government troops, to induce their defection or at least their neutrality (communist term)
Binh Xuyen	A bandit gang operating in the Saigon area in the French period
brigade	A military unit composed of two or more battalions
cadre	Translation of *can bo* (q.v.)
can bo	Cadre; in communist usage, an operative (not necessarily a Party member) in any revolutionary organization; adopted by the Saigon government to refer to its own operatives
Can Lao Nhan Vi Dang	Personalist Labor Party; an elite government party organized under Ngo dinh Nhu; its activities were largely secret and membership was primarily among civil servants
canton	Translation of *tong* (q.v.)
Cao Dai	A reformed Buddhist movement
Central Committee	The supreme continuous policy-making body of the Vietnamese Workers' Party

Central Office for South Vietnam	Mistranslation of *Trung Uong Cuc Mien Nam* (q.v.)
chanh quyen van	Propaganda activities directed toward government officials (communist term)
chi bo	Basic organizational and executive unit of the Party, usually established at the village level in rural Vietnam
Chieu Hoi	A government amnesty program established in 1963
Civic Action	A community development program established in 1955
Civil Guard	Translation of *Bao An* (q.v.)
co nong	Landless peasant (communist term)
Combat Youth	A government paramilitary organization during the Diem period
committee member	A member of a Party committee at any level
Committee of Resistance and Administration	A village organization established by the Vietminh
company	A military unit composed of two or more platoons
Cong An	Police branch responsible for internal security
corps	A military unit composed of two or more divisions; in Vietnam, one of three (later four) regional military commands established under Ngo dinh Diem
COSVN	Acronym for Central Office for South Vietnam, a translation of *Office Central de la Région Sud*, a mistranslation of *Trung Uong Cuc Mien Nam* (q.v.)
counterinsurgency	U.S. military jargon for counterrevolution
dan van	Political agitation and organization among the civil population (communist term)
Dan Ve	Village-level military force during the Diem period
Dang Lao Dong Viet Nam	Vietnamese Workers' Party; name of the communist party in Vietnam
Dang Nhan Dan Cach Mang	People's Revolutionary Party; name adopted by the Workers' Party for operations in the South after 1961
dia chu	In communist usage, one with large landholdings who does not operate his own land but rents it to tenants
district	See *quan* and *huyen*

division	A military unit composed of two or more brigades or regiments
doc phu su	During the French period, the highest civil service grade
doc su	During the French period, the civil service grade corresponding to the office of district chief
don tuyen	Single contact member, i.e., a Party member knowing only a single superior, rather than a superior and fellow cell members
Dong Thap Muoi	Plain of Reeds; a swampy open area to the west of Long An province
enemy	In communist usage, counterrevolutionary elements; in professional military usage, any opposing military force
free strike zone	An area evacuated by the Saigon government, with those remaining presumed to be enemy
gia	A measure of rice equaling forty liters
group	Associations employed by the Party to organize the population; cf. Party-Group system
H & I	Abbreviation for harassment and interdiction (q.v.)
hamlet	Translation of *ap* (q.v.)
Hamlet Evaluation System (HES)	A computerized American reporting system introduced in January 1967 to measure progress in pacification
harassment and interdiction (H & I)	A program of air and artillery strikes against possible revolutionary troop concentrations and lines of communication
hectare	Ten thousand square meters (2.47 acres)
HES	Acronym for Hamlet Evaluation System (q.v.)
Hoa Hao	A reformed Buddhist movement
hoi dong huong chinh	Name of the village council replacing the *ban hoi te* in 1953
huong hoa	Patrimonial land operated to support ancestor worship
huyen	In communist usage, the political and administrative level between village and province, ordinarily translated as district, and corresponding to the level of *quan* in the Saigon political structure

infrastructure	The apparatus at the village and district levels (government term)
International Control Commission	An organization composed of representatives of Canada, India, and Poland, established to supervise the implementation of the Geneva Accords of 1954
interprovince committee	In the Party structure, the committee level supervising several province committees
Labor Youth	The Party youth auxiliary group during the Resistance
landlord	Translation of *dia chu* (q.v.)
Law 10/59	A law promulgated in May 1959, providing harsh penalties for antigovernment activities
MACV	Acronym for Military Assistance Command Vietnam (q.v.)
masses	In communist usage, the working class and the landless and poor peasants
Mat Tran Dan Toc Giai Phong Mien Nam Viet Nam	The National Liberation Front; an organization established by the Party in 1960
middle peasant	Translation of *trung nong* (q.v.)
Military Assistance Command Vietnam (MACV)	The senior American military headquarters in Vietnam, established in 1962
Nam Bo Regional Committee	Translation of *Xu Uy Nam Bo* (q.v.)
National Assembly	A Saigon legislative body established in 1956
National Liberation Front	Translation of *Mat Tran Dan Toc Giai Phong Mien Nam Viet Nam* (q.v.)
National Revolutionary Movement	A government-organized mass party during the Diem period
Nhan Dan Tu Ve	A paramilitary village defense organization established under the rural construction program
NVA	Acronym for North Vietnamese Army, official American term for PAVN (q.v.)
Party branch	Translation of *chi bo* (q.v.)

Party-Group system	Shorthand communist term for the system of disseminating information and directives: downward through the Party hierarchy, then outward to the masses through the system of Party sympathizers in the various liberation associations
PAVN	Acronym for People's Army of Vietnam
People's Revolutionary Party (PRP)	Translation of *Dang Nhan Dan Cach Mang* (q.v.)
People's Self-Defense Force	Translation of *Nhan Dan Tu Ve* or *Dan Ve* (q.v.)
Personalist Labor Party	Translation of *Can Lao Nhan Vi Dang* (q.v.)
PF	Acronym for Popular Force (q.v.)
Phoenix	Translation of *Phuong Hoang* (q.v.)
Phong Trao Giai Phong Nhan Dan Viet Nam	Vietnamese People's Liberation Movement; a front established by the Party in Long An in 1956
phu nong	Rich peasant; in communist usage, one with more than sufficient land for his family, but who probably employs agricultural laborers to operate the land rather than renting it to tenants
Phuong Hoang	Phoenix; an intelligence collection and reaction program established in 1968 and intended to eliminate the communist infrastructure
piaster	Currency of the southern zone; exchanged at the following rates to the U.S. dollar for the period indicated: 35 prior to 1962; 72 from 1962 through 1964; 118 from 1965 through 1970
Plain of Reeds	Translation of *Dong Thap Muoi* (q.v.)
platoon	A military unit composed of two or more squads, totaling about thirty men
poor peasant	Translation of *ban nong* (q.v.)
Popular Force	Village-level military force in the post-Diem period; successor to the *Dan Ve*
province	Translation of *tinh* (q.v.)
province committee	In the Party structure, the committee level supervising several district committees, and responsible for adapting Central Committee policy to local conditions
Provincial Reconnaisance Unit (PRU)	An intelligence collection and reaction force established by the Central Intelligence Agency

quan	In the Saigon political structure, an administrative unit, without the status of juridical person, having supervisory responsibility over several villages
Quoc Hoc	A nationalist school founded in Hue by the father of Ngo dinh Diem
regiment	A military unit composed of two or more battalions
Regional Committee	See *Xu Uy Nam Bo*
regional delegate	During the Diem period, an official responsible to the president, with inspection and advisory powers in one of four administrative regions in the southern zone
Regional Force	District-level military force in the post-Diem period; successor to the *Bao An*
Republican Youth	A government paramilitary organization during the Diem period
Resistance	In communist usage, the period from August 1945 through July 1954
revolutionary development	Official mistranslation of *xay dung nong thon* (q.v.)
RF	Acronym for Regional Force (q.v.)
rich peasant	Translation of *phu nong* (q.v.)
Rung Sat	A swampy jungle to the east of Long An province
rural construction	Translation of *xay dung nong thon* (q.v.)
sector	A military command corresponding to a province
security committee	A committee established to judge those charged with antigovernment activities
strategic hamlet program	A security-oriented resettlement program established in 1961
tam buu phap	In communist usage, the "three instruments" [of revolution]: the Party, the army, and the front
Tet	The Vietnamese Lunar New Year
tinh	In the Saigon political structure, an administrative unit having the status of juridical person, composed of several *quan*; in the communist system, a leadership level composed of several *huyen*; translated in the text as province
tong	In the Saigon political structure, an administrative unit without the status of juridical person, headed by a local notable, responsible for the supervision of several villages under the guid-

	ance of the district chief; no analogous level in the Party structure; translated in the text as canton
troop proselytizing	Translation of *binh van* (q.v.)
tru gian	Extermination of traitors (communist term)
trung gian bao ta	The agent of a landlord charged with enforcing rent collection
trung nong	In communist usage, a middle peasant, one who owns sufficient land to support his family
Trung Uong Cuc Mien Nam	The branch of the Party Central Committee established in the South in 1962 to upgrade the decision-making authority of the *Xu Uy Nam Bo*; ordinarily translated as Central Office for South Vietnam
tu tai	The degree received from a lycée, corresponding to the French *baccalaureat*
USOM	Acronym for United States Operations Mission
Viet Cong	Vietnamese communist; the term applied by the Saigon government to adherents of the revolutionary movement, whether Party members or not; rejected by the Party as misrepresenting the breadth of opposition to the Saigon government; when used in Party publications, invariably with ironic intent
Viet Minh	Abbreviation of *Viet Nam Doc Lap Dong Minh Hoi*, a front established by the Party in 1941
Vietnamese People's Liberation Movement	Translation of *Phong Trao Giai Phong Nhan Dan Viet Nam* (q.v.)
village	Translation of *xa* (q.v.)
village administrative committee	In the Saigon political structure, the village-level administrative organ in the post-1956 period
village administrative council	Translation of *hoi dong huong chinh* (q.v.)
village committee	The Party committee at the village level
village council	A general term for the succession of village government organs under the Saigon political structure

xa	A rural community of from several hundred to several thousand families, sharing a common leadership and communal house; translated in the text as village
xay dung nong thon	Rural construction; a pacification program established in 1966
Xu Uy Nam Bo	From 1955 through 1962, the Party committee responsible for supervising Party operations in the southern region
zone committee	Another term for interprovince committee

Index

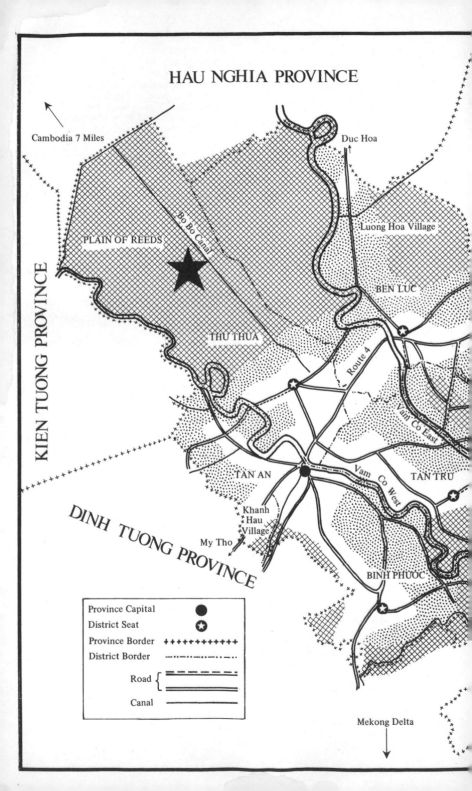

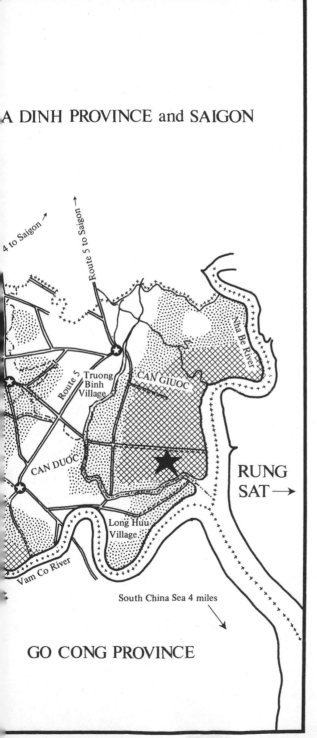

A DINH PROVINCE and SAIGON

4 to Saigon

Route 5 to Saigon

Route 5

Nha Be River

Truong Binh Village

CAN GIUOC

CAN DUOC

RUNG SAT →

Long Huu Village

Vam Co River

South China Sea 4 miles

GO CONG PROVINCE

The security situation in Long An as seen by government officials in late 1968: clear for secure areas, shaded for contested, and crosshatched for insecure. The secure areas were principally along the two major arteries to Saigon, Route 4 and Route 5. The isolated clear areas at the upper left and lower center are two Catholic villages. The two stars represent revolutionary base areas in the west (the Plain of Reeds) and the east (the Tan Tap area of Can Giuoc district adjacent to the Rung Sat).

SOURCE: Long An sector J-2